urban interventions

design ideas for the public space

FLAMANT 11

FLAMANT

C/ Ausiàs March 128
08013 Barcelona, Spain
T. 0034 935 952 283
F. 0034 932 654 883
info@hoakibooks.com
www.hoaki.com

Urban Interventions
Design Ideas for the Public Space

ISBN: 978-84-17084-14-1
D.L. B 23245-2019
Printed in China

Copyright © 2020 by Sandu Publishing Co., Ltd.
Copyright © 2020 by Flamant, and imprint of Hoaki Books, S.L.
for sale in Europe and America

Sponsored by Design 360° — Concept & Design Magazine
Edited, produced, book design, concepts & art direction by
Sandu Publishing Co., Ltd.
www.sandupublishing.com
Chief Editor: Wang Shaoqiang
Executive Editor: Jessie Tan
Designer: Wu Yanting
Front cover project *Pillars of Dreams* by THEVERYMANY, photo by NAARO
Back cover project *The Comedy Carpet* by Gordon Young and
Why Not Associates, photo by Angela Catlin
Cover design by Spread: David Lorente

All rights reserved. The total or partial reproduction of this book,
its transmission in any form or by any means or procedure, whether electronic
or mechanical, including photocopying, recording or incorporation into
an electronic storage and retrieval system, and the distribution of copies of
the work through rental or public lending are not permitted without prior
authorization from the publisher.

Contents

006 — **Preface**

010 — **Emmanuelle Moureaux**

020 — **Gabriel Dawe**

030 — **Quintessenz**

040 — **Chiharu Shiota**

048 — **Janet Echelman**

056 — **Luke Jerram**

064 — **Kurt Perschke**

076 — **Behin Ha**

084 — **Paul Cocksedge Studio**

096 — **THEVERYMANY**

106 — **Florentijn Hofman**

114 — **Coryn Kempster and Julia Jamrozik**

122 — **Moradavaga**

132 — **Gordon Young and Why Not Associates**

140	—	**Yong Ju Lee**
146	—	**Vincent Leroy**
154	—	**Shirin Abedinirad**
162	—	**Gummy Gue**
170	—	**Javier de Riba**
178	—	**Nómada Lab**
186	—	**MOMO**
194	—	**Eltono**
202	—	**Camille Walala**
212	—	**XOMATOK**
218	—	**Reskate Studio**
226	—	**Georgia Hill**
233	—	**Index**
240	—	**Acknowledgments**

Preface

What sets apart the journey of artists who engage in public spaces with an open audience?

Artists seeking to create a public experience, not merely by placing work in public spaces, but by locating the dialogue between audience and artwork at the center of their creative efforts, are at the forefront of a renewal.

Currently, the professional arena most visible to artists is the creation of increasingly expensive objects of acquisition as a mechanism of commodification. While this marketplace rewards some artists and ignores others, it is merely a modern souk, and cannot be conflated with the goal of artistic practice. Commerce is not communion or connection. In the increasingly diverse ecology of public art practice, we are seeing a generative evolution of the connection between artists and public consciousness.

I believe every artist, through their own language of construction, seeks communication. Whether it is broadcast at the moment or buried away for a future viewer, for that work to meet an audience is the propulsive desire that fuels the artist's practice.

The standard, the contemporary metric, by which a renewal of artistic practice through public engagement should be judged is not only imagistic—the lens of a device capturing a cool graphic—but also counts on its capacity for emotional connection via the lens of the body. Spectacle implemented as an aesthetic tool—but not an end in itself—can guide us toward the ephemeral yet profound experience of opening up to joy and wonder, not privately held but communally experienced.

As you witness in this book, we as artists venturing into public spaces have the opportunity to close the gap and engage an unscripted audience. While the risks of leaving the white exhibition cube to work in an unmediated public arena are real, so is the chance to pursue the elusive goal of communal connection.

The greatest challenge, worthy of any artist's endeavor, is to create a transcendent shared experience. In these moments, we exist together as connected humanity—this is the gift.

Kurt Perschke, Artist

"I believe every artist, through their own language of construction, seeks communication. Whether it is broadcast at the moment or buried away for a future viewer, for that work to meet an audience is the propulsive desire that fuels the artist's practice."

"When I saw the cityscape of Tokyo for the first time, I was so impressed by the colors in the city—thousands of colors seem floating in the cityscape, like layers, like three-dimensional elements. It was as if I saw colors for the first time. I was so overwhelmed that I decided to move to Tokyo. Inspired by the colors of Tokyo every day, I realized that colors can create a lot of emotions, create a unique atmosphere felt entirely by the five senses, generating unlimited emotions. They can make people smile, give energy, joy, and, most importantly, make people happy."

Emmanuelle Moureaux

—
Architect
Artist
Designer
—

Born in 1971, Emmanuelle Moureaux is a French architect living in Tokyo since 1996. In Japan, she established "emmanuelle moureaux architecture + design" in 2003. She is also a member of the Tokyo Society of Architects, the Architectural Institute of Japan, and the Japan Institute of Architects.

French Architect in Japan: Giving Emotions through Colors

Emmanuelle Moureaux was very interested in Japanese literature when she was in high school. At that time, there was no internet, so her exploration and interest in Japanese culture came primarily through books and printed media. In 1995 when she was still an architecture student, she decided to go alone to Tokyo for one week. And this one-week trip changed her life. "When I saw the cityscape of Tokyo for the first time, I was so impressed by the colors in the city—thousands of colors seem floating in the cityscape, like layers, like three-dimensional elements. It was as if I saw colors for the first time," recalls Emmanuelle. A year later, she moved to Tokyo and set up her studio called "emmanuelle moureaux architecture + design" in 2003.

Inspired by the layers and colors of Tokyo that built a complex depth and density on the street, along with traditional Japanese spatial elements like sliding screens, Emmanuelle created the concept of "shikiri," which literally means "dividing (creating) space with colors." She uses colors as three-dimensional elements, layers to create spaces, rather than a finishing touch applied on surfaces. By applying colors as a medium to compose space, her wish is to give emotions through colors with her creations, which range from art and design to architecture. "For me, the overflowing effects of colors with 'shikiri' show that colors in public spaces can give more than space, but an area with additional layers of human emotion," says Emmanuelle.

Her representative artwork includes the architectural design for Sugamo Shinkin Bank, the *100 colors* art installation series, a design space for ABC Cooking Studio, art installations for UNIQLO and ISSEY MIYAKE, and *stick chair*, among others. Unveiled in 2013 to celebrate the 10th anniversary of the studio, the *100 colors* series was designed to express the emotions from the colors and layers of Tokyo. Now *100 colors* has evolved as an on-going project and showed up in different cities around the world.

In 2017, Emmanuelle created the installation *Forest of Numbers* at the National Art Center, Tokyo for its 10th-anniversary exhibition. Through the work, Emmanuelle tried to visualize the future decade of the National Art Center from 2017 to 2026, using more than 60,000 pieces of suspended numeral figures from 0 to 9 made of paper. These numbers were regularly aligned in three-dimensional grids, and a section was removed to create a path, inviting visitors to wander inside the colorful forest filled with numbers. This work has become one of Emmanuelle's largest and most acclaimed artwork so far.

Paper, textiles, and threads are often used in Emmanuelle's work. But for her, materials are not important; only colors matter. "The absolute condition in the choice of material is to be able to obtain the beauty of colors I want, by painting, dyeing, and so on," remarks Emmanuelle. She has kept thousands and thousands of colors in her studio, and she collects colors everywhere—it might be a beautiful blue from a page of a magazine. When she starts a project, the first thing is always to decide the number of colors she will use (depending on the function, site, and inspiration). At the same time, she studies the concept by writing and sketching. When the idea is settled, she creates a lot of physical scale models to feel and touch the design in her studio with the help of her teammates. Almost everything is made by hand, and it takes a massive amount of time.

Apart from working as an architect and designer, Emmanuelle is also an associate professor at Tohoku University of Art and Design since 2008. To explore in depth greater possibilities of color, she initiated a project she named "100 colors lab." In her laboratory, she encourages her students to expand on the traditional seven colors of the rainbow to create color palettes from items from their daily lives, like glasses, bubble foam, rice, umbrellas, watches, CDs, chocolate blocks, and so on. With colors, Emmanuelle tries to make people smile, laugh, surprise, react, talk, and in all cases, describe and use colors to create special moments of happiness.

1000 Colors Recipe

For the "IMABARI Color Show" in Spiral Garden in Tokyo, 1000 colors were tailor-made to introduce the Imabari City's dyeing technology. It is a visualization of the delicate and accurate "recipes" required for dyeing: color "C (blue)/M (red)/Y (yellow)," temperature "°C," and time "minute/second." The three elements and their values were dyed in 1000 different colors and cut in the shape of 17,000 symbols (letters and numerical figures from 0 to 9), connected with thread. One thousand colors were then suspended to form a circle at the center, one color for one thread, with the undyed white symbols wrapping the outer circumference to emphasize the existence of 1000 tones.

Photography: **Daisuke Shima** | Material: **Textile, thread** | Location: **Tokyo, Japan**

Forest of Numbers

It is part of Emmanuelle's *100 colors* installation series and celebrates the 10th anniversary of the National Art Center, Tokyo. The 2000-square-meter white space was filled with more than 60,000 pieces of suspended numeral figures from 0 to 9 made of paper. All the figures were regularly aligned in three-dimensional grids with a section removed, leaving a path cut through the installation to let visitors in and wander inside the colorful forest filled with numbers. The installation was composed of ten layers in 100 shades of colors, which represented respectively the next ten years from 2017 to 2026. Each layer contained randomly positioned four digits to stand for the relevant year, for example, 2, 0, 1, and 7 for the layer of 2017.

Photography: **Daisuke Shima** | Material: **Paper, thread** | Location: **Tokyo, Japan**

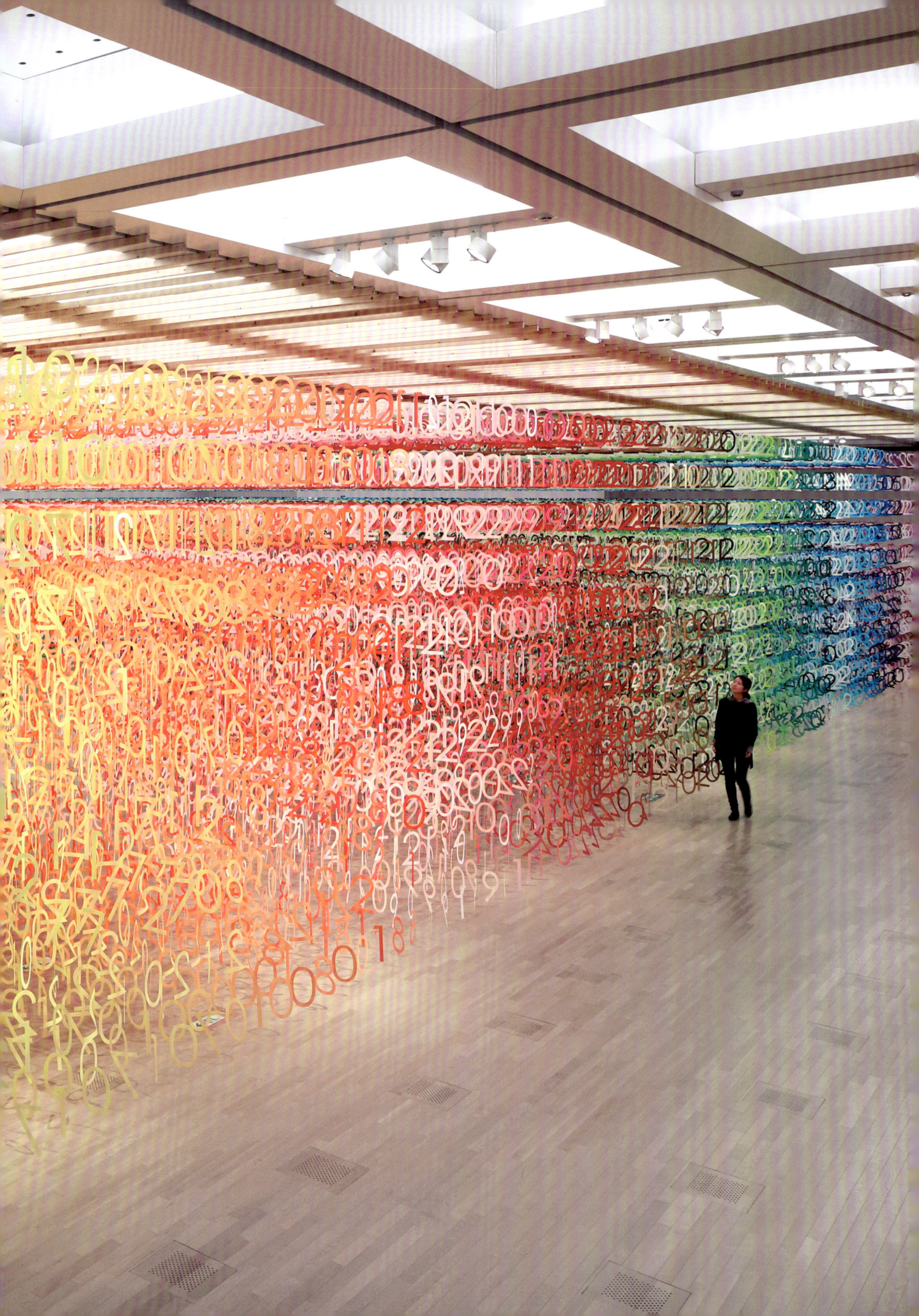

Christmas Forest in 100 Colors

It celebrates the 11th anniversary of Omotesando Hills, a shopping complex in central Tokyo, and it is Emmanuelle's first illumination installation. The work was inspired by the scenery of layers of trees lining up along the main boulevard in Omotesando. Fifteen hundred mini trees in 100 different colors filled the 13.4 meters high space. Each mini tree was created by wrapping a light bulb in colored papers, like a lantern, which emitted a soft and gentle light. Inside the forest, the main tree—formed by a collection of mini trees lit up in white—had a height of seven meters.

Photography: **Daisuke Shima** | Material: **Paper and white LED light for mini trees; white paper, acrylic, and color LED light for main tree** | Location: **Tokyo, Japan**

Interview with Emmanuelle Moureaux

What motivates and intrigues you to stay in Tokyo?

Life in Tokyo is colorful, powerful. Tokyo is my inspiration and source of energy. When I saw the cityscape of Tokyo for the first time, I was so impressed by the colors in the city—thousands of colors seem floating in the cityscape, like layers, like three-dimensional elements. It was as if I saw colors for the first time. I was so overwhelmed that I decided to move to Tokyo.

Inspired by the colors of Tokyo every day, I realized that colors can create a lot of emotions, create a unique atmosphere felt entirely by the five senses, generating unlimited emotions. They can make people smile, give energy, joy, and, most importantly, make people happy.

"Shikiri" is a concept you created. Can you tell us more about it?

The colors and layers I feel in Tokyo were the inspiration for my design concept, "shikiri," which means dividing (creating) space with colors ("shikiri" is a made-up word that literally means "to divide space using colors"). I use colors as three-dimensional elements, like layers, in order to create spaces, not as a finishing touch applied to surfaces. From this experience, I use colors to give emotions to others.

"Shikiri" has adopted its shape and function through every project I designed in the past. It has evolved over time. The concept, inspired by the Japanese traditional screens, first started as surface "shikiri" elements (like the façade of Sugamo Shinkin Bank that I designed). Then it developed into thinner colors and became line "shikiri" elements (like *stick chair*, *Shibafu table*, and *Toge* I made). Now it has evolved in particular items like numbers (*Forest of Numbers*) or letters (*Universe of Words*). I am always on a journey between different scales, from a small art piece to architecture, trying to give emotions to people with colors.

What made you start the first piece of the 100 colors *art installation series?*

I unveiled my first *100 colors* installations to mark the 10th anniversary of my studio in 2013. I made use of a space with the most beautiful 100 colors I created to express the emotion I felt from seeing the colors and layers of Tokyo.

In daily life, people are usually not conscious of color. Although people can distinguish millions of colors, people are living among the limited classification (name) of colors, such as yellow, orange, pink, red, green, blue, and so on. This situation is evident when people are asked to choose their favorite color, as they tend to name one color from the rainbow hue. I wanted to create an installation where people can see 100 shades of colors in one glance. You never have the opportunity to see in one space at the same time 100 colors. Also, 100 is a familiar number (100%, 100 points, etc.). I chose the most beautiful (for me) 100 shades of colors to create my own personal 100 colors palette. I want people to breathe and immerse in 100 shades of colors, to see colors, touch colors, and feel colors with all their senses. I want people to feel color with their entire body.

How long have you spent on Forest of Numbers? *What is the most challenging part of this project?*

All my installations require a lot of time, approximately one year from concept development to production. For *Forest of Numbers*, I decided to use the 2000-square-meter exhibition room of the National Art Center, Tokyo without any partition walls for the first time to create a "forest of numbers" as large as possible. More than 60,000 numbers needed to be perfectly aligned in a three-dimensional grid. All steps of the process were complicated, but the making of this installation was very challenging due to the large number of "numbers" in a limited time frame on site. It was made possible with the cooperation of more than 300 volunteers.

Why did you decide to use colors as a medium to compose space in your artwork? What do you want to convey to the viewers with a combination of colors?

As I said above, I felt a lot of emotions when I saw thousands of colors floating in the cityscape of Tokyo, like layers, like three-dimensional elements.

Using a combination of colors is essential for me in order to feel the depth, rhythm, and of course, emotions. That's why I use a multicolor palette in all my projects. The first thing I decide when I start a new design is the number of colors, for example, 24 colors for the Sugamo Shinkin Bank, depending on the context, function, and inspiration. For me, one color does not represent one meaning or emotion; a multicolor palette represents emotions.

As an established and experienced installation artist, what advice would you give to newcomers?

Trust only your eyes and feelings. Experiment with everything with real-scale mockups. Don't only look but feel with your entire body.

1000 Colors Wave

It is the second installation for the "IMABARI Color Show" to introduce the Imabari City's dyeing technology. Even though the same water, formula, and environment are utilized during the dyeing process, the slightest change in weather and/or temperature can completely disrupt the result of the pigmentation. However, in the skilled hands of the craftsmen of Imabari, the dyeing process is so precise that 1000 unique colors of fabrics are made possible. One thousand pieces of textile specially dyed in 1000 different colors covered the 1002 seats of the Imabari City Auditorium, designed by the famous architect Kenzo Tange. The bright palettes created an astounding wave of colors, echoing the ceiling of the public hall.

Photography: **Daisuke Shima** | Material: **Textile** | Location: **Imabari City, Japan**

"After making the first two installations, I realized that the resulting structures were very ethereal, and they looked like rays of light floating in mid-air. To reinforce the idea of light, I decided to use the full spectrum of fragmented light intentionally. Since then, using this idea of fragmented light is at the point of origin for every installation. From there, I play around with those colors, depending on what feels right for each installation. Sometimes I use only half or even a third of the colors, and sometimes I use all of them in different orders."

Gabriel Dawe

Artist
Designer

Originally from Mexico City, Gabriel Dawe creates site-specific installations that explore the connection between fashion and architecture, and how they relate to the human need for shelter in all its shapes and forms. His work has been exhibited worldwide and published on-line and in print.

Colorful Rays of Light: Illuminating Intricate Social Norms

As an artist with Mexican rooting, Gabriel Dawe is deeply influenced by the country's culture. One of the most prominent influences is the use of color in his work. In Mexico, the use of color is uninhibited, and one can find colors in every corner. Furthermore, his mother is a collector of high-quality handicrafts, so at his early age, he was exposed to some fantastic artifacts, giving him a rich sense of color, textures, materials, and craftsmanship.

Another subtle influence on him is the machismo that plays a pervasive role in shaping Mexican culture. When Gabriel was a boy, he was desperately wanted to learn to embroider. Still, his grandmother only taught that to his older sister because the embroidery was considered a definite no-no for boys. "I grew out of that frustration, but the memory of it led me to explore this technique as an adult, and in doing so, to question the many social constructs that we sometimes presume to be permanent, rigid, and inflexible," said Gabriel. Thus, the choice of thread becomes a natural extension and symbolic representation of these social constructs that he wants to shed light on. Today, Gabriel has become an artist known for his work that is centered in the exploration of textiles, aiming to examine the complicated construction of gender and identity in his native Mexico and attempting to subvert the notions of masculinity and machismo.

Before working as an artist, Gabriel has worked as a graphic designer in Montreal, Canada, for seven years. His career as an artist started from Dallas, Texas, where he pursued his MFA at the University of Texas at Dallas (UTD). When he studied at the UTD, his work was often small to medium scale, and the limitations of the size of the medium left him somewhat unsatisfied. There was a growing desire within him to create work in a grander scale. Along with the desire came the chance. An architect approached him for an exhibition that aimed to explore the links between fashion and architecture. The theme of the first show was related to the human's need for shelter. Gabriel forced himself to think outside the bounds of his work, and as the ideas developed, he decided to create an architectural structure by using the core material of the clothing, that is, thread. Eventually, he succeeded in creating the installation work that later became the shape of his famous *Plexus* series.

Plexus literally means the network of nerves or vessels informing and sustaining the body. "It was the perfect name because it not only refers to the connection of the body with its environment, but it also relates directly to the intricate network of threads forming the installation itself, and to the tension inherent in the thread, vibrating with an almost tangible luminosity," remarked Gabriel.

Plexus series expresses Gabriel's desire to use gradations of color. The fineness of the thread makes these installations ethereal, almost immaterial. "This color mist alludes to a symbolic quest to materialize light," Gabriel said, "to give it density, so that I can offer the viewer an approximation of things otherwise inaccessible to us—a glimmer of hope that brings us closer to the transcendent, to show that there can be beauty in this messed up world we live in."

Plexus NO. 35

Site-specific installation at the Toledo Museum of Art.

Photography: **Toledo Museum of Art** | Material: **Thread, wood, hooks** | Location: **Toledo, Ohio, USA**

Plexus NO. 29

Site-specific installation at the Brigham Young University Museum of Art.

Photography: **Gabriel Dawe** | Material: **Thread, wood, hooks** | Location: **Provo, Utah, USA**

Interview with Gabriel Dawe

Thread is an essential medium in your art. Why did you choose it?

I have always had a fascination with textiles, and when I was a kid, I desperately wanted to learn to embroider. Unfortunately, embroidery is not something that boys are encouraged to do in a macho culture, so it became a frustration. When I grew up and became an artist, I remembered that frustration and decided to teach myself to embroider. In doing so as a grown man, I aimed to challenge the notions of gender identity that oppressed me when I was an eight-year-old boy.

Do you think you have succeeded in challenging such stereotypes through your artworks?

I think that my early work is definitely successful in challenging those norms and ideas. When my work evolved into the installations, that narrative shifted to the background. Because of my history, that challenge of gender norms is still there, albeit in a subtler way.

Differences caused by traditional gender models are still prevalent in social and professional structures. What do you think we can do to bridge such gaps?

I think there is definitely some progress, and it is very noticeable in younger generations in terms of both sexual and gender expressions, which gives me a lot of hope despite some seemingly reversal of progress we have seen in recent years. I think we are experiencing the final blows of a dying patriarchal system that is struggling to hold on to power. It might be a loud and deceivingly terrifying death, but I have no doubt it is indeed dying.

Plexus NO. 34

Site-specific installation at the Amon Carter Museum of American Art.

Photography: **Amon Carter Museum of American Art** | Material: **Thread, wood, hooks** | Location: **Fort Worth, Texas, USA**

Plexus C14

Site-specific installation at Facebook's headquarters in New York City.

Photography: **Gabriel Dawe** | Material: **Thread, steel** | Location: **New York City, New York, USA**

Plexus *series is your significant installation collection. Why did you name it "plexus?" When and why did you make the first piece of* Plexus?

The first installation came out of my experiments that were part of the collaboration with an architect who worked for his exhibition that aimed to explore the links between fashion and architecture. That exhibition led me to ponder the question: What would happen if I cover this whole wall in my studio with sewing thread? So I took a ladder and proceeded to stretch thread from floor to ceiling. It was a painfully slow process, but the results were fascinating because it was obvious that it had endless possibilities. Throughout my career, I like working with series that carry one name, followed by a number. In looking for a name that could work for this new series, I dived to the dictionary and thesaurus trying to find words that could be adept at describing the network of thread I had created. When I landed on the entry "plexus," which is the name of a network of nerve endings or blood vessels in the human body, it felt like a right match.

What do colors mean to you? How do you decide on the color scheme?

After making the first two installations, I realized that the resulting structures were very ethereal, and they looked like rays of light floating in mid-air. To reinforce the idea of light, I decided to use the full spectrum of fragmented light intentionally. Since then, using this idea of fragmented light is at the point of origin for every installation. From there, I play around with those colors, depending on what feels right for each installation. Sometimes I use only half or even a third of the colors, and sometimes I use all of them in different orders. It all depends on what I want to explore with the colors.

Can you tell us the process of how you create an installation? What is the most challenging part?

It is a very straightforward process. I come into a space to have a dialog with it and get a sense of what it is asking of me. I go back to the studio to sketch and do lots of logistical planning, and then I go back to the space and install using a tool I have developed that enables me not to go up and down a ladder hundreds of times a day.

It varies from installation to installation. Sometimes the sketching process is swift; I get an image in my head immediately upon visiting a space. But sometimes some spaces pose a particular challenge that requires a lot of reflection on how to proceed. Other times, the logistics can be the tricky part, given individual characteristics of a space that might pose a problem to my usual way of working. Finally, depending on what each installation requires, the difficulty can lay on the actual installation of the thread. Sometimes, it is the most natural part. It all comes down to the space itself.

"Our installations are always temporary and are always between architecture and nature that have been there for years. If we place an installation just for a short time into such an area, it will be part of people's daily life there. If they stop for a while along the way, it makes a difference to the installation. Even if people don't understand our installation, it probably evacuates an unexpected feeling. We really enjoy seeing our installations spread worldwide, for young and old people, for men and women, and for everyone who can understand our colorful language."

Quintessenz

—
Artists
—

Quintessenz is a duo founded by Hannover- and Berlin-based artists Thomas Granseuer and Tomislav Topic. With roots in graffiti culture, they developed a unique work style combing painting, installation, and conceptual art in public spaces.

When Color Meets Space: It Becomes Art Itself

Thomas Granseuer and Tomislav Topic met each other when studying at the University of Applied Arts in Hildesheim in 2006. Thomas received his Master's degree in graphic design and advertising, while Tomislav studied color design and earned a diploma in chromatics. Employing their background in applied arts, they not only got to know both the theoretical and practical part of arts but had a chance to attend courses taught by professors with a fine art background, which prepared them for their career as an artist.

Graffiti culture was the common ground for Thomas and Tomislav, and in 2008, they established Quintessenz with some of their friends—or better said—their former graffiti crew from the past. Back then, their work of style was strongly influenced by graffiti and hip-hop culture with typical graffiti and letters. As time passed, they began to find it hard to define themselves because they fell in between designers and artists. But one thing was clear: They want to create something else, to develop their language and style.

Later, they separated with their previous crew, and in those days, they had a hard time with no clear direction or plausible solution. Eventually, they made a bold decision: Just let it go. "When we look back, we think it was a good decision because even today, people can't define us and our work neither," says Tomislav. "This is a nice big playground. It is challenging but also fun to explore the limit again and again." Now it has been more than ten years since their first collaboration, and they have finally discovered a playground on which they can both express themselves and, more importantly, make both of them satisfied and delighted.

In school days, Thomas and Tomislav were interested in collecting all sorts of materials and experimenting with them as they did not have much money for brand new materials and colors. They gathered every material they could get for free, for example, hem string used as the stuffing in seat sacks. They kept some bags of the abandoned hem string and thought they might use it one day. The day did come three years later when they were invited by an urban art festival called IBUG, a festival that often takes place in abandoned places, to create an installation. Thomas and Tomislav brought the hem and constructed their first installation. They stretched the fabric straight up from the ceiling to the floor, and it was the first time they discovered the moiré pattern and fell in love with it instantly. Since then, they began experimenting with translucent mesh fabric to get the moiré pattern and visual effect.

For Quintessenz, space is a fundamental source of inspiration. Their work not only uses shapes and patterns found in architecture, but it also interferes with its environment, changing the spectator's perception of space. With every medium they use, both in public areas and galleries, their abstract work shares one thing in common: It creates space for its color. To them, color is more than form. It is the content itself. Most of their installations are site-specific, so every time they start a new work, they will visit the space and get inspiration. They analysis the forms and colors from the space, site, or architecture and take several attempts until they find the right combination and composition. "In a more general way, space/form and color are the key 'ingredients' of our work: We create forms, be it building installations, paper-works, murals, or canvases. These art-formats give us empty spaces and blank forms that we then use as the sub-surface, as the ground for our colors. The combination of forms and colors is what our art reduces itself to."

Carme Genesis

Quintessenz created *Carme Genesis* for C.A.R.M.E, an art space based on a former church in Brescia, Italy. It was Quintessenz's first church art installation. By arranging the pastel panels in petrol, ochre, and red into a rainbow gradient that starts low above the floor and rises to the arched ceiling, Quintessenz aimed to emphasize the vacant space in the nave and symbolize the installation as a bridge between ground and heaven. In doing so, they wanted to reflect and respect the site's previous life. The structure of the church allows the spectator to appreciate the artwork from different angles.

Photography: **Quintessenz** | Material: **Mesh, paint, aluminum, wood, ropes** | Location: **Brescia, Italy**

Kagkatika's Secret

Quintessenz created *Kagkatika's Secret* for the Paxos Contemporary Art Project held in Paxos, a small island in the Ionic Sea in Greece. All the invited artists were asked to choose a site to create their artworks. Quintessenz eventually found a 400-year-old ruin in a village called Kagkatika. They colorized the fabric into 120 color shades, and each layer was getting bigger as the viewers walked towards the window with a view of the sea. As the wind caressed the layers, and the sun shed its light on them, the installation appeared like a digital body in the real world, connecting the analog and digital, the old and new.

Photography: **Quintessenz**
Material: **Mesh, spray paint, metal ropes, wood**
Location: **Kagkatika, Paxos, Greece**

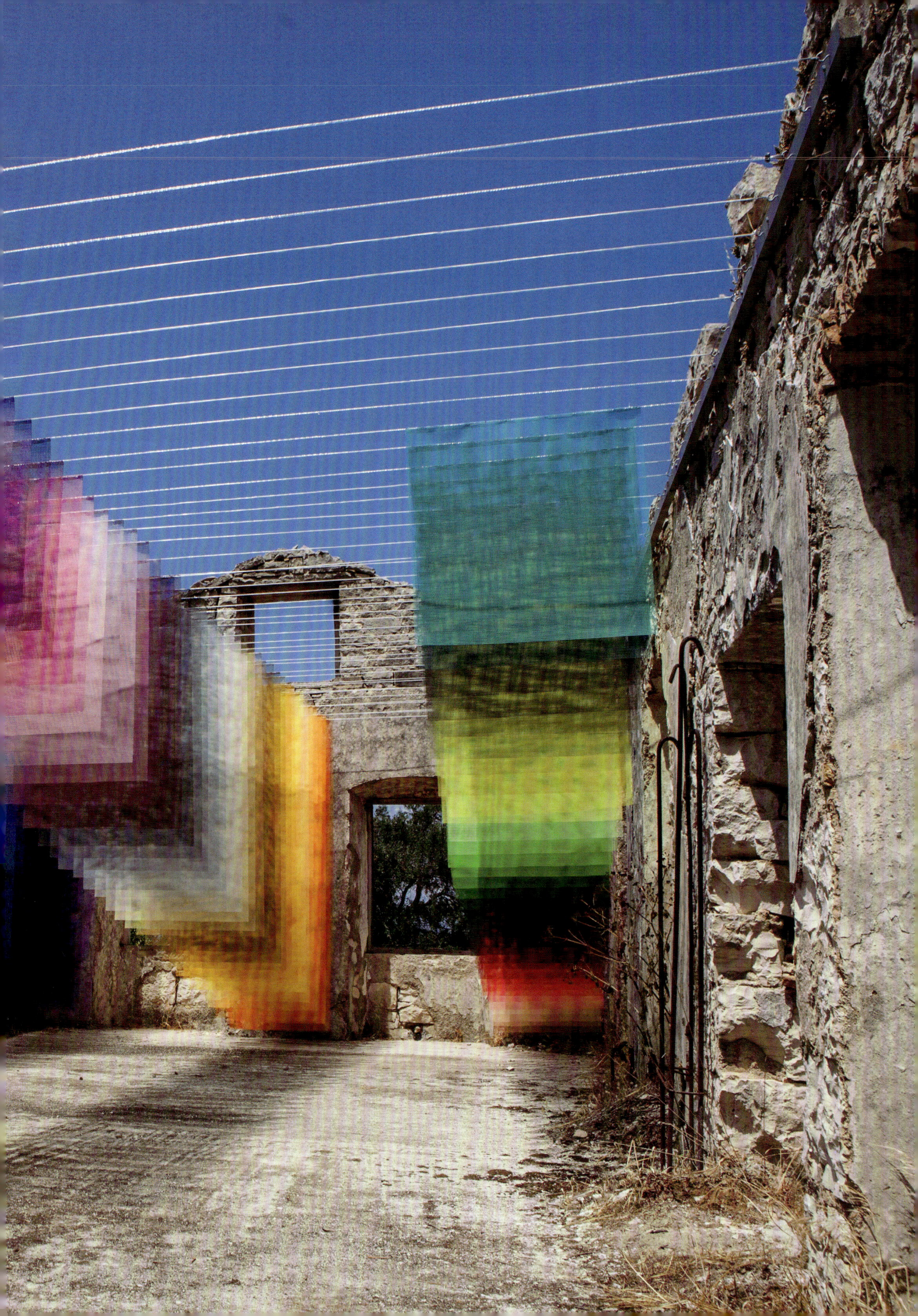

Interview with Quintessenz

Colors in different shades are the signature feature of your work. Why is color so important to you?

Color is so typical in our everyday life. People don't really think about color; it is just there. We also don't talk about color unless we see an incredible sunset or an ugly color used in a building or car. Besides that, color is, in many cases, just a subconscious impression. The first conscious impression we have for color refers to the shape of an object. Color in its raw appearance can bring joy to everyone, either young or older people. It is worldwide understandable, and it can make a difference in people's everyday life. The fact that seeing color is so natural brought us a feeling that we have to present color differently and give the color a stage where its appearance is not secondary. It is the first impression that leads us to an emotional reaction because this is what color is doing—it creates an emotional feeling that is worldwide understandable.

Kagkatika's Secret is one of the most successful artworks you have made so far. How did you find that place and make things go perfect?

This project gave us freedom but also restrictions to create something powerful. As I mentioned before, this is one of the most spontaneous projects we have ever done, and this is probably because of the power it emits. Finding the place/site on our own was probably the most crucial part. Most places are beautiful, and of course, we decide if we do a project or not depending on the sites that we are proposed. But for this project, it is very different because we got on a scooter and found the site by ourselves on one of the most beautiful islands we had ever been to.

Nothing really went perfect during the production of our installation. We even didn't have a hammer to push in the dowels for our construction. But the festival organizers and curators were warmhearted and tried to help us with all the problems. Our artist friends were there; the weather was good; the food was delicious. What I want to say is, all these little things come together and will affect your creation if you are working and creating directly on site. It is the perfect condition for a site-specific installation, we think.

Nenuphar de Molitor

The Molitor is an iconic Parisian place known for its 60-year reign as the most popular swimming pool in the city for its avant-garde ambiance. Quintessenz tried to capture the soul and heart of the historic space by using 29 layers with three rows of colored fabric, each mounted above the atrium of the outdoor pool.

Photography: **Quintessenz**
Material: **Mesh, paint, metal ropes, wood**
Location: **Paris, France**

Will you use computer-aided design for the palettes? Can you tell us the process of how you create an installation?

Well, the computer is a helpful device, but in the first stage, there is always the inspiration from the space we are working in. We scan the space to get an idea of the color scheme that could work in it. We ask questions like: Do we want to create a contrast between the color and space? Or do we instead want the color to melt with the environment? Following this step are composition sketches and color studies. If the gallery, art show, festival, or clients expect a proper design, the last step will be working with the computer. But we have to admit that we are really not into 3D modeling. Sometimes it's annoying when people expect a proper 3D rendering from us because we don't want any of our artwork to become one hundred percent predictable. Our installation concepts are actually based on color codes, measurements, and rough analog sketches—that is to say—the final installation comes as a big surprise. Our production plan seldom shows a rendering of our vision. Primarily, it is more about cutting and coloring methods. We produce on site or in our studio. When we start to hang the parts, everything comes together, and a work that fits in the form of codes and numbers just comes to life. A new baby is born, and this brings us the happiest feeling, the unexpected joy. A good friend and talented artist Rene Wagner once said to us, "If I know how it will look, I don't have to do it anymore." This is quite true, we think.

What do you expect your public installations to bring to the location and the people there?

Our installations should bring a temporary value to the place where it is installed. Our installations are always temporary and are always between architecture and nature that have been there for years. If we place an installation just for a short time into such an area, it will be part of people's daily life there. If they stop for a while along the way, it makes a difference to the installation. Even if people don't understand our installation, it probably evacuates an unexpected feeling. We really enjoy seeing our installations spread worldwide, for young and old people, for men and women, and for everyone who can understand our colorful language.

Are there any artists whom you admire?

There are several artist we look up to: Frantisek Kupka, pioneer of the early phases of abstract art, Mark Rothko, who was not only an artist but totally a genius in paintings, Olafur Eliasson for his experiments and variety, Anish Kapoor for his megalomania, and of course, Christo & Jeanne-Claude for their vision and the way they create temporary work.

Paradis Perdus

Quintessenz created *Paradis Perdus* for the A-Part contemporary art festival held in Les Baux de Provence, a majestic town in Southern France. Tones of violet, grey, and red were used to form the palette of the installation to reflect the plants growing in the local gardens. The wind that blew softly on the painted transparent fabric highlighted the moiré patterns, the signature style of Quintessenz's work.

Photography: **Quintessenz**
Material: **Mesh, spray paint, metal ropes**
Location: **Les Baux de Provence, France**

2 AUSSTELLUNGEN
EXHIBITIONS
KONFERENZRAUM
CONFERENCE ROOM
1 AUSSTELLUNGEN
EXHIBITIONS
0 AUSSTELLUNGEN
EXHIBITIONS
TICKETS
TICKETS
BUCHHANDLUNG
BOOKSHOP
RESTAURANT
RESTAURANT
-1 GARDEROBE
KINO
CINEMA
TOILETTEN
TOILETS

"Normally, when people experience public artwork, they are mesmerized at first; their breath is taken away by the size or the technique. Only afterward will they think about the meaning. But the viewer should reflect on the meaning of the artwork as soon as they see it; good public art should give a strong emotional impression immediately. The purpose of art is to affect the viewer emotionally."

Chiharu Shiota

Artist

Born in Osaka, Japan, in 1972, Chiharu Shiota lives and works in Berlin, Germany. She explores fundamental human concerns such as life, death, and relations through large-scale thread installations, drawings, sculptures, photography, and videos. Her work has been displayed at international institutions and exhibitions. Portrait photo by Sunhi Mang. © VG Bild-Kunst, Bonn, 2019, and the artist.

Weaving New Worlds:
An Ode to Life and Memory

Chiharu Shiota always wanted to become an artist. She studied painting at an art school in Japan, but in the second year of her study, she felt restricted and stuck in the painting. "Painting has such a long, profound history, and I had the feeling that this art practice did not belong to my history," questioned Chiharu. "There was no meaning in painting for me. It was just color on a canvas." In search of change, in 1993, Chiharu decided to participate in a one-year exchange program at the Australia National University of Canberra in Australia. One day, she had a dream: She was inside a two-dimensional painting and overwhelmed by the paint. Drawing inspiration from her dream, she did her first performance art called *Becoming Painting*, in which she was covered by red enamel paint. The paint is toxic to human's skin, so after the performance, she had to cut her hair, and her skin stayed discolored for months. However, she enjoyed the performance because she felt herself in control, and unlike in her dream, she could move in the painting. Since then, she began experimenting with other materials and her body to create artwork. In 1996, she furthered her art studies in Germany and eventually settled down in Berlin. Now, Chiharu is renowned internationally for her thread installations intertwined with objects like keys, chairs, letters, pianos, or boats, all kinds of objects that she collected to wrap memories and shed light on human relationships.

String is a prominent material used in Chiharu's work, which allows her to extend the line from the painting into space. "Creating these installations is like drawing in the air. There are no limitations," Chiharu explains. When she starts a new work, she will visit the space first, imaging the possibilities to perform within the area. Every time when she walks in an empty space, she feels as if her body and spirit transcended into another dimension, which allows her to create a new world. "The weaving process is a way of conveying existence in the absence," adds Chiharu. By creating complex networks of string that are interlaced between daily objects, Chiharu narrates the stories of the past—memories stored within these objects—and the present, a new visual plane full of possibilities, emotions, and imagination.

In *Beyond Memory*, Chiharu collected 6000 sheets of photocopies of books from the archive of Gropius Bau. The Gropius Bau is one of the most important exhibition venues in Europe, which used to be a shared space between a school and museum. In 1911, they curated an exhibition called "Art History of Silk Weaving," in which thousands of fabric samples from all over the world were displayed. Chiharu tried to reveal the glory of the venue by using 6000 sheets of photocopies from the books about the history of the Gropius Bau and the architectural plans of the building. The sheets of paper function as a conjunction between the past with the present. "When you walk through the building, you can feel specific energy, a presence of people, and time. With the installation, I wanted to reflect this feeling," Chiharu says.

Among the objects featured, boats are recurrent images in Chiharu's installations, which carry different symbols, yet overall, reflect people's journey in life. "I think we all struggle to define a purpose because our life has become too convenient. We like to follow a certain path marked by our education and cultural background, which will lead us in a clear line to comfort. But we don't know where we are going," explains Chiharu. In the installations, the boats seem to have a defined direction. Still, while floating upwards in a prevailing direction, the destination remains unknown, just like a journey of life for most people.

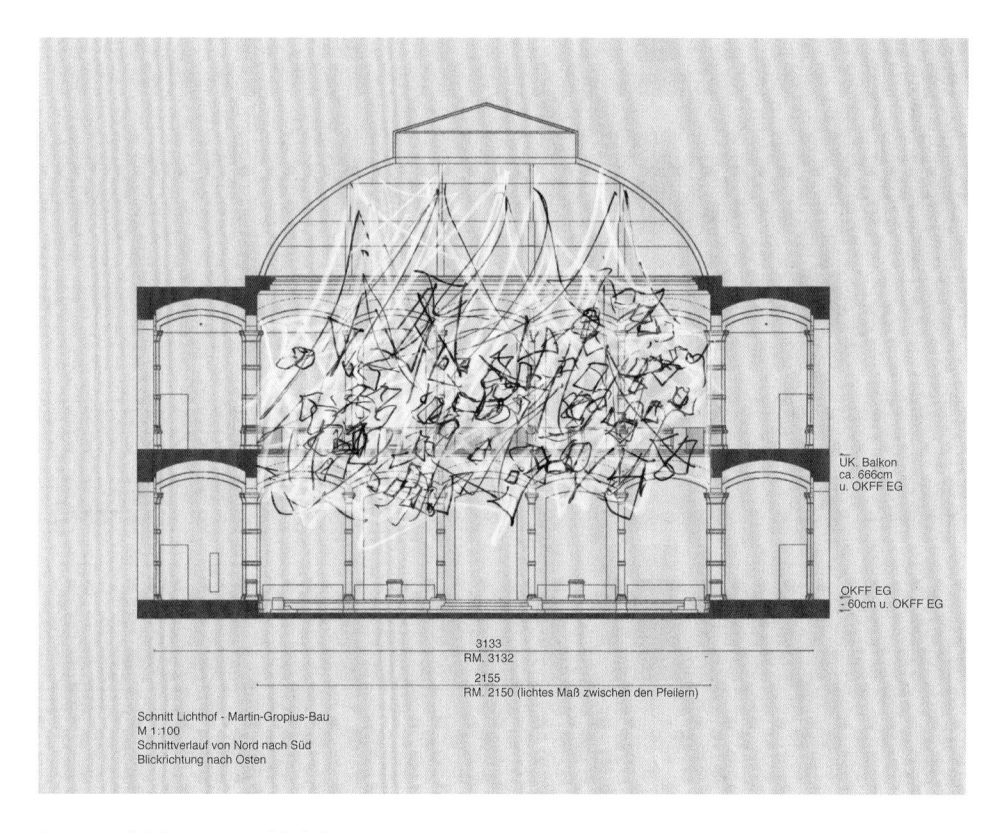

Beyond Memory, 2019

Beyond Memory connects the past of the Gropius Bau with the present. Chiharu tried to reveal the story of the venue by using 6000 sheets of photocopies of books from the Gropius Bau's archive. The white thread is interlaced like neurons in the brain, transmitting information and making connections.

Photography: **Sunhi Mang** | Material: **White wool, paper** | Location: **Berlin, Germany**

Six Boats, 2019

Six Boats was an installation for Ginza Six, Tokyo. The boats symbolize the bearers of one's dreams and hope along his/her journey of life. The white thread shrouds the boats, resembling a mist of uncertainty that blurs one's vision.

Photography: **Ken Kato** | Material: **Felt, white rope, metal frame** | Location: **Tokyo, Japan**

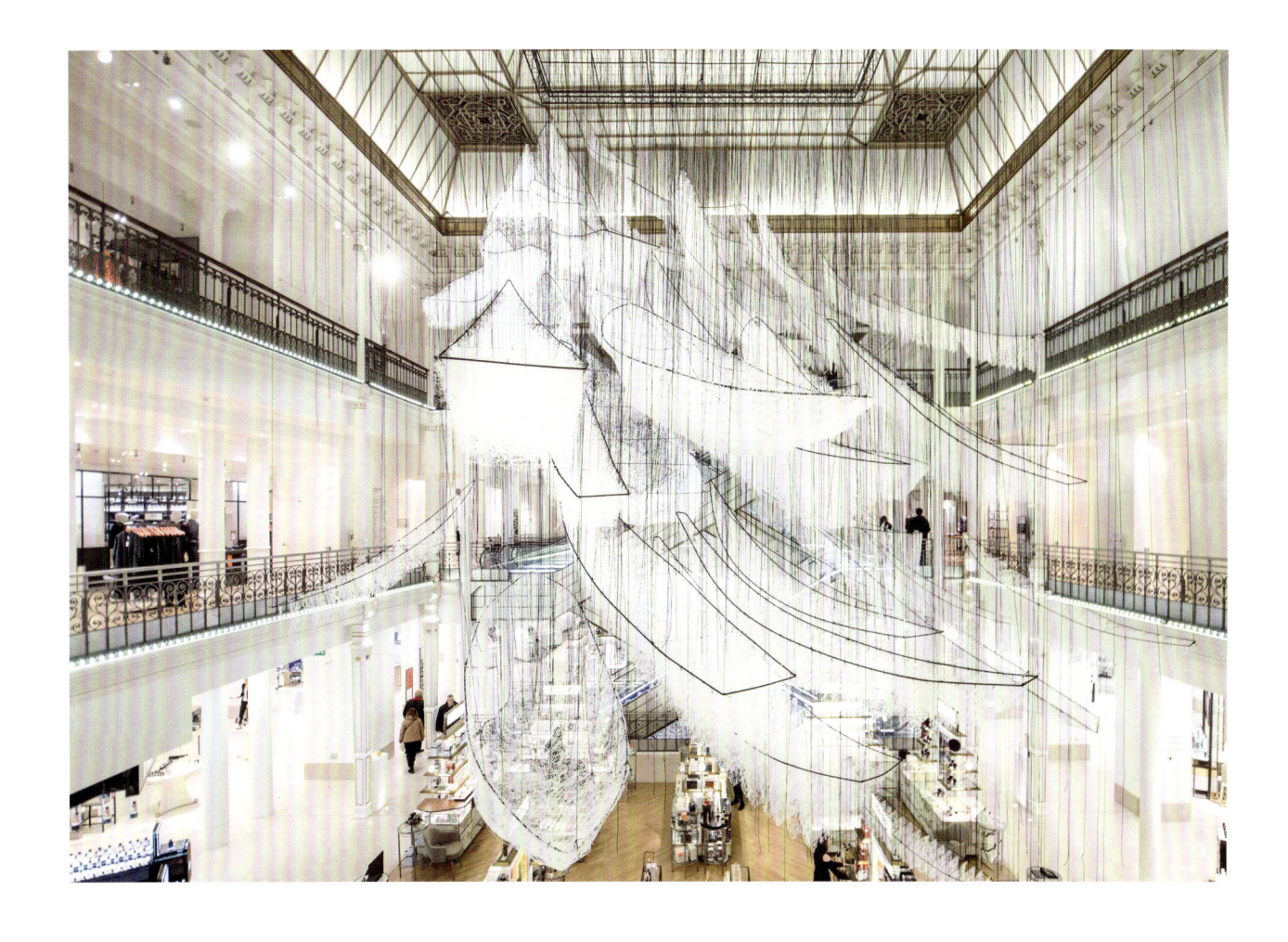

Where are we going?, 2017

Chiharu created *Where are we going?* for Le Bon Marché Rive Gauche in Paris. Life is a journey with no determined destination. People are ready to go but have no idea where they are heading to exactly. The more comfortable life is, the more challenging it is to stay sober and be aware of the purpose of life.

Photography: **Gabriel de la Chapelle**
Material: **Wire, string, white wool**
Location: **Paris, France**

Accumulation of Power, 2017

St. Joseph's Church is a space where power, thoughts, wishes, ideas, and prayers assemble. In this sense, the red whirlwind construction embodies the accumulation of the spiritual power present in this church. Every idea, thought from the prayer is collected and gathered in this storm-like construction.

Photography: **Philippe Bréard** | Material: **Red wool, metal rings** | Location: **Le Havre, France**

Boats sailing in the sky, 2017

It was created for the Open Art Biennale in Örebro, Sweden. The red color symbolizes blood and furthermore, human relations. The ropes hold everything together, and each rope is made of many pieces of thread, suggesting the connections within society. The boats are featured in a defined direction and have no choice but to keep moving, but no one knows the destination, nor can anyone stop.

Photography: **Sofia Isaaksson** | Material: **Red wool, metal frame** | Location: **Örebro, Sweden**

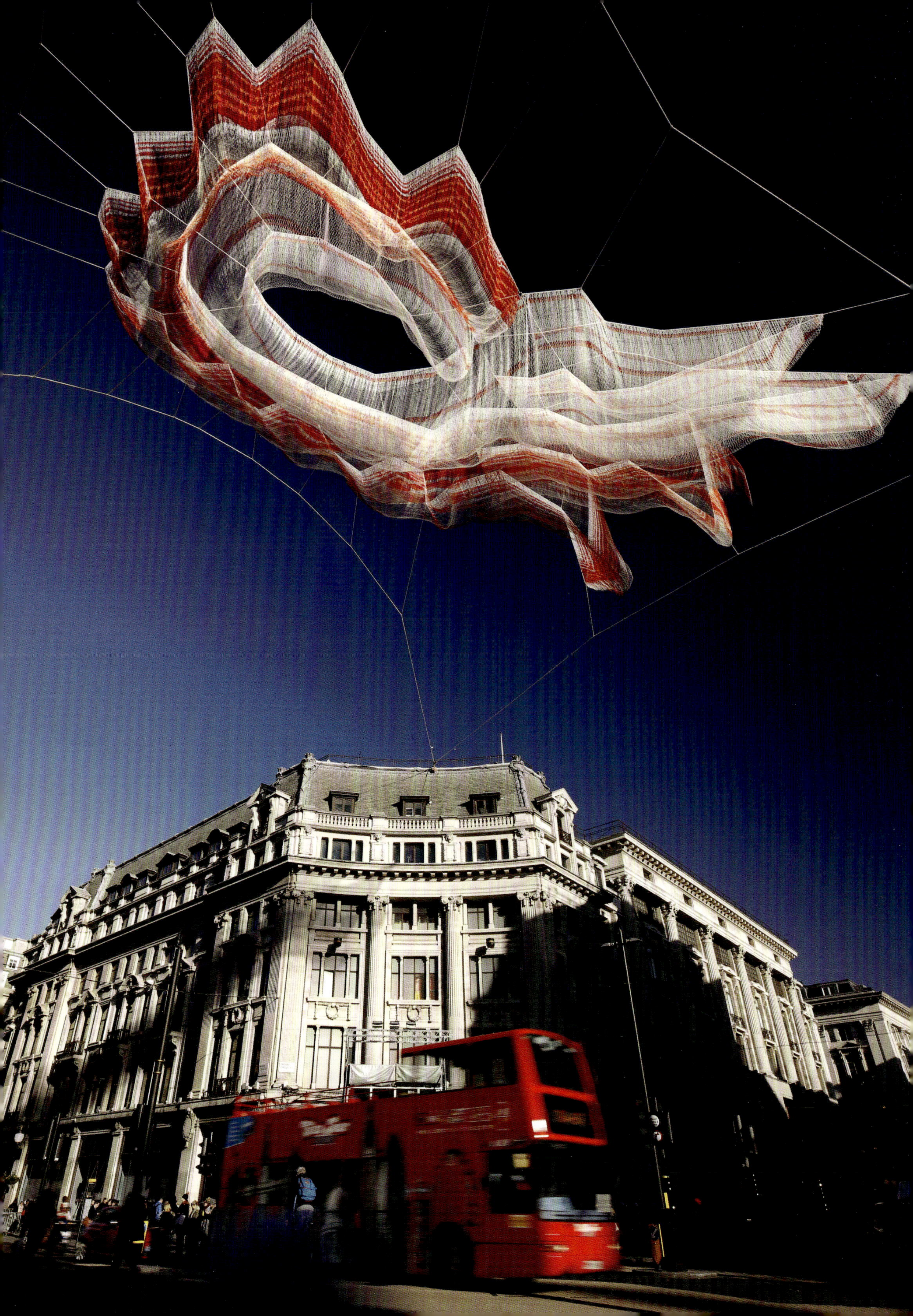

"I see art, architecture, and landscape as interwoven elements that we can design in a way to improve our cities. They can be fused to create a unified experience much greater than each entity can do alone. Each artist has different standards for how they measure success in their work. I choose to spend my life creating art in cities around the world, inviting people to experience underneath the sculpture and form a relationship with it. If someone pauses to notice the interaction with wind and sunlight as my work changes in the midst of their daily life, then it has achieved my personal artistic goal."

Janet Echelman

—
Artist
Sculptor
—

Janet Echelman is an artist who creates experiential sculpture at the scale of buildings that transform with wind and light. The art shifts from being an object people look at to something people can get lost in. Her TED talk "Taking Imagination Seriously" has been translated into 35 languages with more than two million views.

Everything Is Interwoven:
Art that Interacts with Nature

Janet Echelman had never really made art until she entered the university and stumbled into an elective drawing course. At that time, she had a chance to take one more art course before graduation, after taking the course, she realized being an artist was the only thing she wanted to do. When she finished her study, she applied to seven art schools and was rejected by all of them. "It took ten more years before I found my voice as a sculptor and another ten years before I figured out how to build my sculpture at the scale of buildings. I never studied sculpture, engineering, or architecture, so I may seem like an unlikely person to be doing what I'm doing—creating monumental, billowing forms in cities around the world," recalls Janet. She never let the rejections stop her, and instead, she went off on her own to become an artist.

In 1992, Janet moved to Bali, Indonesia, with 300 dollars in her pocket and started painting there. A decade later, she received the opportunity to teach painting in India on a Fulbright Scholar Program, and it was where she discovered sculpting. Janet was a young painter then and promised to hold her painting exhibitions around India on behalf of the US Embassy. For the shows, she shipped her special paints and equipment to create new paintings. Unfortunately, the deadline for the shows arrived, but her paints did not. "I was in a terrible bind, with no materials to make my art. I was staying in a South Indian fishing village, and each afternoon, I walked the long beach, watching the fishermen bundling their nets into mounds on the sand. I had seen it every day, but this time I saw it differently—a new approach to sculpture, a way to make volumetric form without heavy solid materials," Janet explains. Janet's first satisfying sculptures were handcrafted in collaboration with those fishermen. She brought the sculptures to the beach and lifted them into the air to photograph them. "It was then that I discovered their soft surfaces revealed every ripple of wind in constantly changing patterns and was mesmerized."

Janet looks for inspiration from everything around her, ranging from the forms of the planet in macro and micro scale to the patterns of life within it to the measurement of time, weather patterns, or the paths created by fluid dynamics. She always turns to the unique site as a guiding force for each artwork. "When I make the first site visit, I get a feel for its space and explore its history and texture to understand what it means to the space and its people," Janet says.

When Janet embarks on a specific project, she works with her colleagues to brainstorm, sketch, and explore all ideas without censoring their ideas in the early stages. As the sculpture designs begin to unfold, their studio architects, designers, and model-makers collaborate with an external team of aeronautical and structural engineers, computer scientists, lighting designers, landscape architects, and city planners to bring the initial sketches into reality. The netted sculptures used to be entirely fabricated by hand, and now, all of her recent work is a combination of machine and handwork. "My studio uses handwork to create unusual, irregular shapes and joints, and to make lace patterns within the sculpture. We utilize machines for making rectangular and trapezoidal panels with stronger, machine-tightened knots that can withstand intense hurricane-force winds, the heavyweight of snow, and ice storms," says Janet.

Collaborating with her team, Janet selects different fiber types depending on the role the fiber plays in the sculpture, whether it is for structural strength or expressiveness of color. "Constraints can push creativity. I design art to withstand typhoon winds, ice, and snow. I try to approach these design challenges and solutions as features rather than artistic limitations," Janet remarks.

Janet has gained public recognition for her art in recent years. As a recipient of the Guggenheim Fellowship, Harvard Loeb Fellowship, Aspen Institute Henry Crown Fellowship, and Fulbright Sr. Lectureship, in 2014, Janet received the Smithsonian American Ingenuity Award in Visual Arts, honoring "the greatest innovators in America today."

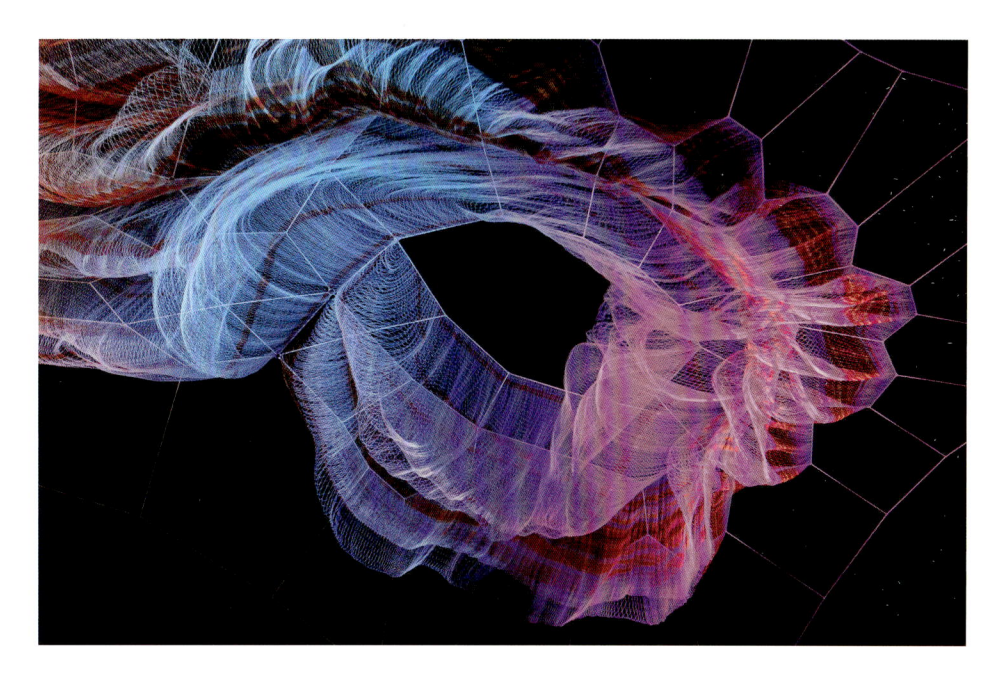

1.8 London

Earth Time series is a project that Janet has been working on for the last eight years. It includes a set of sculptures that focus on people's concept of time. The number within the title (1.26, 1.78, and 1.8) refers to the number of microseconds that the day was shortened when a single earthquake shifted the planet's mass, thus speeding up the earth's rotation of one day. It calls upon people's complex interconnectedness with larger cycles of time and the systems of the physical world. In *1.8 London*, the soft, voluminous net sculpture surged 180 feet through the air between buildings above Oxford Circus, the busiest pedestrian area in all of London.

Photography: **Ema Peter** | Material: **Fiber, colored lighting** | Location: **London, UK**

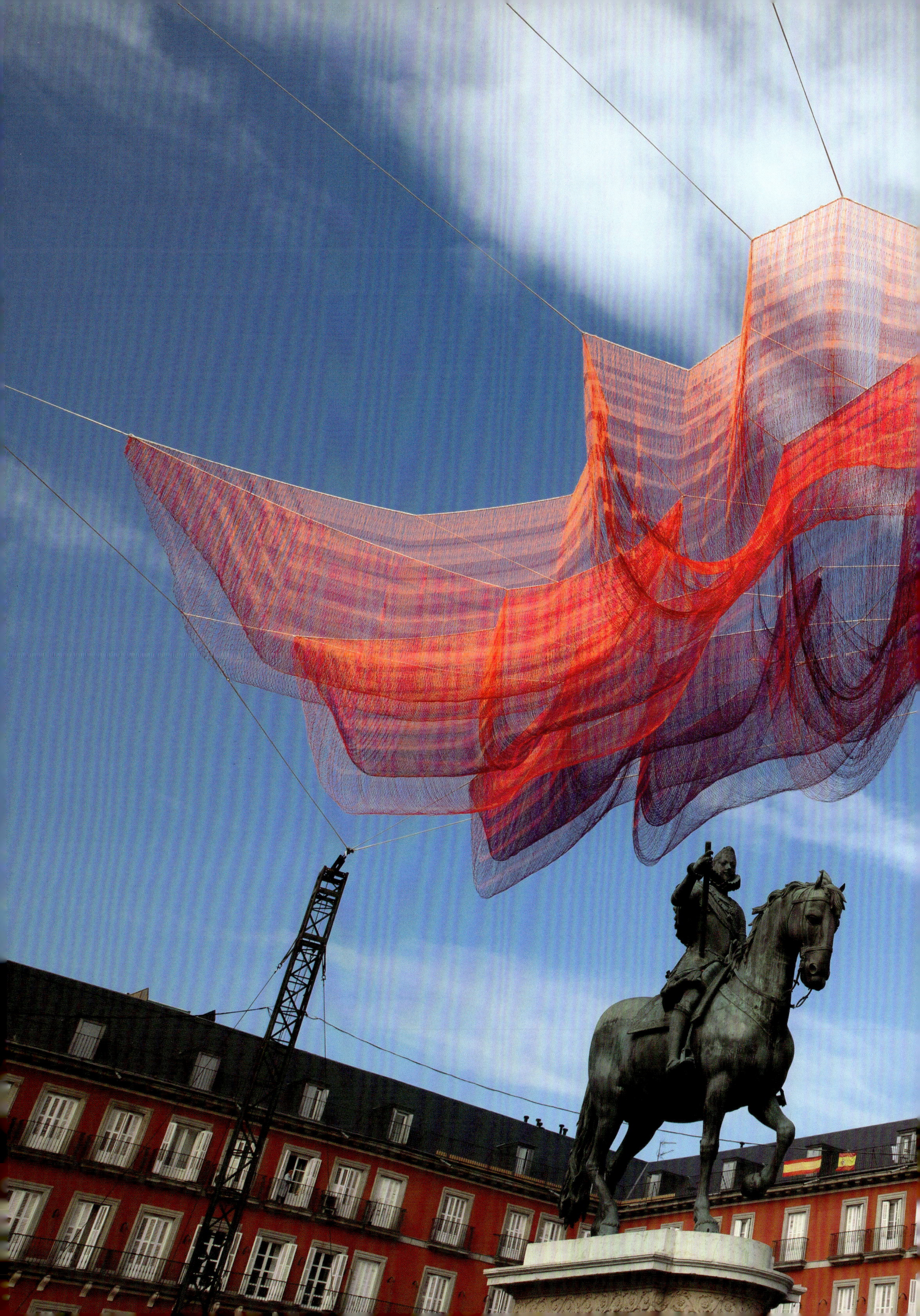

1.78 Madrid

The City of Madrid celebrated the 400th anniversary of the Plaza Mayor with a commission by Janet Echelman that explores the cycles of time. As part of her *Earth Time* series, the Madrid sculpture reminds the viewers of the many periods of time at various scales, ranging from a single day to the past four centuries when people have gathered in the Plaza Mayor. When anyone element in the sculpture's network moves, every other element is affected, suggesting people's interconnectedness with larger cycles of time.

Photography: **Joao Ferrand**
Material: **Fiber, colored lighting**
Location: **Madrid, Spain**

1.26 Durham

The concept of the artwork stems from the series of *Earth Time*: the interconnectedness of human beings and the natural world. At night, the sculpture came to life with projected colored light. The precise colors and patterns were created interactively based on the involvement of the pubic members, who were invited to use their smartphones to select colors and tap out patterns with the touch of a finger. The patterns were projected onto the monumental surface of the sculpture, creating ripple effects for all to see.

Photography: **Melissa Henry (upper photo), Matthew Andrews (bottom photo)**
Material: **Fiber, colored lighting**
Location: **Durham, UK**

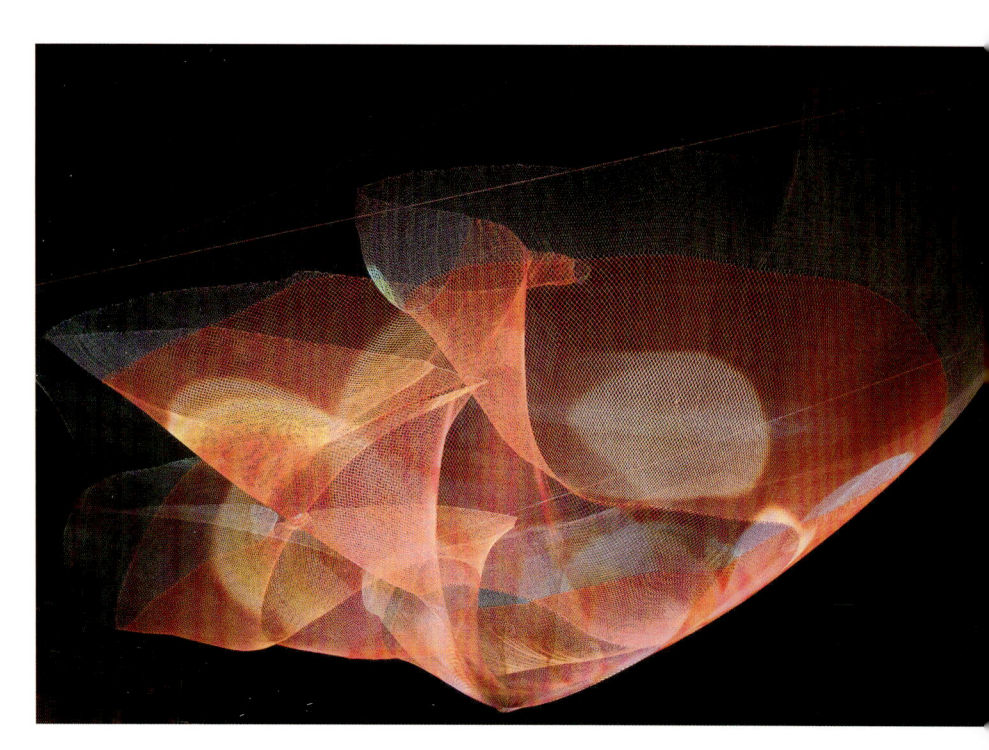

Dream Catcher

Inspired by dreams, this artwork on the Sunset Strip in West Hollywood is constructed with four horizontal structural layers suspended between two hotel towers. Between these structural layers float colorful sculptural elements that combine tensioned and draped form. These forms were inspired by the mapping of brainwave activity during REM (Rapid Eye Movement) sleep.

Photography: **Benny Chan** | Material: **Fiber, colored lighting** | Location: **West Hollywood, California, USA**

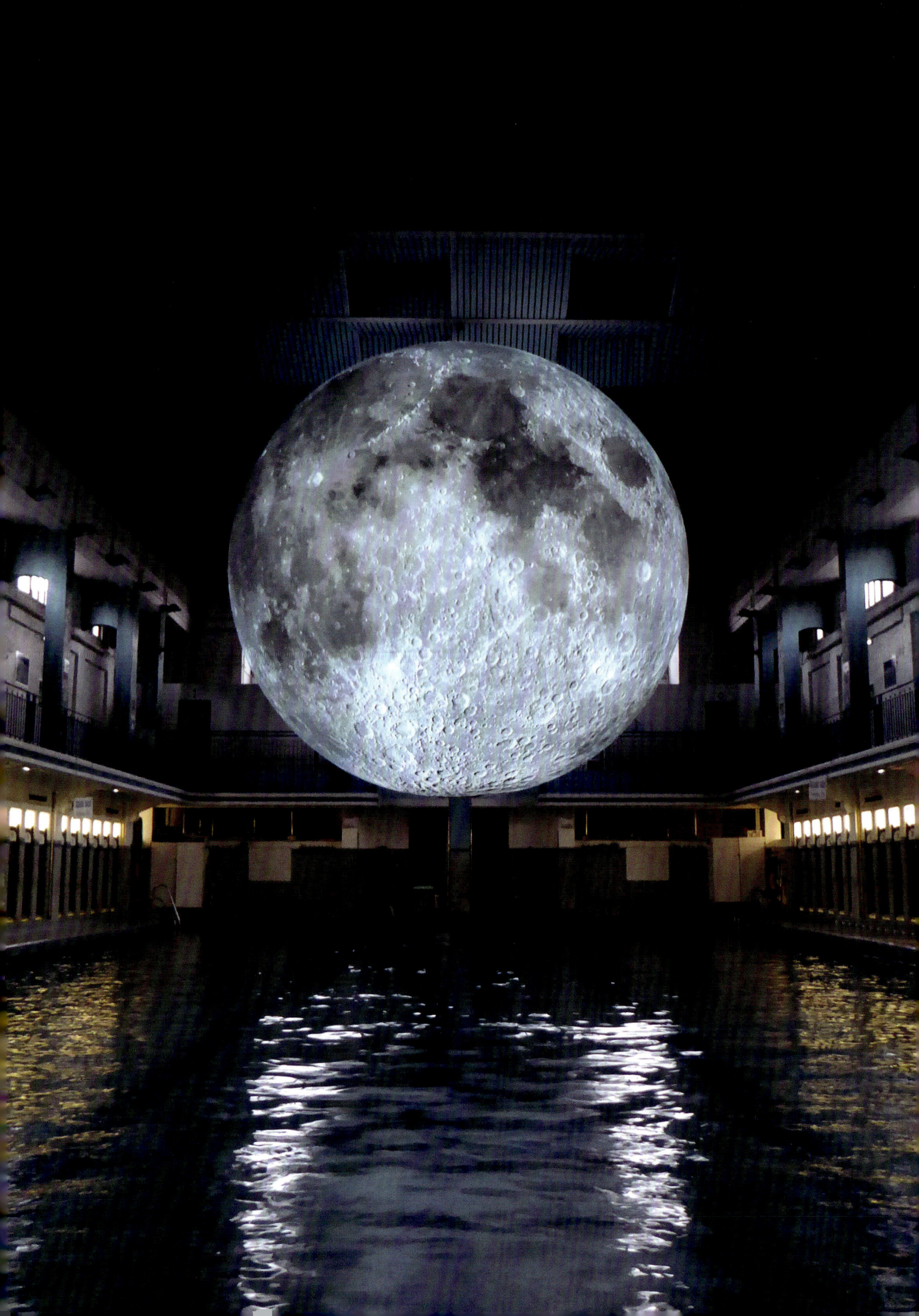

"It's been wonderful to witness the public's response to the artwork. Many people spend hours with the Moon exploring its every detail. Some visitors lie down and moon-bathe. At the Natural History Museum, a man in a suit came up to me in tears. He explained how he was a space scientist from the European Space Agency and had spent his career studying the surface of the Moon. I hugged him, and he left the exhibition a very happy man! In Leicester, one young girl asked, 'Will you put the Moon back afterward?' She thought I had stolen the real Moon! I reassured the young girl that I would definitely return the Moon after the exhibition."

Luke Jerram

Artist
Sculptor

Luke Jerram is a British installation artist. His multidisciplinary practice involves the creation of sculptures, installations, and live arts projects. Living in the UK but working internationally since 1997, Luke has created many extraordinary art projects which have excited and inspired people around the globe. Portrait photo by the National Environment Research Council.

A Closer Look at Space: Interacting with the Moon and the Earth

British artist Luke Jerram is known globally for his innovative arts practice and large-scale public artwork. With many of his artwork in permanent collections, including the Metropolitan Museum of Art in New York City and the Wellcome Collection in London, he also tours his art installations at art festivals and museums worldwide.

Luke has created many well-received public works of art that leave space for the public to interact with one another and participate in a communal shared experience. Since 2008, his celebrated street pianos installation *Play Me, I'm Yours* has been presented in over 70 cities and been enjoyed by more than ten million people worldwide. This art project created a global movement of pianos being installed in public places around the world by organizations and individuals, for people to play and enjoy. The concept (of street pianos) has now become part of the world's culture. In 2014, his giant installation *Park and Slide* made international headline news, creating 500 news stories reaching an estimated one billion people worldwide. As a consequence of the success of this artwork, several commercial companies sprung up (not affiliated with Luke Jerram), installing temporary waterslides in cities throughout the United States, Europe, and Australia.

Museum of the Moon is one of Luke's latest art projects that have caught the public's imagination, which so far has been presented in different ways, more than 100 times in 30 different countries. Luke had the idea to create the *Museum of the Moon* some 15 years ago, but it was only until very recently that the date for generating the Moon imagery was made available by NASA. "As a child, I always wanted a telescope so I could study the Moon and the night's sky. Now with my own Moon, I can fly there, study every detail, and share this experience with the public. We can explore the far side of the Moon, which is never visible from the Earth," remarks Luke.

Measuring seven meters in diameter, the moon features 120 dpi detailed NASA imagery of the lunar surface. At an approximate scale of 1:500,000, each centimeter of the internally lit spherical sculpture represents five kilometers of the Moon's surface. The installation is a fusion of lunar imagery, moonlight, and surround sound composition created by BAFTA and Ivor Novello award-winning composer Dan Jones. Luke has been working with Dan for over 15 years, commissioning him to create music for a number of his art installations.

Following *Museum of the Moon*, Luke created another critically acclaimed touring artwork called *Gaia*. Created in partnership with the Natural Environment Research Council (NERC), Bluedot, and the UK Association for Science and Discovery Centres, *Gaia* premiered at the Bluedot Festival in July 2018. Measuring seven meters in diameter, *Gaia* features 120 dpi detailed NASA imagery of the Earth's surface. With this artwork, Luke hopes to create a sense of the overview effect, a term and concept coined in 1987 by author Frank White. The concept transforms astronauts' perspective of the planet and humanity's place upon it.

Common features of the experience are a feeling of awe for the planet, a profound understanding of the interconnection of all life, and a renewed sense of responsibility for taking care of the environment.

The artwork is 1.8 million times smaller than the real Earth, with each centimeter of the internally lit sculpture describing 18 kilometers of the Earth's surface. By standing 211 meters away from the artwork, the public will be able to see the Earth as it appears from the Moon. Over its lifetime, *Gaia* will be presented in many different ways, both indoors and outdoors. Whether *Gaia* is displayed in a museum, science center, or parkland, the experience and interpretation of the artwork will change.

Learning from each artwork and moving on, Luke is continually reinventing his art practice. Over time, however, narratives connecting these different artworks have emerged and continue to evolve. Many of Luke's most successful artworks leave space for either the public, curators, or other artists to be creative. He builds and manages specialist teams of engineers, craftsmen, and technicians to help him realize his works, from composers to glassblowers, medieval musicologists to hot air balloonists. In this way, he says, "I'm only limited by my imagination in what can be produced. Anything is possible."

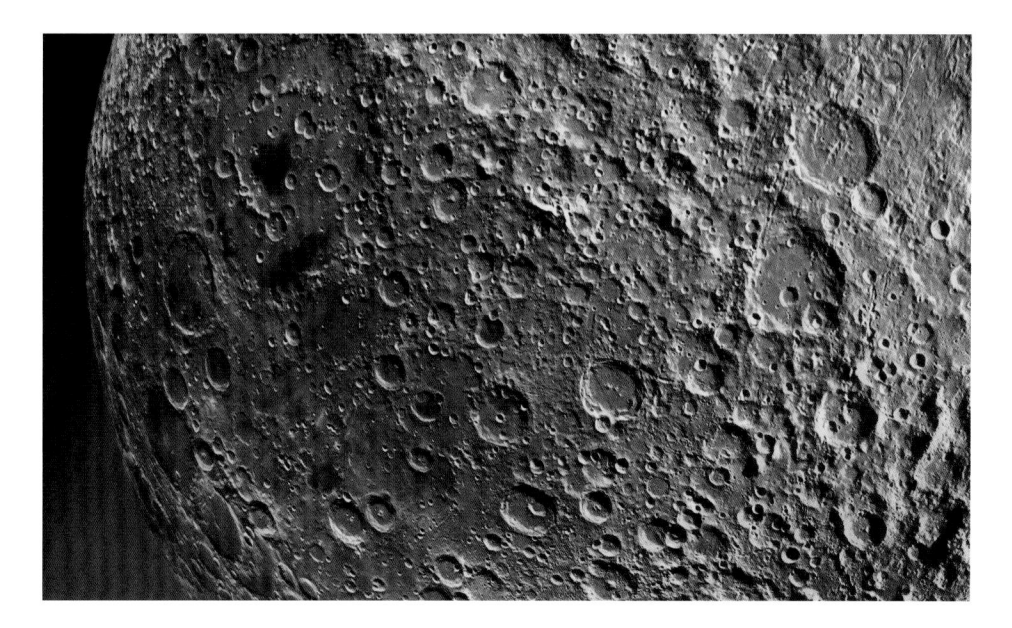

Museum of the Moon

Measuring seven meters in diameter, the Moon features 120 dpi detailed NASA imagery of the lunar surface. At an approximate scale of 1:500,000, each centimeter of the internally lit spherical sculpture represents five kilometers of the Moon's surface. It has been presented so far in different ways, more than 100 times in 30 different countries.

Photography: **Luke Jerram (photos on page 056, 058–059), Andrea Cherchi (photo on page 060–061)** | Material: **Nylon balloon** | Location: **Worldwide**

Museum of the Moon at Milanosport, 2019. Photo by Andrea Cherchi.

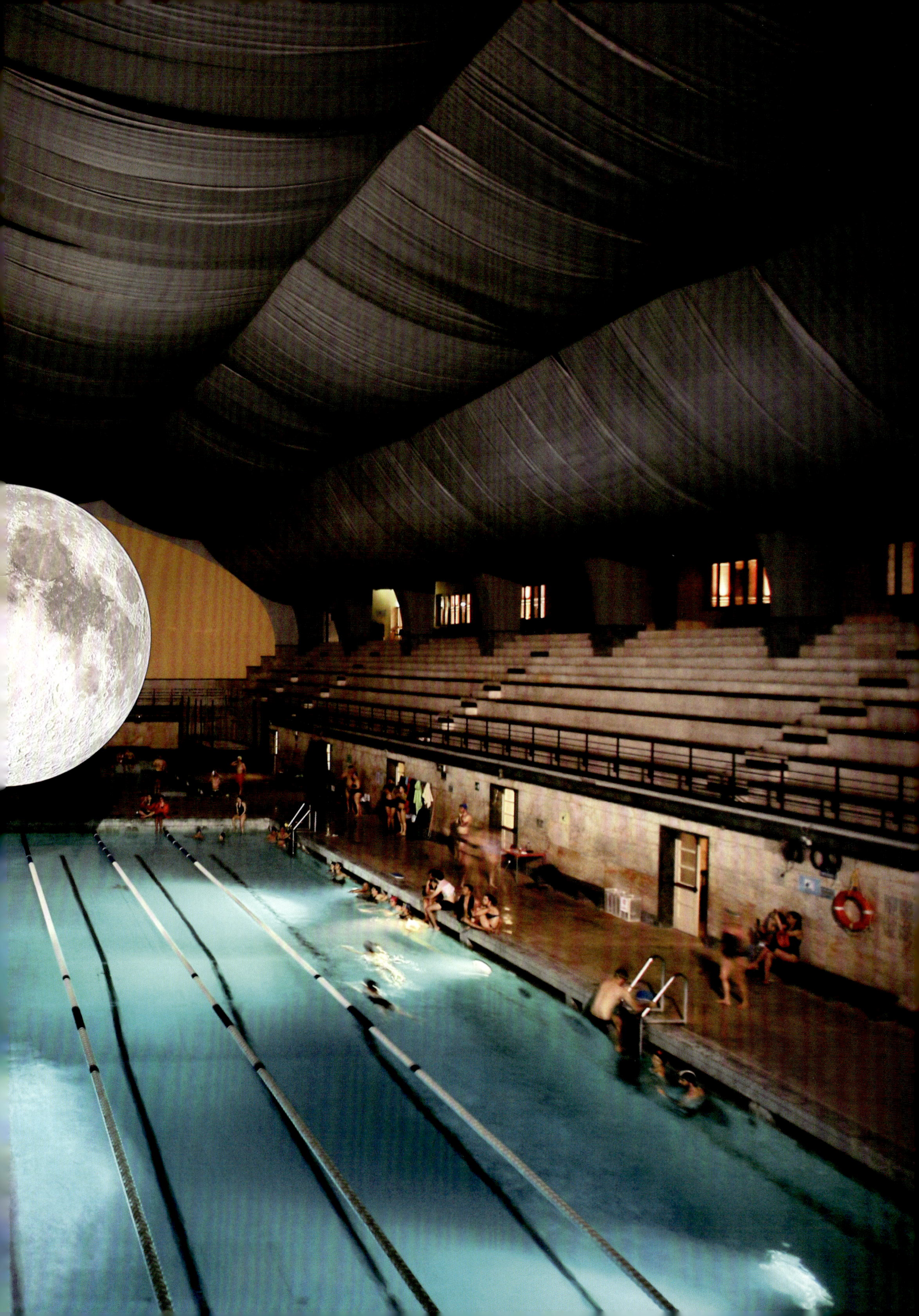

Gaia

Measuring seven meters in diameter, *Gaia* features 120 dpi detailed NASA imagery of the Earth's surface. The artwork is 1.8 million times smaller than the real Earth, with each centimeter of the internally lit sculpture describing 18 kilometers of the Earth's surface. By standing 211 meters away from the artwork, the public will be able to see the Earth as it appears from the Moon. Over its lifetime, *Gaia* will be presented in many different ways, both indoors and outdoors. Whether *Gaia* is displayed in a museum, science center, or parkland, the experience and interpretation of the artwork will change.

Photography: **Luke Jerram** (photo on page 062, upper photo on page 063), **The Hype Factory** (bottom photo on page 063) | Material: **Nylon balloon** | Location: **Worldwide**

· 063 ·

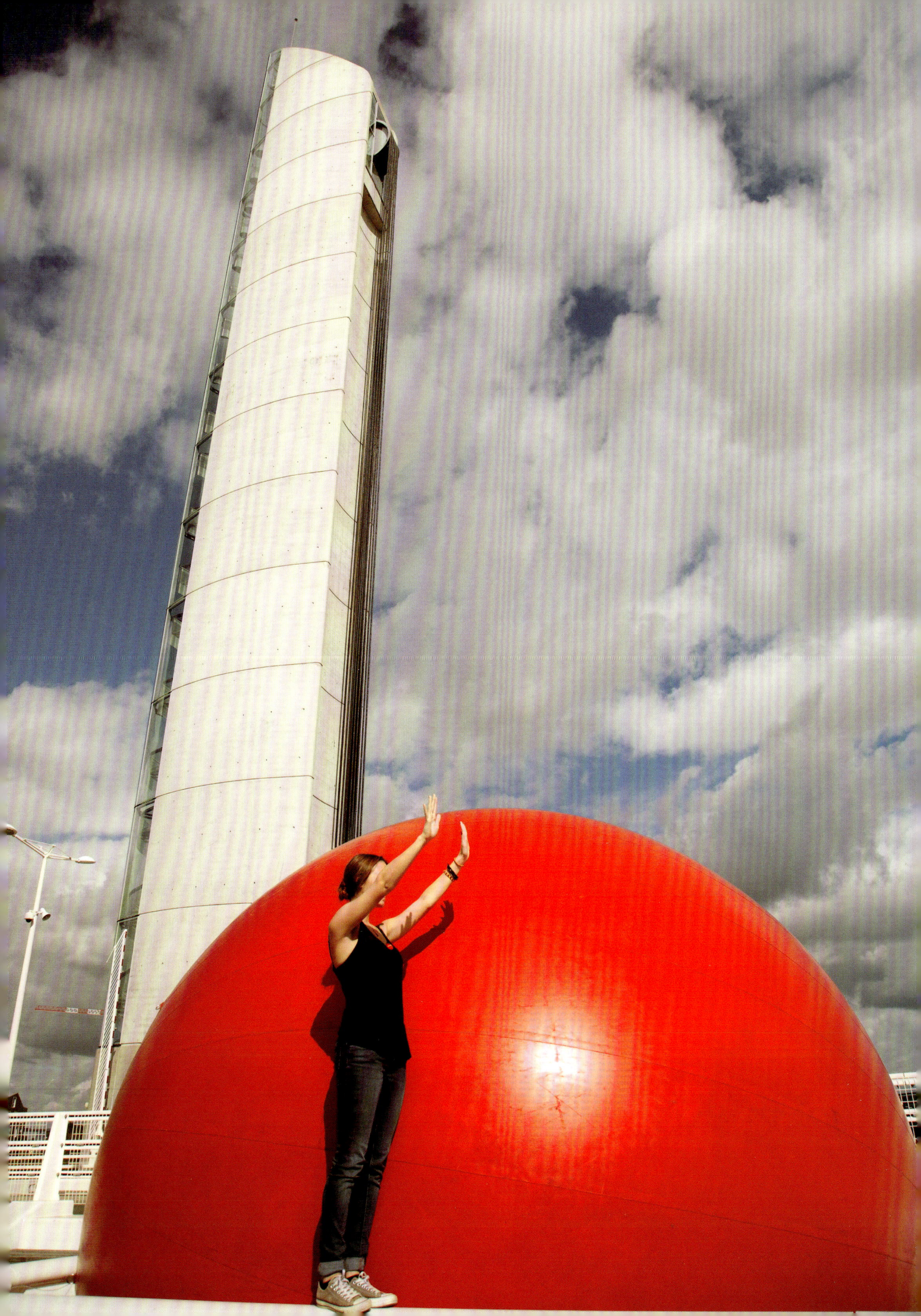

"As RedBall travels around the world, people approach me on the street with excited suggestions about where to put it in their city. At that moment, the person is not a spectator but a participant in the act of imagination. I've witnessed this from people young and old, from diverse cultures, speaking hundreds of languages across continents—all naturally responding to RedBall's invitation. That invitation to engage, to collectively imagine, is the true essence of RedBall. The larger arc of the project is how each city responds to that invitation and, over time, what the developing story reveals about our individual and cultural imagination."

Kurt Perschke

Artist

Kurt Perschke is an artist who works in sculpture, video, collage, and public space. His most acclaimed work, *RedBall Project*, is a traveling public art project that has taken place worldwide and received a National Award from Americans for the Arts Public Art Network.

RedBall without Borders:
An Invitation to Imagination

Growing up in Chicago, a city with abundant architectural legacy, Kurt Perschke was always interested in building things with his hands, although his family was not artistically focused. From his childhood, his mother's first ambition for him was to be an architect, but Kurt was personally bent towards visual aesthetics. In the end, being an artist came to him as a natural choice. Now, Kurt is an artist renown for his iconic work, *RedBall Project*, with which he plays with architecture, space, and interact with a wide range of audience.

The first *RedBall* was born in 2001 in St. Louis, but it was in 2002 in Barcelona that it finally carried its current concept and traveled around the world. It has been to many cities, such as Abu Dhabi, Taipei, Perth, England, Barcelona, St. Louis, Korea, Portland, Sydney, Arizona, Chicago, Toronto, and among others. *RedBall* has been avidly followed by the media, appearing in thousands of media outlets, including magazines, television, newspaper, and radio.

The *RedBall* made of PVC fabric weighs 120 kilos (250 lbs), unpacked, and measures 4.6 meters (15 ft.) high. When *RedBall* is not on tour, it stays in its big red crate in Kurt's studio, waiting for the next city. When Kurt prepares for *RedBall's* journey, he travels to each city far in advance to find the sites. "The selection of sites is the creation of the artwork. The ball is only an object; the performance is the joining of "site + audience" to it. As a process, I go to each city, a year in advance usually, and literally walk and bike along the streets. I carry a camera, a sketchbook, and a laser meter and go exploring a city, getting very lost, over and over," explains Kurt.

In making a public work, Kurt is very conscious of the history of sculpture in public places, its origins in monuments, and how that leads—for better or worse—into a perception of what public art should be today. Kurt believes that the urban environment is overbuilt and full of possibilities, and the project is about seeing and playing with the sculptural spaces of a city. "The humor and charisma of the piece allow it to access to the city and invite others into its story." Kurt continues, "I think it is essential for public work to do more than be 'outdoors'—it needs to live in the public's communal imagination." Ultimately, Kurt considers that art is about people. That is why he always aspires to see how each city responds to the invitation *RedBall* offers. "The project is not about a ball; it's about what the combination of the site, the piece, and everyone's energy creates together in that day," says Kurt.

In addition to *RedBall*, Kurt creates modern dance set designs for the Kate Weare Company in New York City. He has completed commissions for several institutions, including the Barcelona Museum of Contemporary Art, the Vienna Technical Museum, and the Contemporary Art Museum St. Louis. His video work has been screened in Europe, the US, and at the Bronx Museum of the Arts during his time for the Artist in the Marketplace (AIM) program.

RedBall Project: Bordeaux

RedBall Project: Bordeaux was presented by the Novart International Festival in Bordeaux. It started from Opéra de Bordeaux and traveled to other amazing sites throughout the city.

Photography: **Brit Worgan** | Material: **PVC fabric** | Location: **Bordeaux, France**

RedBall Project: Bordeaux. Photo by Brit Worgan.

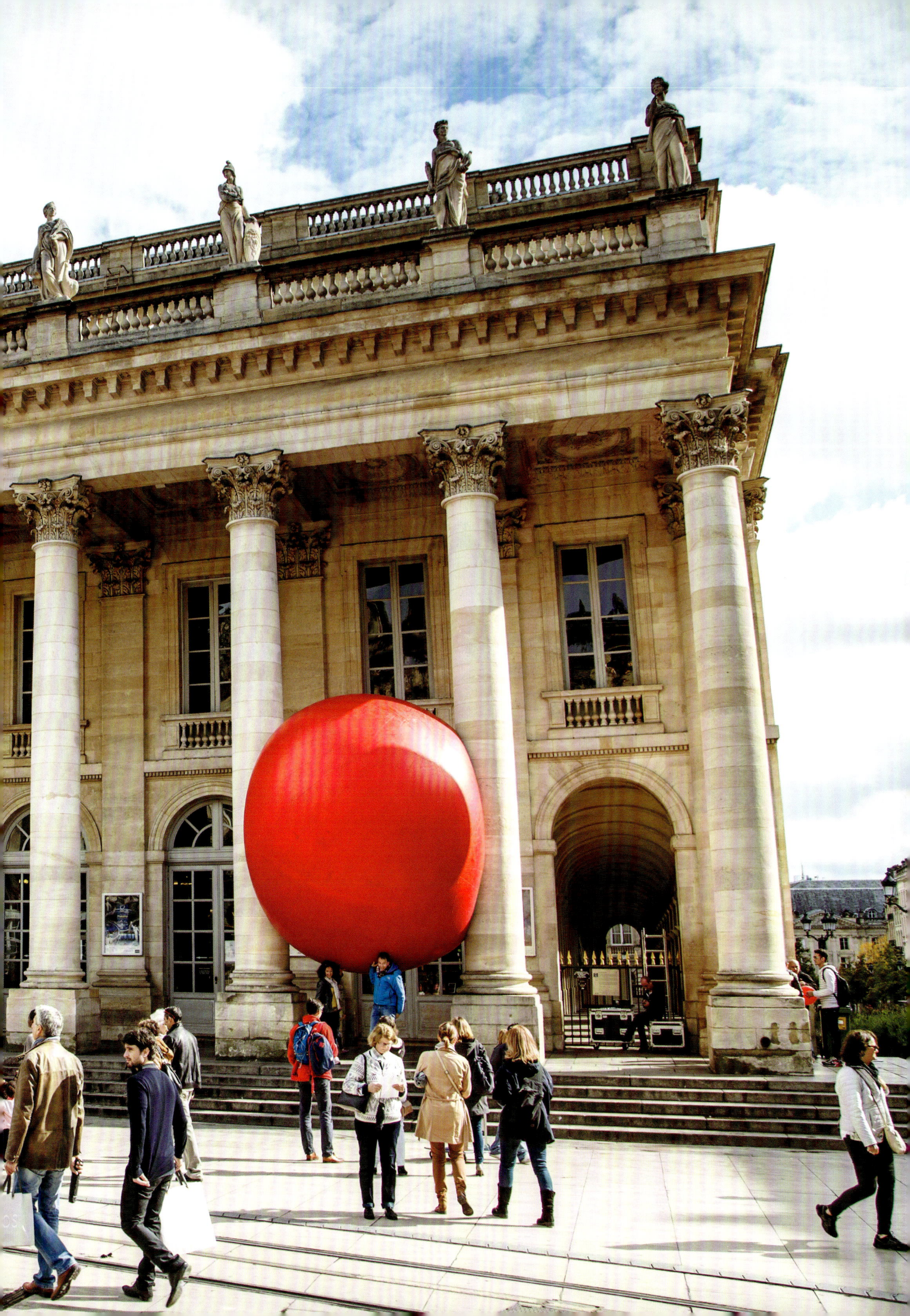

Interview with Kurt Perschke

What drew you to create RedBall? When and where was the first time RedBall enter the public spaces?

I was given the opportunity to develop an idea for one of three sites in St. Louis through the Art in Transit Program (AIT) in 2001. I kept coming back to this ugly area underneath an overpass with a bit of gravel on the ground. It had clearly been offered up because it was one of those leftover spots in a city, but I was drawn to the way the concrete bridge merged into the earth and the compressed space it created. RedBall came out of my musing about that space, and how to create an experience for others of what I was seeing.

Was it your intention to make it a long-term and traveling project? What motivated you to keep it on?

The piece was first installed in St. Louis on September 9th, 2001, but how it exists now was born in Barcelona the following summer. I mapped the city for locations and then installed it on the streets of Barcelona illegally with some friends. We kept moving the RedBall to a different site each day over a week.

A few years after the work was launched, I was told I needed to end it. These were well-intentioned art world insiders who used the calendar of art fairs as a framework. I made a decision that I would serve the work, rather than focus on how the work would serve my career. It was clear to me RedBall grew stronger as it built its story, so I decided to see where that would lead.

Is it hard to select a location for RedBall when it comes to a new city? What do you take into consideration when choosing the site?

What I am looking for is a collection of sites that together create a shared experience for the audience. Some sites offer architectural excitement or history; others are at a nexus of pedestrian energy. I am always hunting for great sun and the chance for surprise. When I did my first international commission in Sydney, I walked the city for a month! Now I'm a bit quicker.

RedBall Project: Roppongi

It was *RedBall's* premiere in Tokyo, Japan, presented by Roppongi Art Night Executive Committee in collaboration with the Mori Art Museum in Tokyo. Landing in the nightlife center of Tokyo for an expected audience of over 500,000 is a fantastic introduction of *RedBall* to a Japanese audience.

Photography: **Brit Worgan** | Material: **PVC fabric** | Location: **Tokyo, Japan**

How do you think RedBall affects the people who look at it or interact with it?	The humor and charisma of the piece allow it access to a city and invites others into its story. I think it is essential for public work to do more than be "outdoors"—it needs to live in the public's communal imagination. I do seek to create that experience, but I don't wish to mediate it.
Any cities that you'd like RedBall to visit in the future? Why?	There are so many places to explore. I learned a lesson in Norwich, England, at the Norfolk & Norwich Festival (NNF). The best experiences of the work are not always found in the shiniest spots but the most connected communities.
	I do dream of working in places where diverse cultures mesh together in daily life and the physical environment of the city. Istanbul and Singapore are two examples that I hope to work in someday. Still, I don't doubt that I will get the chance to discover through *RedBall* a fantastic city or town I haven't even thought of yet, but more importantly, a great audience.

RedBall Project: Fargo

Fargo may be known for the movie, but the arts and culture destination continues to roll. Plains Art Museum and Minnesota State University Moorhead teamed up with Kurt Perschke to bring the *RedBall* to Fargo (ND) and Moorhead (MN). The seven-day installation traversed the cities, bringing attention to its history, people, and geography. The project was truly collaborative with a diverse group of sponsors, including Fargo Arts and Culture Commission, Minnesota State University Moorhead, Insight to Action, Fargo-Moorhead Convention and Visitors Bureau, Fargo Parks District, and Plains Art Museum.

Photography: **Brit Worgan** | Material: **PVC fabric** | Location: **Fargo, North Dakota, USA**

RedBall Project: Antwerp

Kurt and his team were invited by Zomer van Antwerpen to bring *RedBall* to Antwerp as their last city of the 2016 season. Zomer van Antwerpen is an amazing festival that runs all summer, and *RedBall* was part of the grand finale of 2016.

Photography: **Brit Worgan**
Material: **PVC fabric**
Location: **Antwerp, Belgium**

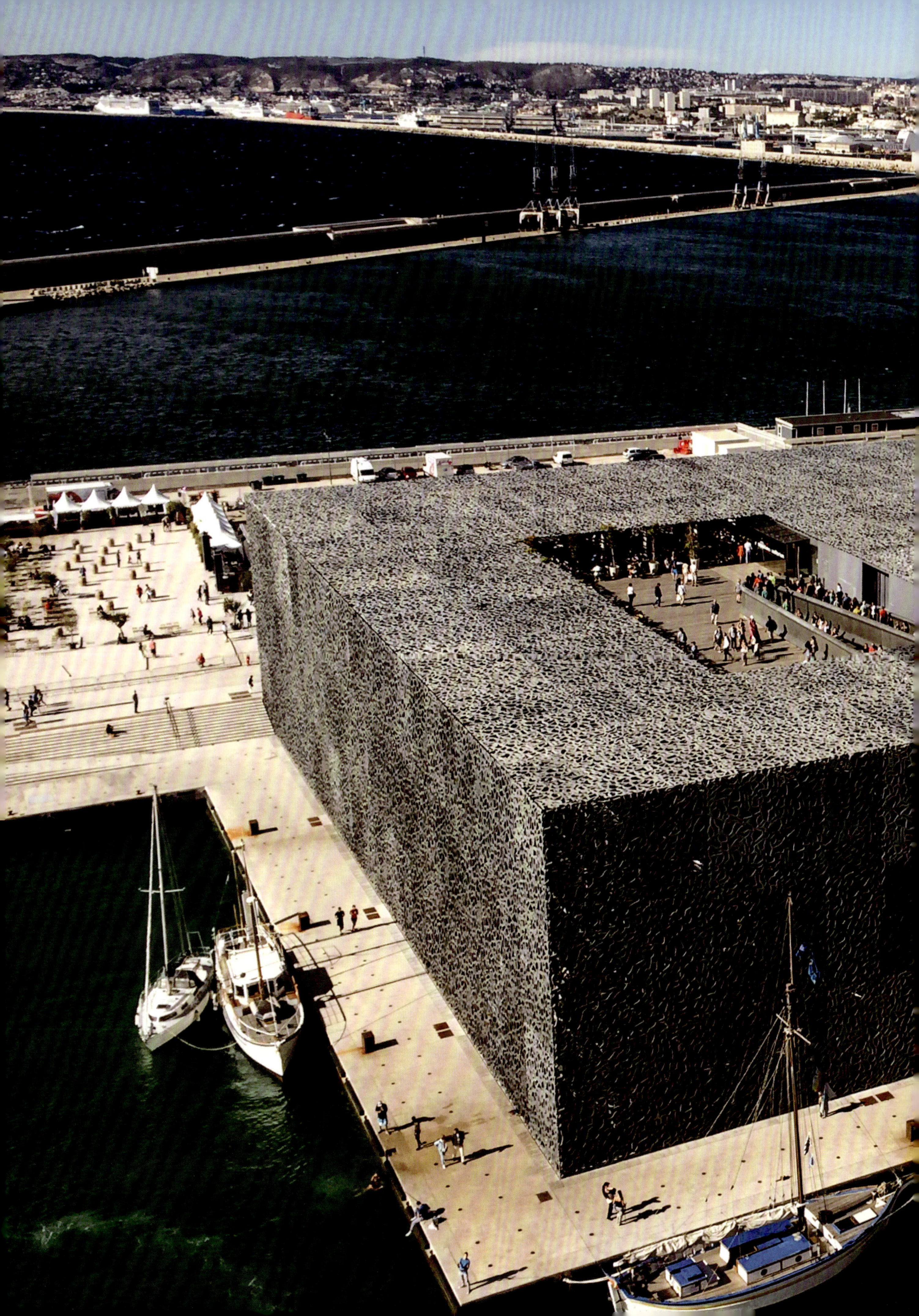

RedBall Project: Marseille

Presented by Lieux Publics, *RedBall* was chosen by Pierre Sauvageot, art director at Lieux Publics, the French national center for art in public spaces in Marseille, to be part of 2015's Travellings Festival in Marseille, and to lead into the IN SITU gathering of European artists and curators. IN SITU is the European platform for artistic creations in public spaces led by Lieux Publics. *RedBall Project: Marseille* made its debut at the top of the MuCEM, the Museum of European and Mediterranean Civilisations.

Photography: **Brit Worgan** | Material: **PVC fabric** | Location: **Marseille, France**

ANS CETTE EGLISE 1566 M DE SALES
AYANT PAS D'ENFANT VINT DEMANDER
A DIEU UN FILS QUI FUT S FRANCOIS
DE SALES LE 8 SEPTEMBRE 1614 TANDIS
QUE LE SAINT EVEQUE PONTIFIAIT UNE
OLOMBE BLANCHE DESCENDIT SUR LUI

"We feel that work in the public sphere should give you what a consumerist experience cannot. More and more, our identities and our shared experiences with others revolve around consumption and commercialism. What we buy as consumers is an indication of our individual tastes (and our means), and this form of conspicuous consumption has become a way for society to stratify itself along economic lines and into silos of like-minded identities. Art in the public space has the potential to counteract this pattern and bring people together. As such, we feel it should have a broad appeal, invite interaction, and ultimately provide people with a communal experience."

Behin Ha

―
Artists
Architects
―

Behin Ha is an architectural design studio founded by Behrang Behin and Ann Ha in 2009. Based in the New York City area, the studio works with a variety of scales and typologies, including ground-up buildings, interior renovations, and public art installations.

Public Work Matters: Bridging Differences and Building Connections

Both Behrang Behin and Ann Ha were born and raised in immigrant families. Ann was born to first-generation immigrants from Vietnam and grew up in Tampa, Florida, while Behrang immigrated to the US from Iran as a child and grew up in Teaneck, a New Jersey suburb of New York City. In many ways, their upbringing reflects the typical American immigrant story: hard-working parents, an emphasis on education, and a childhood that bridges between the culture of their origin countries and adopted homes.

They both wanted to be architects from a young age. Ann took a direct path and received a pure architectural education and background; Behrang took a detour into physics and engineering before becoming an architect. What drives them together is that they are both keen on building things. As an engineer, Behrang was once designing and building microelectromechanical devices, which required plenty of creativity but lacked connection to human experience and culture—a major reason that drove him to become an architect eventually.

Before they founded Behin Ha, they were working for architecture firms in New York City. From time to time, they took on specific projects and worked together as a team under the name of Behin Ha. Then the time was ripe for moving forward as they gave up their fulltime jobs and eventually dedicated themselves to their own studio. In addition to working together, they are married to each other and are now raising two children. As a married couple, they seem to be well aligned in their thoughts about design. "For every idea that we put out, we have made dozens of iterations that don't see the light of day. We rely on each other's critique for this culling and reformulating of design iterations," says Behrang.

As architects, they approach their work with the public realm in mind. Whether it is about how a private residence relates to and interacts with the street, or how a museum building promotes communal experience in its visitor spaces, their work relies on the notion of "the public" as a driving factor. In addition, they search out and receive opportunities to build temporary installations that operate directly in the public realm. These projects have been an excellent way for them to experiment with design ideas on much shorter time scales than a typical building project, and to see the public interact with their creations. "We feel that work in the public sphere should give you what a consumerist experience cannot." Behrang continues, "We feel it should have a broad appeal, invite interaction, and ultimately provide people with a communal experience."

One of their typical projects is *Living Pavilion*, which is a low-tech, low-impact installation that employs milk crates as the framework for growing a planted surface similar to a green wall. *Living Pavilion* aspires to create a synthesis of form, structure, light, and life. The pavilion's surface is planted with hanging shade-tolerant plants that provide an environment maintained at a cooler temperature through a combination of shading and evapotranspiration. The grounding point of *Living Pavilion* was to reconsider technologies such as green roofs and green walls, which are being integrated into the city to reduce the heat-island effect and mitigate stormwater runoff. While these technologies have a positive impact on the city's environmental footprint, they wanted to explore how they can also enrich the lives of city dwellers by adding a new dimension to the urban experience.

Growing up as beneficiaries of great public school systems with diverse populations, Behrang and Ann want to express their appreciation for public institutions, both in terms of the benefits they provide, and the role they serve as a common ground for building a civic society. "As adults, it's easy to forget who your fellow citizens are since our lives are so focused on the narrow silos of our day-to-day and the group of immediate friends and family we most associate with. It's within public spaces where one rubs elbows with strangers and gets this sense of shared and communal destiny. Public space reminds us that despite all our differences, we are all in the same boat," Behrang explains.

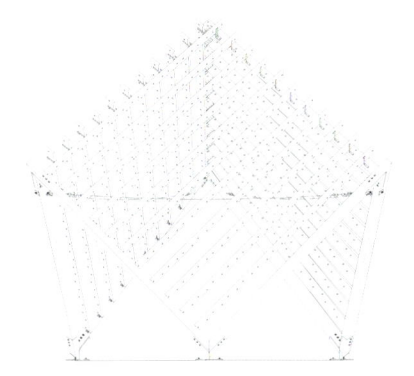

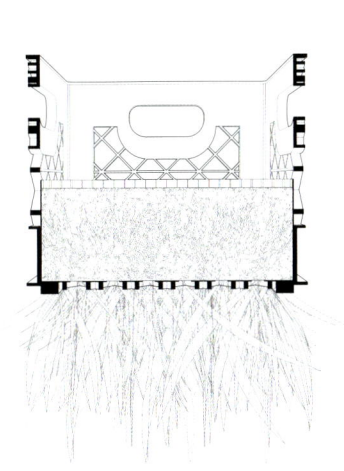

Living Pavilion: Annecy

Installed for the annual Annecy Paysages Festival, *Living Pavilion: Annecy* suspends an inverted garden overhead at the Notre Dame Plaza in the old city center of Annecy, France, with plants growing on the underside of a three-sided open wooden structure. The modular design allows the plants to continue growing elsewhere after the pavilion has been disassembled, and the pavilion to be regenerated in future years.

Photography: **Behin Ha** | Material: **Wood, plastic, growth medium, liriope plants** | Location: **Annecy, France**

Interview with Behin Ha

Do you have a philosophy that drives your work?

We are primarily an architecture firm focused on making thoughtful interventions in the built environment through the design and implementation of residential, commercial, cultural, and institutional buildings and interiors. We approach each project with an open mind and embark on a design process attuned to the project's specific and unique challenges.

In addition to conventional building projects, we have been fortunate to work on several temporary installation pieces. While the production of buildings is a very permanent undertaking, temporary installations, by nature, occupy the other end of the spectrum. These installation projects have been a liberating way for us to experiment with concept and form, without some of the contingencies that usually factor into a building project.

Whether it's a building project or a temporary installation, we are very much interested in how things are put together, and in the interplay of construction and assembly processes with built form and human experience. Though we don't feel that every project we do has to explore these issues, we find ourselves drawn to them frequently.

How do you get the concept to create Living Pavilion?

We are intrigued by the idea of using everyday objects and materials (the dairy crate in the case of *Living Pavilion*) in uncommon ways. It is a physical form of "hacking" that appeals to us in its unabashed pragmatism, which we feel is ripe for exploration. It is a way of "piggy-backing" onto existing manufacturing processes to build something of significant scale and complexity without the exorbitant costs of custom fabrication. It has the added benefit that a temporary structure made out of common, useful objects and materials can be reused or repurposed after the structure is disassembled. Perhaps more importantly, people automatically relate to instantly recognizable objects, and using these objects in unusual ways can encourage them to imagine possibilities lurking just beneath the surface of everyday life.

Coshocton Ray Trace

Behin Ha's *Coshocton Ray Trace* employs scrap material from a coated mesh fabric manufacturer to create a temporary installation at a community park in Coshocton, Ohio. The installation engages the community both by involving its members in its construction, and by creating an unexpected point of attraction near the town square. The bright orange color of the installation invites curious passers-by to come into and explore the park. The installation has also been used for various formal gatherings, including city council meetings and music performances.

Photography: **Brad Feinknopf**
Material: **Coated mesh**
Location: **Coshocton, Ohio, USA**

***Can you tell us the process of how you create the latest* Living Pavilion: Annecy?**

We were given an opportunity to adapt our *Living Pavilion* project to a new site in Annecy, France. We decided to keep the module of the planted crate but to explore a new structural and formal expression. We were intrigued by the hipped and gabled roofs in the historic city center and explored how the individual unit of the crate could be aggregated to create an enclosure that recalled that geometry. The design turns three sides of a 12 × 12 × 12 cubed assembly of crates on its corners to create an overhead enclosure with a planted surface underside. The corners which rest on the ground are offset towards the center, warping the faces of the assembly while keeping a linear structural frame.

How do you think your work affects people who look at it or interact with it?

We need to acknowledge the cultural and community organizations that are behind the public installation work we have done. The work can only be understood within the context created by these organizations. The first *Living Pavilion* was created for FIGMENT, a participatory arts organization that holds a festival every summer in New York City and elsewhere. The second *Living Pavilion* was designed for Bonlieu Scène Nationale Annecy as part of their annual arts festival in Annecy. *Coshcoton Ray Trace* was installed in Coshocton's ArtPark, the site of a burned-down hotel in a rural Ohio town, which was turned into a public park by the Pomerene Center for the Arts, a community arts organization. In each case, these organizations have cultivated a space for art in their communities, gathered the resources necessary to fund it, and created the context in which the public can interact with the work.

We mention these organizations because we feel that at the most basic level, public art is a barometer of the health of public space. It is a sign that organizations and institutions exist to invest in open space and cultivate a notion of the "public good." We have been fortunate to work within the space created by these organizations. Our hope for the work is that it appeals to a wide range of people, and in that sense, acts as a mutual experience for a diverse set of people and reinforces their relationship with public spaces. Additionally, we would like visitors to find the work approachable, but to also encourage visitors to dig a bit deeper than the first impression and be challenged by it.

Living Pavilion: Governors Island

The participatory arts organization FIGMENT joined forces with The Emerging New York Architects Committee of the American Institute of Architects New York Chapter (ENYA) and the Structural Engineers Association of New York (SEAoNY) to co-host a competition to design and install an architectural pavilion for the 2010 summer season on Governors Island. Behin Ha's *Living Pavilion* was selected as the winning entry. *Living Pavilion* is a low-tech, low-impact installation that employs milk crates as the framework for growing a planted surface similar to a green wall. It aspires to create a synthesis of form, structure, light, and life.

Photography: **Behrang Behin**
Material: **Wood, plastic, growth medium, liriope plants**
Location: **New York City, New York, USA**

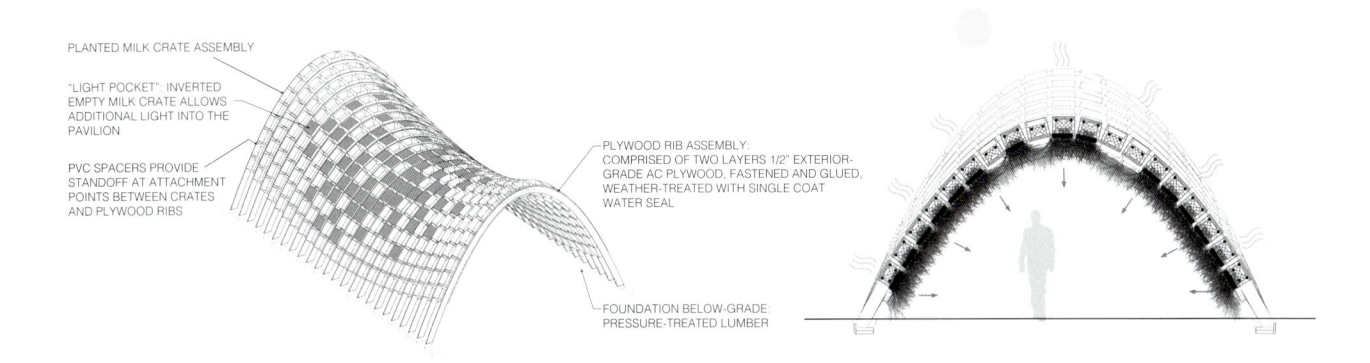

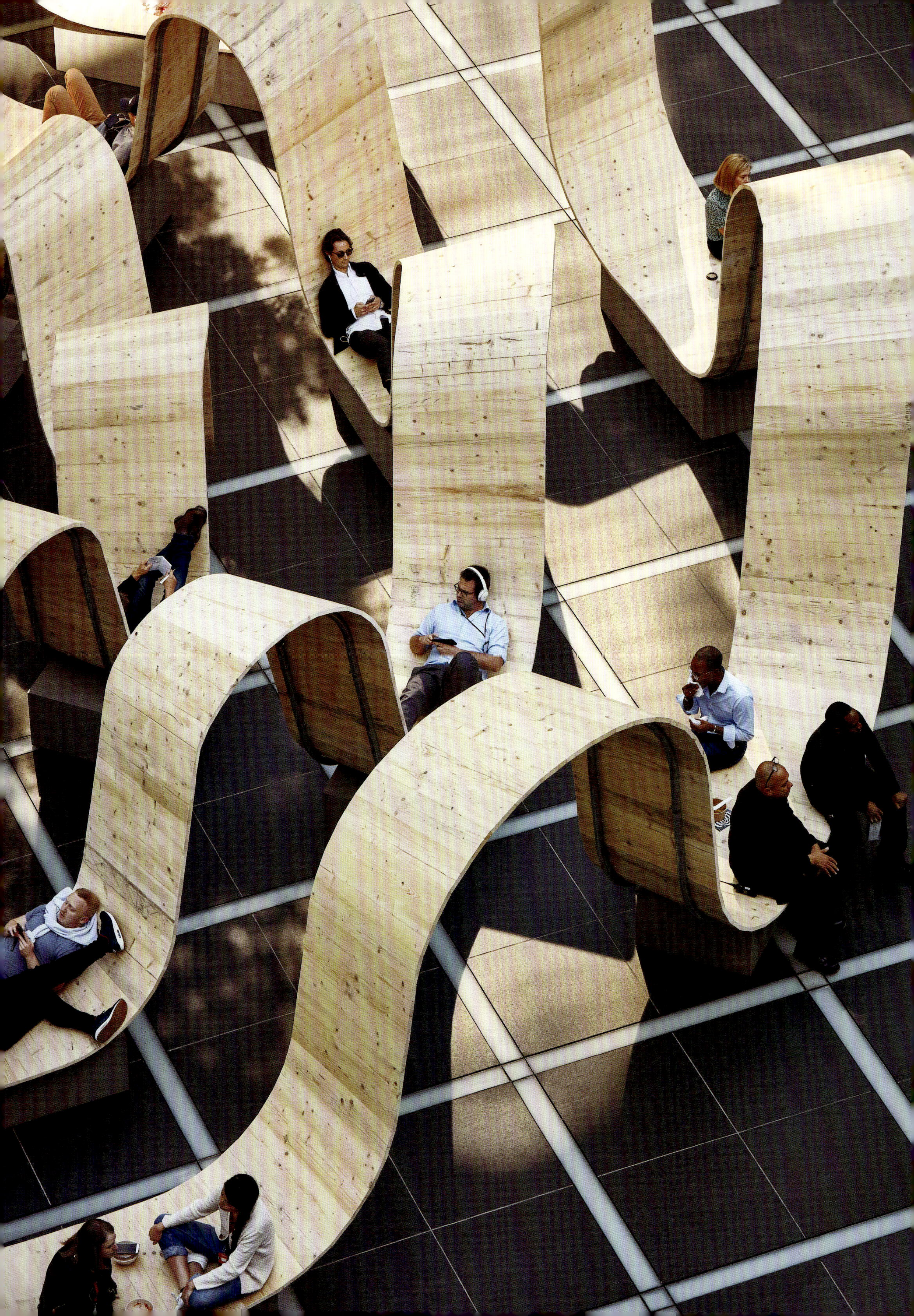

"I think it is important that people can talk about it and describe it—either in simple words or a more complex, poetic way. The other side is through photos and social media. For Please Be Seated, we were able to get up high and photograph it from the top down, which made for amazing images. But we also had some lovely photos capturing people chatting, kids enjoying it, and those images were equally as powerful. That said, creating something 'Instagrammable' is too obvious. If this is a project's only focus, you end up with something that looks good in a photo but lacks something when it comes to the human experience."

Paul Cocksedge Studio

—

Artist
Designer

—

Paul Cocksedge Studio was founded in 2004 by Paul Cocksedge and Joana Pinho. With a strong and dedicated team of collaborators, the studio has won national and international acclaim for its original and innovative design, underpinned by research into the limits of technology, materials, and manufacturing processes.

Design Is Not Set in Stone: Carry on Being Creative

Throughout his childhood, Paul Cocksedge had a lot of freedom since his family never steered him down one path. In his teens, he got a glimpse of what a creative career was like and started getting into design. "I think growing up with a family that was down to earth has been really beneficial for me, creatively speaking. It kept me aware that creativity and design should be helpful and create benefit and beauty for all kinds of people," recalls Paul. At secondary school, he was keen to design technology and graphic design and later moved on to art. Fascinated by science, he buried himself in physics and mathematics and enjoyed the fun of mixing different disciplines. He felt that there was a connection between art and science, rather than tension.

Paul learned the nuts and bolts of industrial design at Sheffield Hallam University and gained problem-solving skills. Later on, he attended advanced studies at the Royal College of Art (RCA), where he was surrounded by artists and designers who had a real thirst for what they were doing. He also met Joana Pinho at the RCA, who later became his business partner and co-founder of Paul Cocksedge Studio. After graduating from the RCA, Paul was on a roll, as he said. He made many projects and had lots of ideas in mind waiting to be realized. The idea of founding a studio became clearer and stronger. "I had no responsibility or money and nothing to lose. The only thing that made sense was to carry on being creative. After meeting my business partner Joana Pinho, we started to collaborate on projects and then co-founded the studio," explains Paul.

Paul and Joana are well-aligned in what they are doing. Rather than setting one fixed path for the studio, they endeavor to explore different paths and let them intertwined and united. Joana gives Paul the freedom to be creative and continue his creations while she focuses on the structure and business side of the studio. "It has been important for us that the studio doesn't compromise," Paul says, "and that we stay true to the things we believe in."

Since 2004, the studio has been working on projects across the world, dealing with a variety of different objectives, budgets, and regulations. A key feature of their work, in everything from product design and architectural projects to installations and sculpture, is a focus on simplicity and imagination in order to create unique people-centered designs. At the core of this focus lies an unrelenting attention to detail, a willingness to question previous assumptions about design, and an eagerness to take on a wide-ranging array of projects. Besides some notable projects like the studio's *KISS* installation that has traveled worldwide, Paul has created some impactful installations with his team in recent years, just to name a few, the landmark installation for London Design Festival 2019 called *Please Be Seated*, typographic installation for *Make Blood Cancer Visible Campaign, Spectrum* lounge for Swire Properties at Art Basel Hong Kong, and among others. To Paul, he holds a view that design is not just for a niche audience, but a chance to show that it can carry a message to the broader public. Their work attracts people not only by the ingenious design but the more profound concept within the project and a more humane view of the world.

Throughout the years, Paul Cocksedge Studio has collaborated with many big names, including V&A, London Design Festival, NHS, Swarovski, BMW, Hermès, City of Lyon, Wellcome Trust, Sony, and many more. In 2018, the studio was shortlisted to design the UK Pavilion at Expo 2020 Dubai. Paul has received a number of awards and prizes for his designs and is regularly invited to speak at key design events around the world.

Please Be Seated

Partnered with high-end interior company White & White London and Arup, Paul Cocksedge Studio created a landmark installation *Please Be Seated* for London Design Festival 2019 at British Land's Broadgate, located in the busy thoroughfare of Finsbury Avenue Square. It was designed as a rippling wave of wood rising to form arches for people to walk through, and curves serving as spaces for people to sit, lie, and relax. It is made from 1152 reclaimed scaffolding boards. Each one has been planed, sanded, and cut to become part of a series of huge curves and concentric circles.

Photography: **Mark Cocksedge** | Material: **Recycled wood planks, steel** | Location: **London, UK**

"The project solved the practical problem of creating an artwork that fills a public square and engages passers-by, without obstructing the space," says Paul.

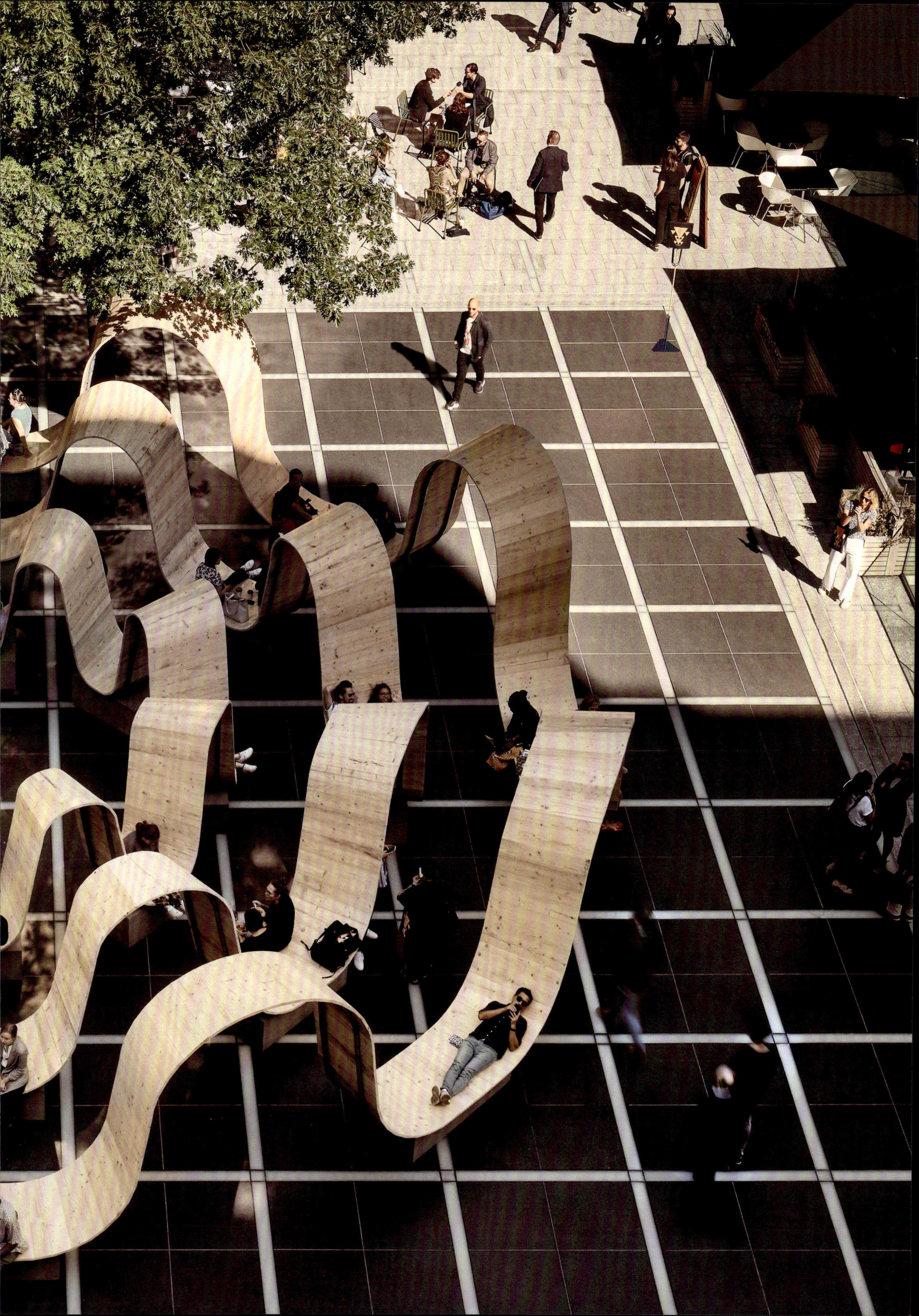

Interview with Paul Cocksedge

Do you have a philosophy that drives your work?

When you are creating something, you are pushing and pulling against a feeling that is hard to put into words. You know it is there, though, and you instinctively know if something works or not, if a composition is right, or if an idea makes sense. It is a silent voice inside you that moves you, and it feels like you are collaborating with something internal. There are complexity and beauty in that.

How do you think* Please Be Seated *affects people who look at it or interact with it?

The essence of this idea was about interactivity, on many different levels. We wanted it to be visually exciting, organic, and free-flowing to contrast the straight lines of the city architecture. Our phones are such a distraction from the physical world, and a piece like this really needs to be something you haven't seen before to keep your attention. It was all about tactility, getting people sitting together in a public space, relaxing, and looking at the sky.

How do you think can a temporary public artwork become significant and memorable?

I think it is important that people can talk about it and describe it—either in simple words or a more complex, poetic way. The other side is through photos and social media. For *Please Be Seated*, we were able to get up high and photograph it from the top down, which made for amazing images. But we also had some lovely photos capturing people chatting, kids enjoying it, and those images were equally as powerful. That said, creating something "Instagrammable" is too obvious. If this is a project's only focus, you end up with something that looks good in a photo but lacks something when it comes to the human experience.

Bourrasque

In this installation, Paul Cocksedge combined his interest in the nature and morphology of paper with a subject that has long been an essential element of his design work: light. Paul explains: "I have been fascinated for a long time by the various properties of light: How it emanates; how it diffuses, bends, reflects, and scatters." Designed for the City Council of Lyon, *Bourrasque* shows an acute sense of the role of technology in design, combined with a characteristic lightness of touch, with elegance and joy.

Photography: **Mark Cocksedge**
Material: **Electroluminescent material**
Location: **Lyon, France**

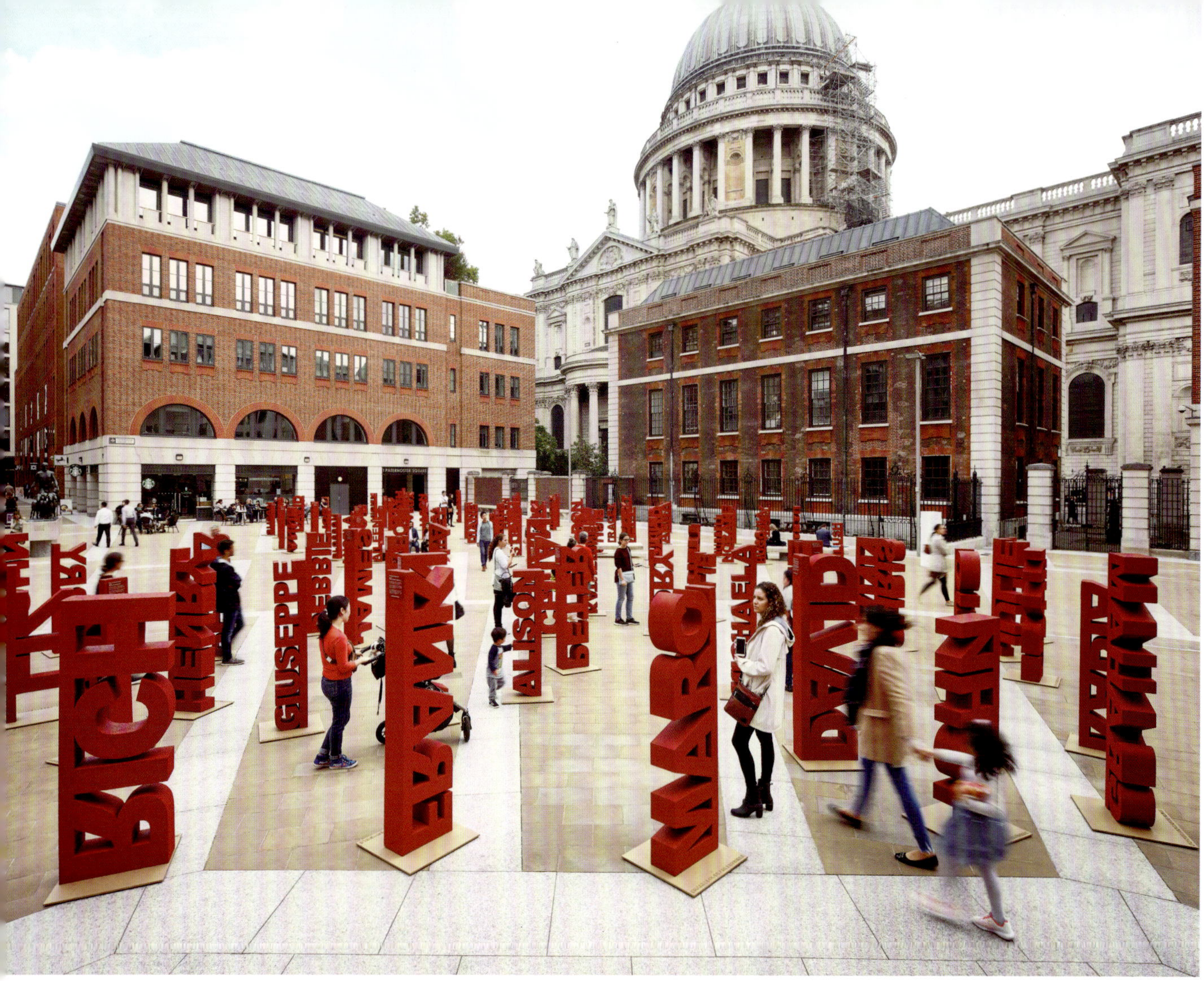
GIUSEPPE
ALISON
MARC
DAVID

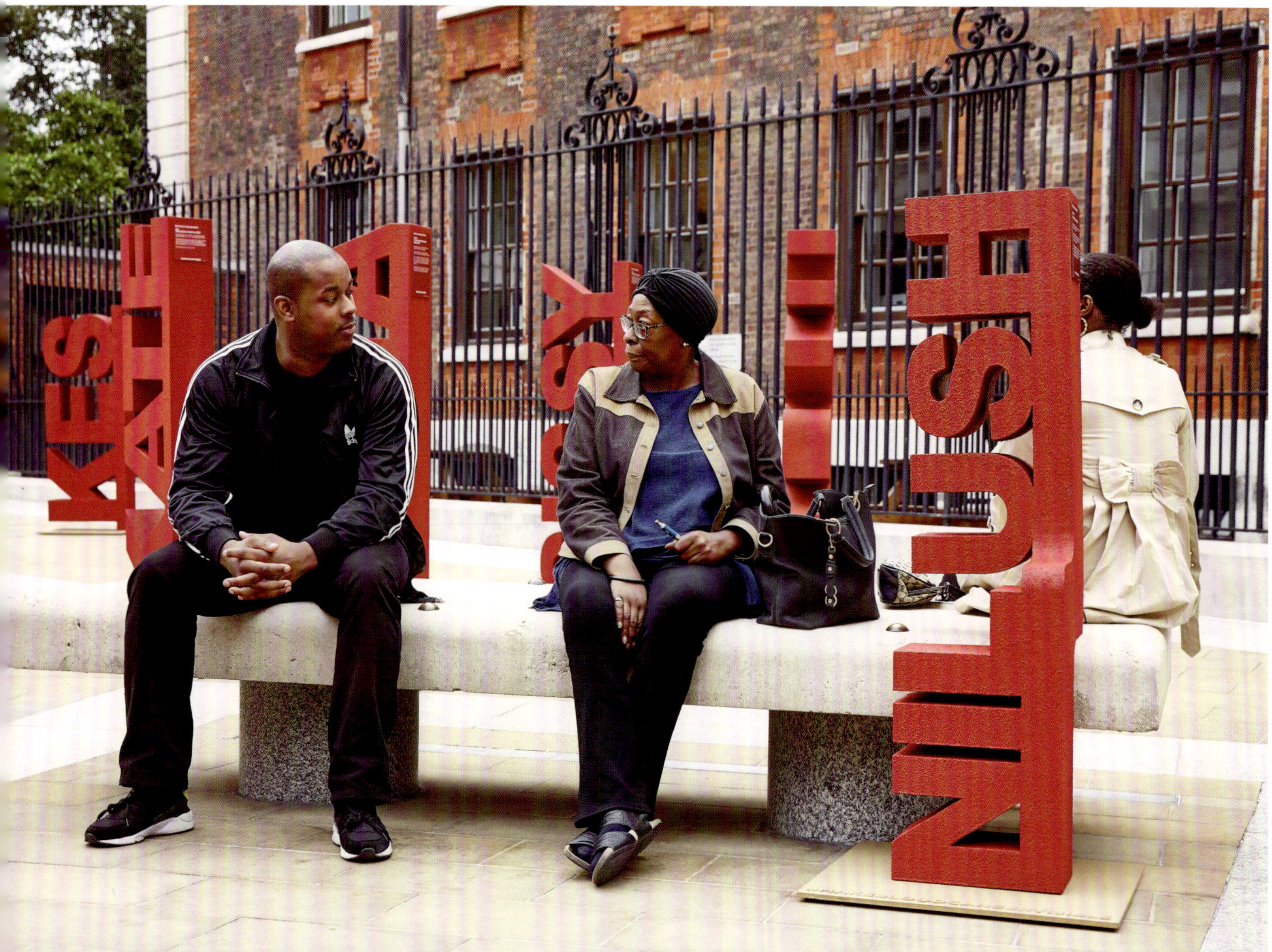

Where did you get the idea to express Make Blood Cancer Visible Campaign using typographic installations? What's been the public's response to this work?

It was an exciting project for us because it stretched the studio in a direction we are not used to. We were dealing with an incredibly emotional subject, but it also had positivity and hope in it. We had a statistic of 104 people being diagnosed with blood cancer every day, and we were thinking about how to illustrate that and show it to the public. It went beyond statistics and into emotion. Suddenly, the idea of the installation came about, where we took the name of a patient and turned it into this quite playful, sculptural installation in London.

When people saw it, they were running over and hugging their own name, and taking selfies, and on that level seeing it as something quite fun. Later on, they became intrigued by why it was there, and what the stories behind the names were—it became a totally different experience. That flipping of understanding is something I enjoy doing with our work. You think it is one thing, and it turns out to be something else.

Any artists whom you admire?

The late Ingo Maurer has always been a major influence for me, both creatively and personally, and I was hugely saddened to hear that he had passed away. I respect his uncompromising approach, as well as his warmth and kindness.

Any advice for newcomers in this field?

My advice for others would be not to compromise on your own creativity. Work out the ingredients and materials, and give yourself space to understand what you are about. Learn from your teachers, as well as the people you meet. Be open-minded and challenge yourself, and appreciate the early years of your creative journey as a place to experiment, succeed, fail, and everything else in between. The other thing is to remember that if money is holding you back, be inventive. There are value and worth in all kinds of things, not just expensive materials.

Make Blood Cancer Visible Campaign

To support the launch of the Make Blood Cancer Visible Campaign, Paul Cocksedge Studio designed a three-dimensional typographic installation comprised of 104 separate sculptures—giant names placed at intervals around the square, which together represented the 104 people diagnosed with blood cancer every day. Each monolith was the real name of someone who had been diagnosed and was sized to match their height perfectly. Individual stories were engraved into the sculptures, to raise public awareness of the experiences of those with blood cancer.

Photography: **Mark Cocksedge** | Material: **Polystyrene, steel** | Location: **London, UK**

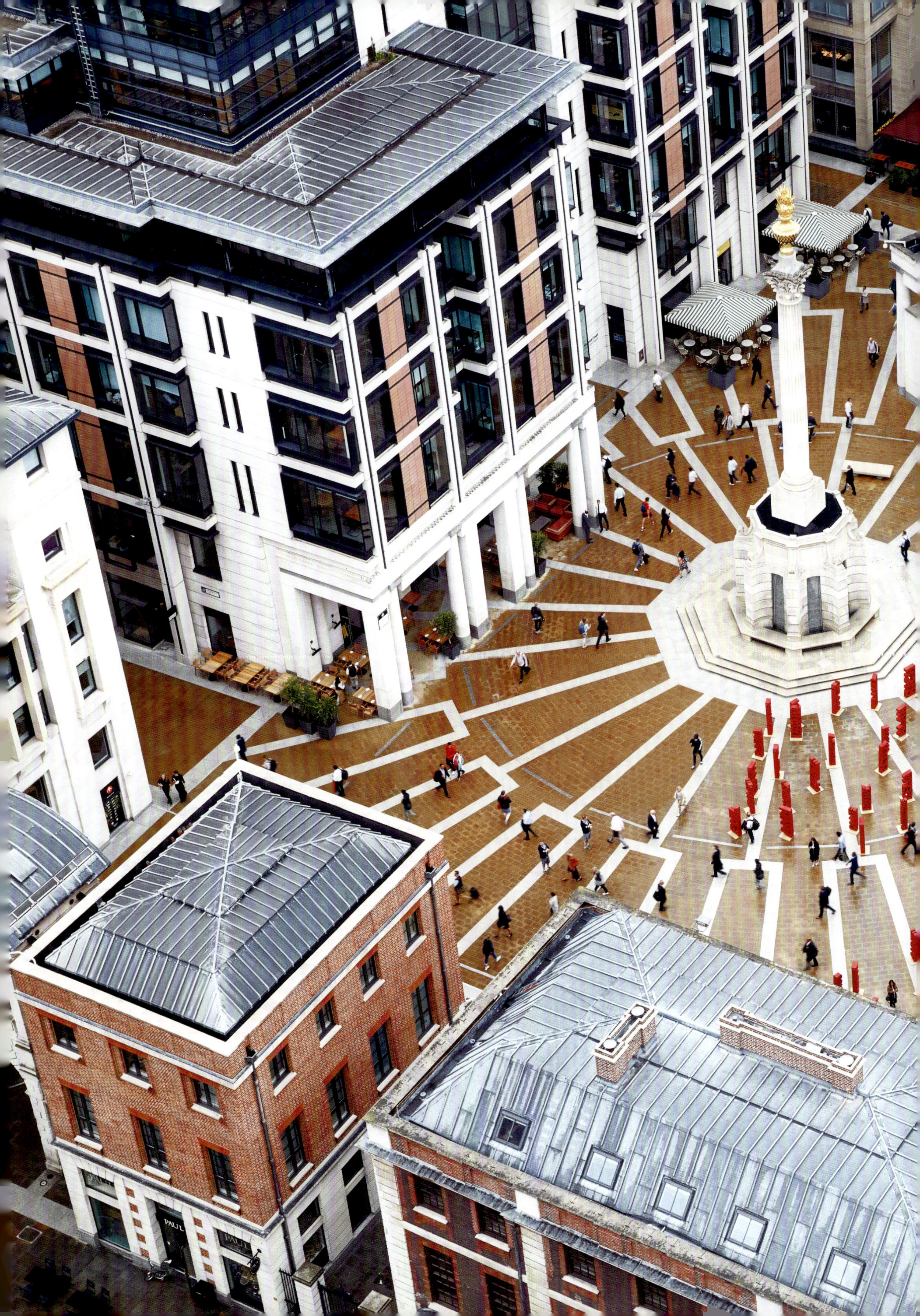

The installation was sponsored by Janssen UK and endorsed by Bloodwise, Leukaemia CARE, Myeloma UK, CLL Support Association, Waldenstrom (WM) UK, Anthony Nolan, MDS Foundation, Lymphoma Association, and CML Support. "We feel that this piece communicates in a way that is engaging, accessible, and, most importantly, leaves a lasting impact. It has also been an opportunity to use design to tell the stories of individuals who have experienced blood cancer and make sure they are shared with as many people as possible," said Paul.

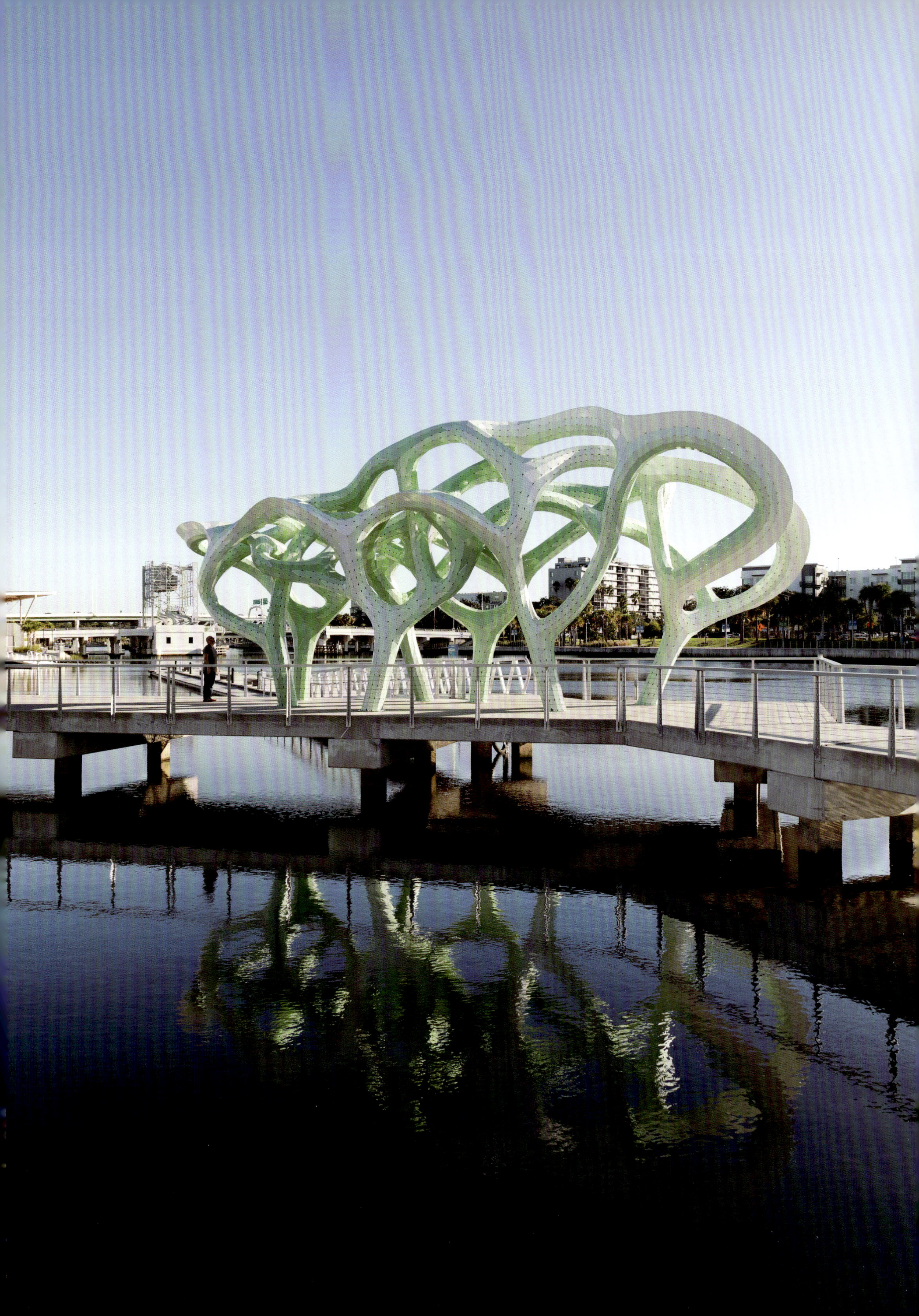

"Over the last ten years, we have designed and built a number of thin-shell pavilions and installations that push the limits of form, structure, and space. Somewhere between architecture and art, each public project aims to provide an otherworldly experience for its visitors, while also contributing to the visual identity and social life of its place."

THEVERYMANY

Architect

Marc Fornes, registered and practicing architect, leads THEVERYMANY, a New York-based studio specializing in large-scale, site-specific structures that unify skin, support, form, and experience into a single system. Their work is based on the belief that a public project creates meaningful experiences in a diverse audience.

The Beauty of Science: Creating Art with Codes

Born in Strasbourg, France, Mark Fornes grew up in this border city to Germany and was more likely to understand things from many sides and embrace different values. In the early 2000s, Marc worked at Zaha Hadid Architects (ZHA) as a project architect for an experimental Mediatheque in Pau, France. He directed the extensive material research and geometrical development to explore the largest self-supported carbon fiber shell to date. During his time at ZHA, Marc became fascinated with materials research and geometric forms, and to work out optimum solutions, he studied mathematics. With cumulative knowledge and rich experiences, in 2004, he founded his own studio, THEVERYMANY, in Brooklyn, New York City. He led a team of ten persons, exploring computational protocols and applying them to ever bigger and more complex curvilinear structures.

The name of THEVERYMANY comes from two simple things. "First, you can understand anything in nature or the built world if you break it apart and study its many elements. Second, the design process depends on a team, not one single person. Everyone is important, from the designer to the coder to the fabricator," Marc explains.

The design research of the studio is deeply rooted in the development of computational protocols and means of digital fabrication. It represents a body of research that continues to advance new parametric outcomes and implement complex techniques in architecture and beyond. Each project evolves previous inquiries and further investigates design though codes and computational protocols, addressing new ways to describe complex curvilinear self-supported surfaces into a series of flat elements for efficient fabrication.

Form of Wander

Commissioned by Hillsborough County Public Art, *Form of Wander* plants a winding structural network on a pier. Columns straddle the extension of the Tampa Riverwalk, inviting visitors to walk around and through it on a winding path. From the ground, these columns thrust upward into a tangle of branches, like the native mangroves which take root along Florida shorelines. Over the water, the piece becomes a floating, forest-like canopy, which provides shade and ambiance to those beneath and within. A moiré pattern of shadow and light projects through the lattice overhead to create a dynamic space at all times of the day.

Photography: **NAARO**
Material: **Painted aluminum**
Location: **Tampa, Florida, USA**

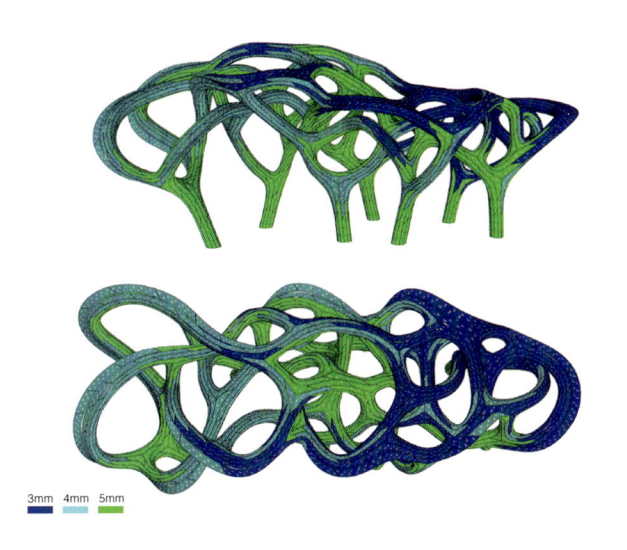

3mm 4mm 5mm

Over the last fifteen years, Marc has designed and built a number of organic, thin-shell constructions that push the limits of form, structure, and space. This body of work is situated between the fields of art and architecture, with a particular focus in the realm of public art. Each public artwork aims to provide a unique spatial experience for its visitors, while also contributing to the visual identity of a place and catalyzing community engagement.

The studio has invented and further developed "structural stripes," a building system by which custom-designed parts form complex, self-supporting curvilinear surfaces. Applying their unique approach to design, engineering, and construction, the studio has designed and built a collection of "crawling assemblies" across United States, Canada, and Europe. They are fantastical structures at a scale between art and architecture, which unify surface, structure, and spatial experience into a single system. Calling to mind different organic references depending on the viewer, the undulating, often brightly-colored structures craft unique spaces that manipulate light and their typical understanding of depth.

Some of these prototypical architectures have acquired and displayed by institutions and galleries, including the Centre Pompidou (Paris), where *Y/Surf/Struc* is part of the permanent collection, the FRAC Centre (Orleans, France), and the Storefront for Art and Architecture (New York City). Marc has also exhibited at the Guggenheim, GGG Art Basel Miami, Art Paris.

Marc has shared his research as a TED fellow, in public lectures and through academic appointments, artist residencies, and workshops. With Francois Roche, he co-founded "(n)Certainties," a graduate studio at Columbia University with visiting semesters at the University of Southern California and Die Angewandte in Vienna. He has taught at the University of Michigan, Princeton University, and Harvard Graduate School of Design with Patrik Schumacher, a partner at ZHA.

Marquise

Commissioned by the City of El Paso, *Marquise* transforms a standard building entrance into a spatial experience and visual icon. Gridded curvilinear petals comprise the brightly-colored canopy and its self-supporting structural system. This billowing structure opens up when it touches the ground, forming a seating area with benches and turning the entry into a welcoming social space. Marked by a two-way Cheshire gradient, the lightweight aluminum structure entirely transforms the approach and initial experience of its host building, the Westside Natatorium.

Photography: **NAARO** | Material: **Painted aluminum** | Location: **El Paso, Texas, USA**

101

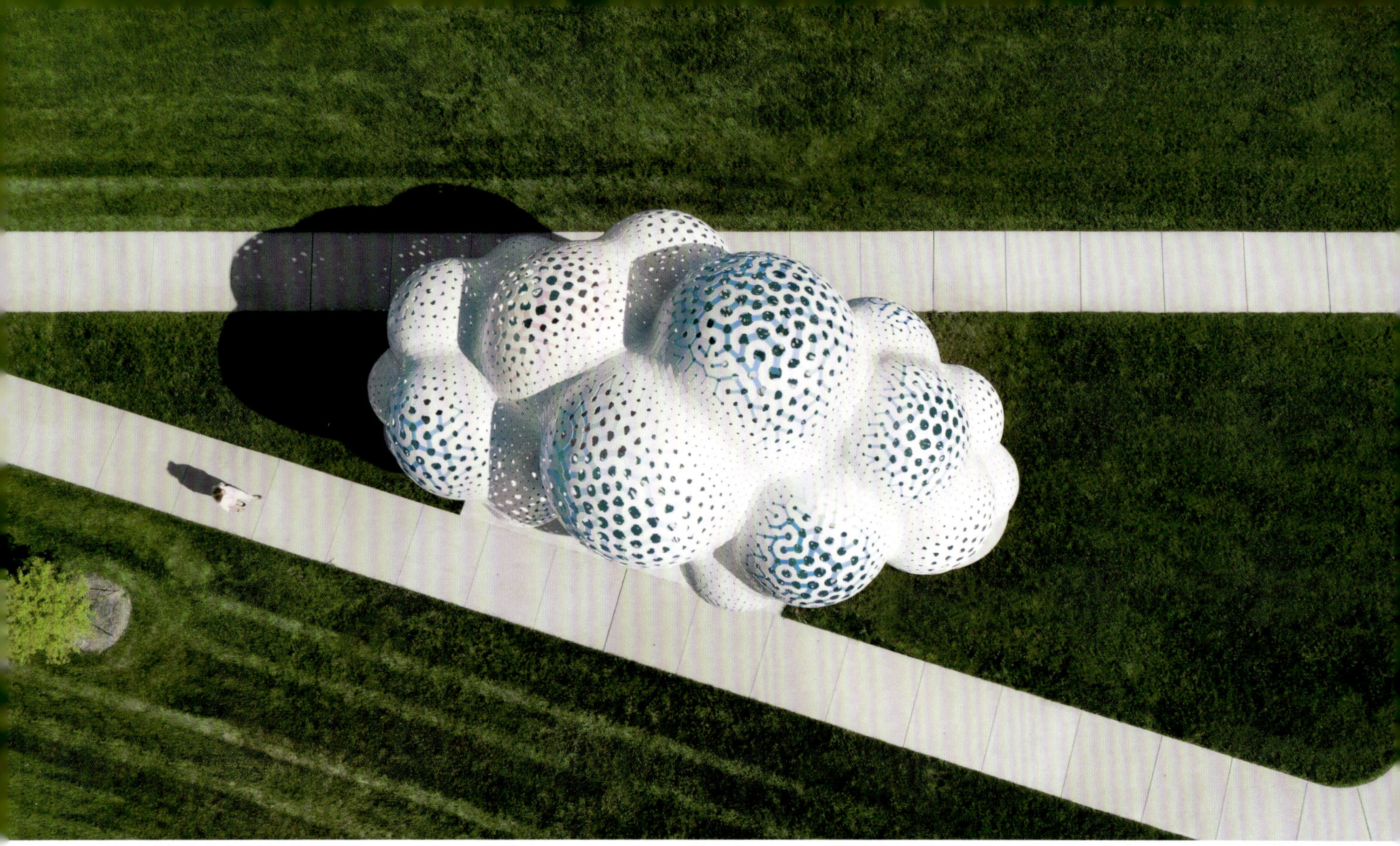

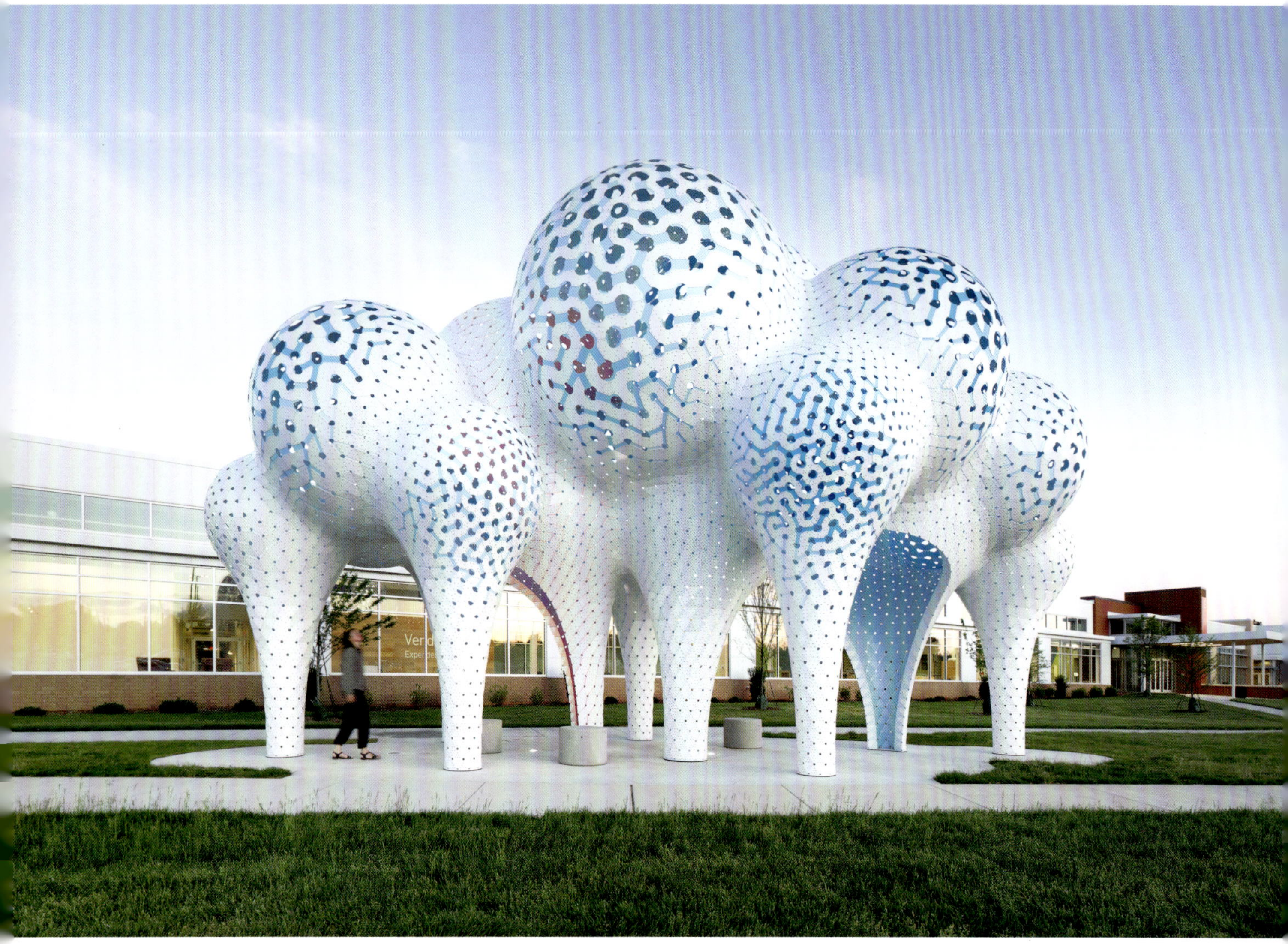

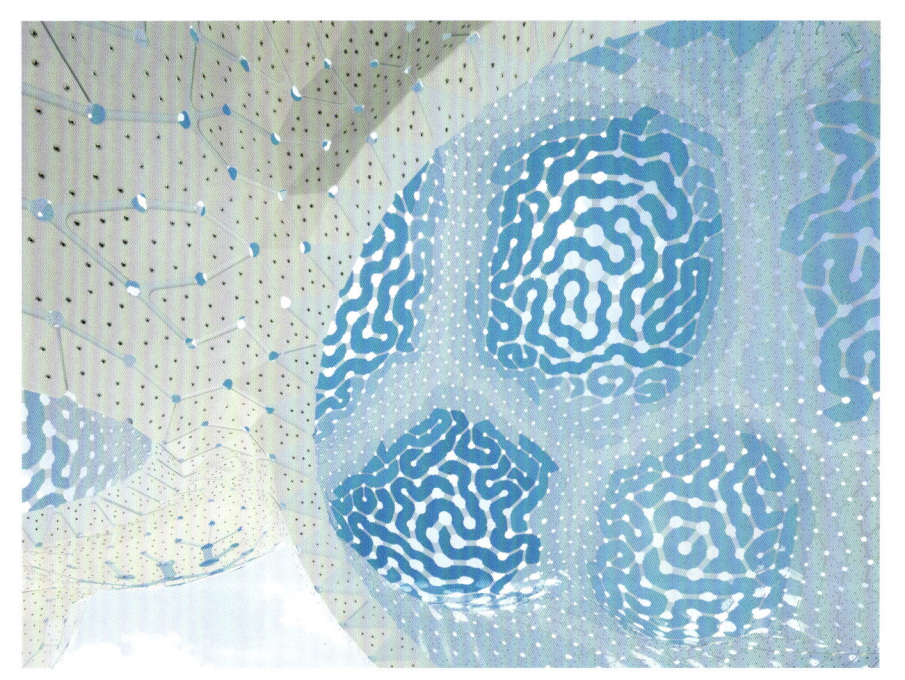

Pillars of Dreams

Commissioned by Mecklenburg County and Mecklenburg Public Art Commission and Arts and Science Council, this permanent pavilion for the Valerie C. Woodard Center is the stuff of dreams; its open volumes appear to be filled with air, yet the floating form is held up by a continuous structural skin in ultra-thin aluminum. A unique system of computationally generated "structural stripes" accumulates to produce an experiential veil that is also self-supporting. This labyrinthine arrangement of unique parts unfurls across the surface in two layers of three millimeters aluminum.

Photography: **NAARO**
Material: **Painted aluminum**
Location: **Charlotte, North Carolina, USA**

Minima | Maxima

Commissioned by Epazote Sa. Vladislav Sludskiy for World Expo 2017, three sandwiched layers of ultra-thin, lightweight aluminum stripes accumulate to create complex geometry, flowing form, and overwhelming spatial experience. These notions of efficiency model the theme of Expo 2017, "Future Energy."

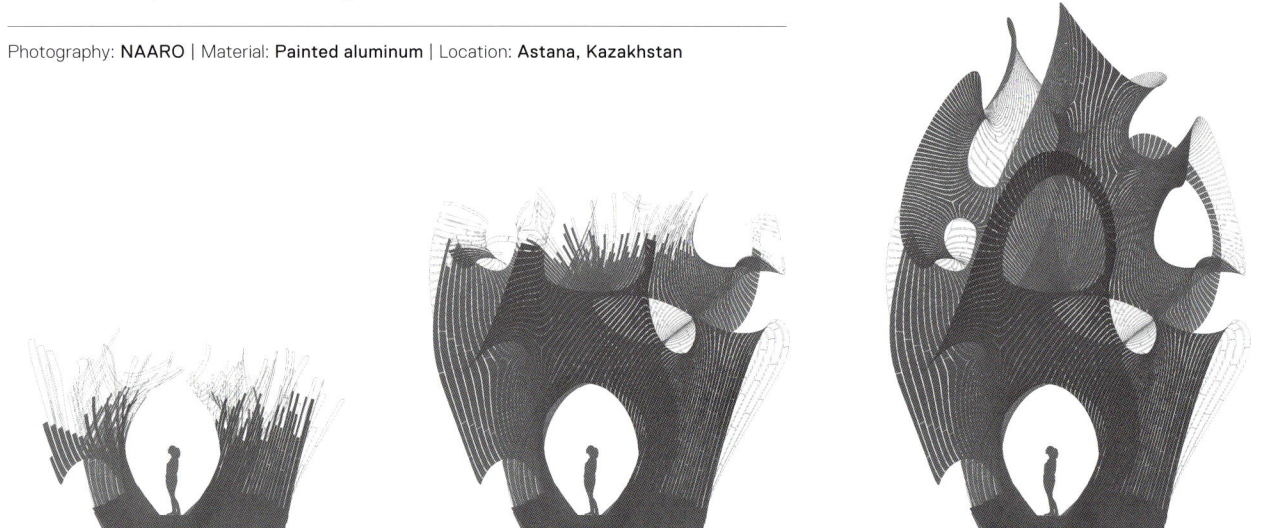

Photography: **NAARO** | Material: **Painted aluminum** | Location: **Astana, Kazakhstan**

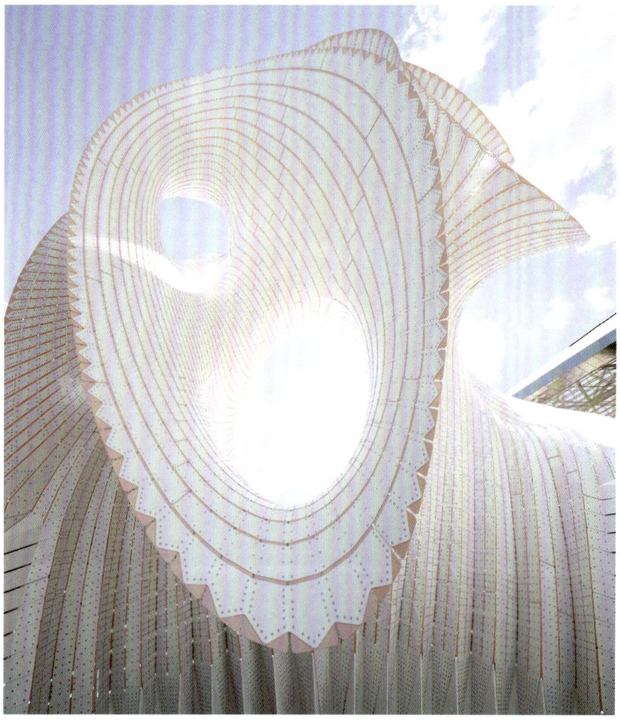

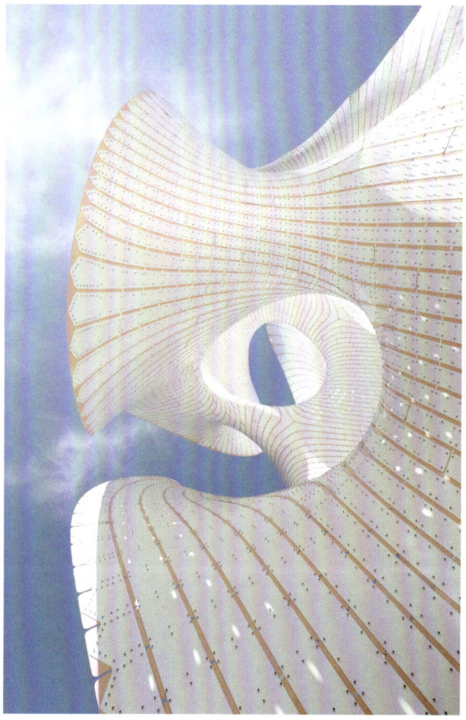

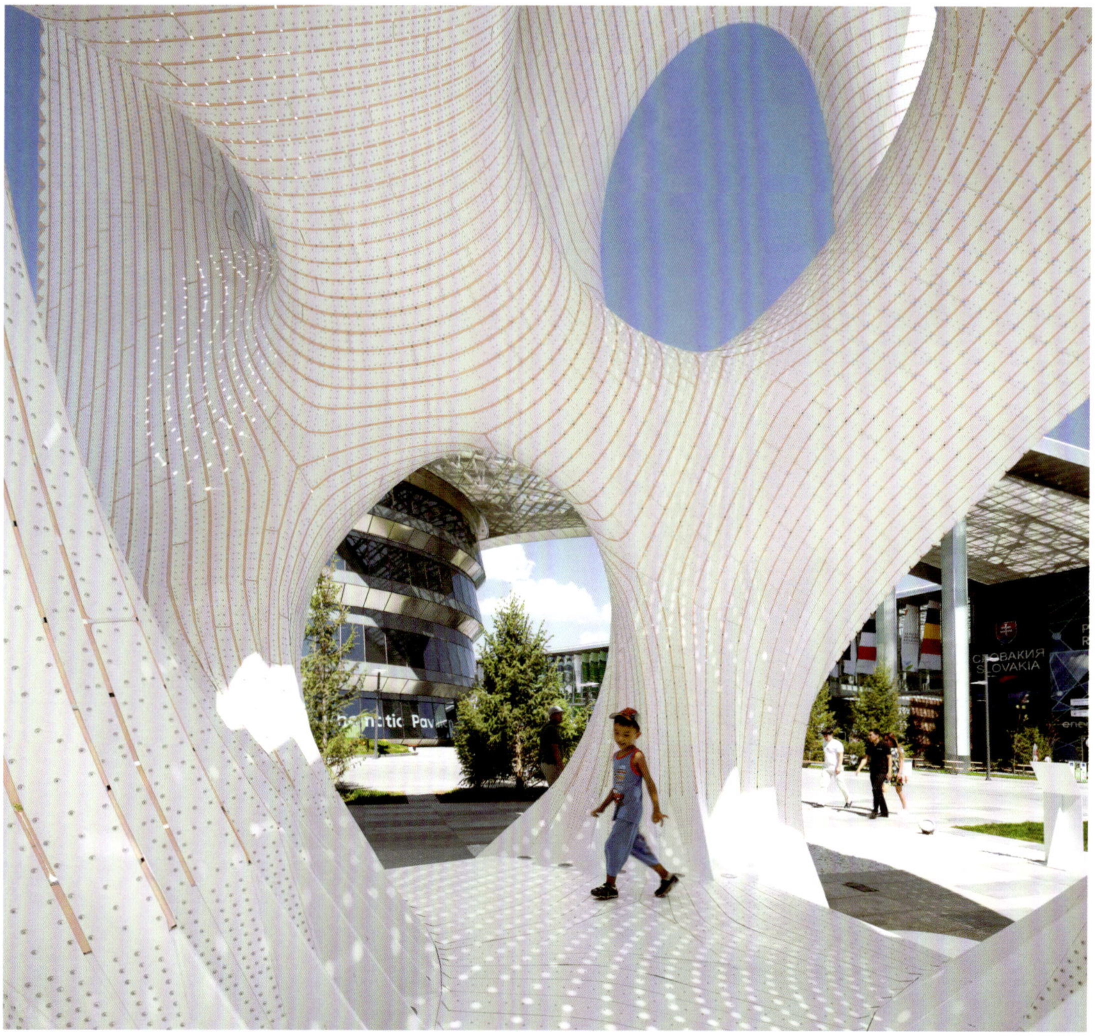
СЛОВАКИЯ
SLOVAKIA

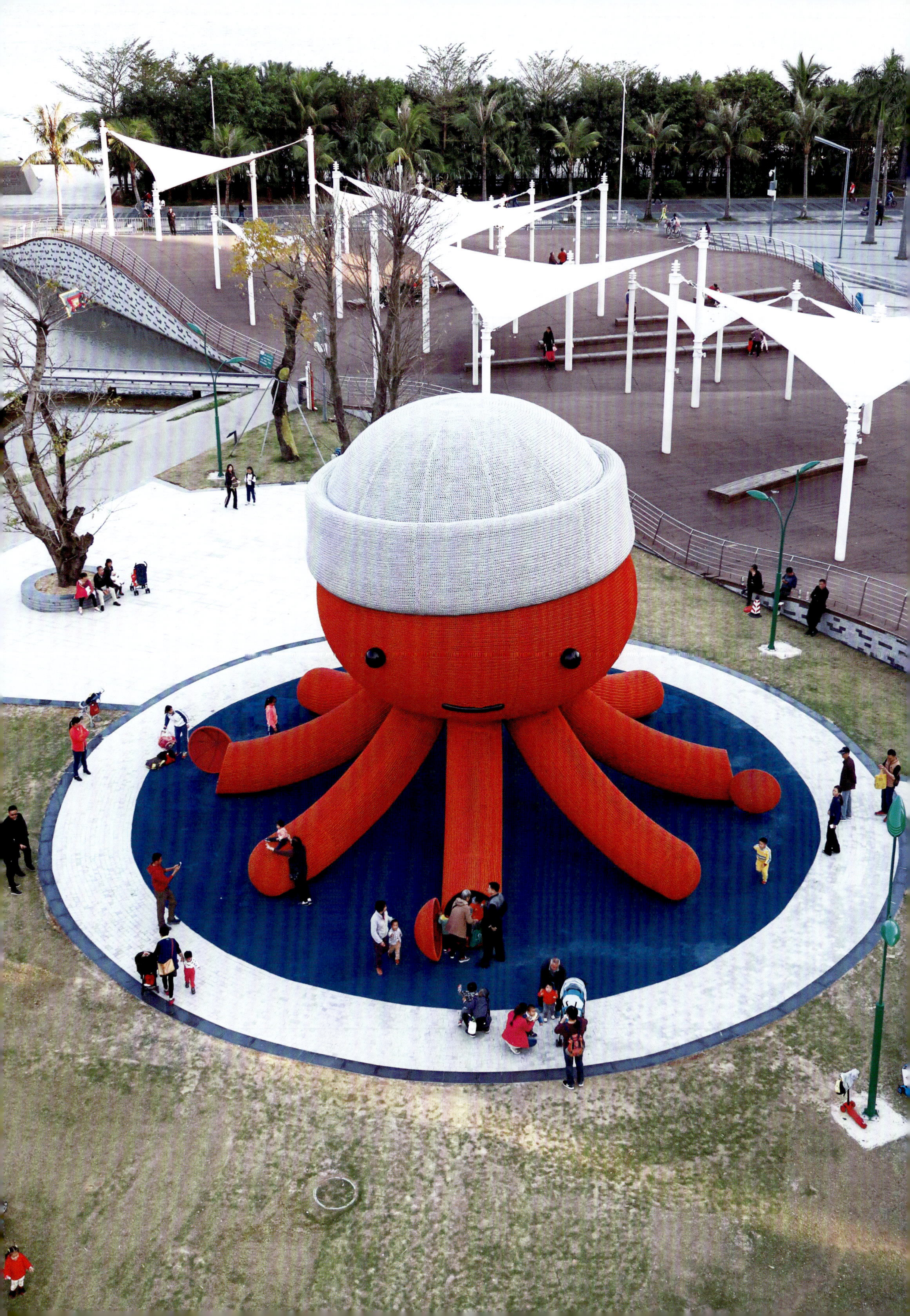

"My sculptures cause an uproar, astonishment, and put a smile on your face. They give people a break from their daily routines. Passers-by stop in front of them, get off their bicycles, and enter into conversation with other spectators. People are making contact with each other again. That is the effect of my sculptures in the public domain."

Florentijn Hofman

Artist

Florentijn Hofman is a Dutch artist renowned for his playful, scaled-up urban installations and animal sculptures. His most famous projects include the monumental floating *Rubber Duck* that traveled worldwide, the vast *HippopoThames* that made its way down the river Thames, and many others. Portrait photo by Alexey Snetkov.

Play Around the World: Having Fun with Giant Animals

Humour, sensation, maximum impact, internationally renowned artist Florentijn Hofman does not settle for less. His sculptures are large, gigantic, and are bound to make an impression. Take *Rubber Duck*, for example, a gigantic 26-meter-high yellow rubber duck. It is an inflatable, based on the standard model that children from all four corners of the world are familiar with. The impressive rubber duck travels the world and pops up in many different cities—from Auckland and São Paulo to Osaka—a very positive artistic statement that immediately connects people to their childhood. Another example is *Fat Monkey*, a huge monkey tied together from 10,000 brightly colored flipflops, the Brazilian shoe par excellence. The monkey is lying stretched out in the park, where his 15-meter length makes passers-by stop dead in their tracks.

Florentijn's sculptures often originate from everyday objects. A straightforward paper boat, a pictogram of an industrial zone, or mass-produced little toy figures can all serve as sources. They are all ready-mades, selected by Florentijn, for the beauty of their forms. Subsequently, he crafts these into clear and iconic images, cartoonish blow-ups of reality that alienate and unsettle through their sheer size and use of materials. Nevertheless, they are immediately identifiable and have an instant appeal. Inflatables, window stickers, agricultural plastic sheeting: for Florentijn, any material is suitable for turning into art. The skin of *Big Yellow Rabbit*, for example, consisted of thousands of Swedish shingles. A wooden frame was covered in reed for *Muskrat*. For *Lookout Rabbit*, he screwed together many wooden planks, and for *Fat Monkey*, he used the flip-flops as mentioned above.

Florentijn's projects are often very labor-intensive. Gravity is being defied though by his love of materials and craft.

Next to temporary and permanent sculptures in the public domain, Florentijn has realized several other projects. In *Beukelsblauw*, he brought attention to a block of houses, destined for demolition, by painting the buildings bright blue from top to bottom. For *Zirkus Zeppelin*, on the occasion of the opening of motorway N470, Florentijn chose 470 people to fly with him on the world's largest zeppelin and view their everyday surroundings from the air. In these specific projects, Florentijn invites spectators to reconsider things that at first appear to be a matter of course.

Although artists do not always tend to value reactions of passers-by, for Florentijn, the audience is an essential part of his work. He takes due care of embedding his images in their surroundings. For *Steelman*, he, therefore, engaged in conversation with young residents of the Staalmansquare, a formerly rough neighborhood in Amsterdam Slotervaart. Subsequently, he conceived of an 11-meter high bear with a pillow under its arm. Florentijn says: "The bear is tough and is standing straddle-legged. Those who live in this neighborhood have to stand their ground. At the same time, the bear is a symbol of fraternization. People socialize at the foot of the sculpture."

An encounter with one of Florentijn's extraordinary sculptures invites the viewer to stand still for a moment and to look, to really look and to take a picture. Florentijn: "My sculptures cause an uproar, astonishment, and put a smile on your face. They give people a break from their daily routines. Passers-by stop in front of them, get off their bicycles, and enter into conversation with other spectators. People are making contact with each other again. That is the effect of my sculptures in the public domain."

Kraken

Commissioned by Vanke group's One City development, *Kraken* forms an engaging and inhabitable space for children and adults alike. The enormous octopus subtly draws from the history of the site, which—until recently—was occupied by a former Soviet aircraft carrier turned theme park. Providing an imaginative space for families to explore, visitors enter the playscape through the character's tentacles, where they climb through a netted abyss. Upon arrival to the top, a sizeable playable space awaits within *Kraken*'s rounded head.

Photography: **Charlie Xia**
Material: **Rope, steel**
Location: **Shenzhen, China**

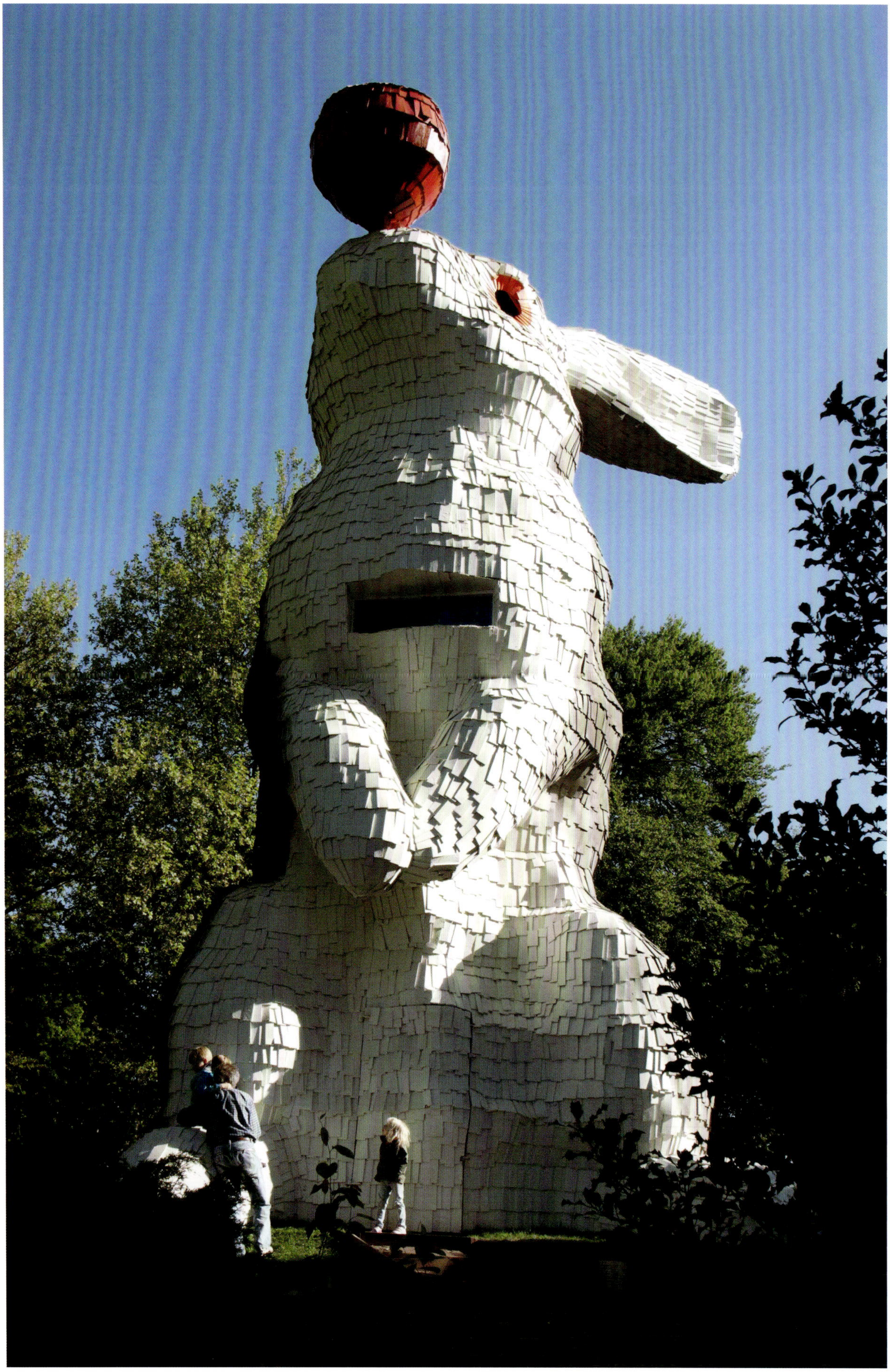

Lookout Rabbit

The Lookout Rabbit is a temporary 12-meter-high sculpture. It is a rabbit with a red dot where the audience can enter and have a lookout over the river the Waal. The work was situated at the Valkhofpark at Nijmegen.

Photography: **Monique Zoon (photo on page 110, upper photo on page 111), Nico van Hoorn (bottom photo on page 111)** | Material: **Wood, steal, cement coating, paint** | Location: **Nijmegen, the Netherlands**

Moonrabbit

The site-specific installation was inspired by a Chinese cultural myth of Chang'e and the Jade Rabbit. It is a myth depicting a story about a rabbit making elixirs on the moon. The tale is widely associated with the Mid-Autumn Festival in China. The sculpture features a rabbit relaxing on a retired aircraft hangar in the breeze and thinking about its future, dreams, and life after death.

Photography: **Lee Chia-yu** | Material: **Wood, Tyvek (waterproof paper)** | Location: **Taiwan, China**

Rubber Duck

Visiting various locations over the world since 2007, the *Rubber Duck* knows no frontiers. It does not discriminate against people and does not have a political connotation. The friendly, floating *Rubber Duck* has healing properties: It can relieve mondial tensions and define them. It is soft, friendly, and suitable for all ages.

Photography: **AllRightsReserved** | Material: **Inflatable structure on metal barge** | Location: **Worldwide**

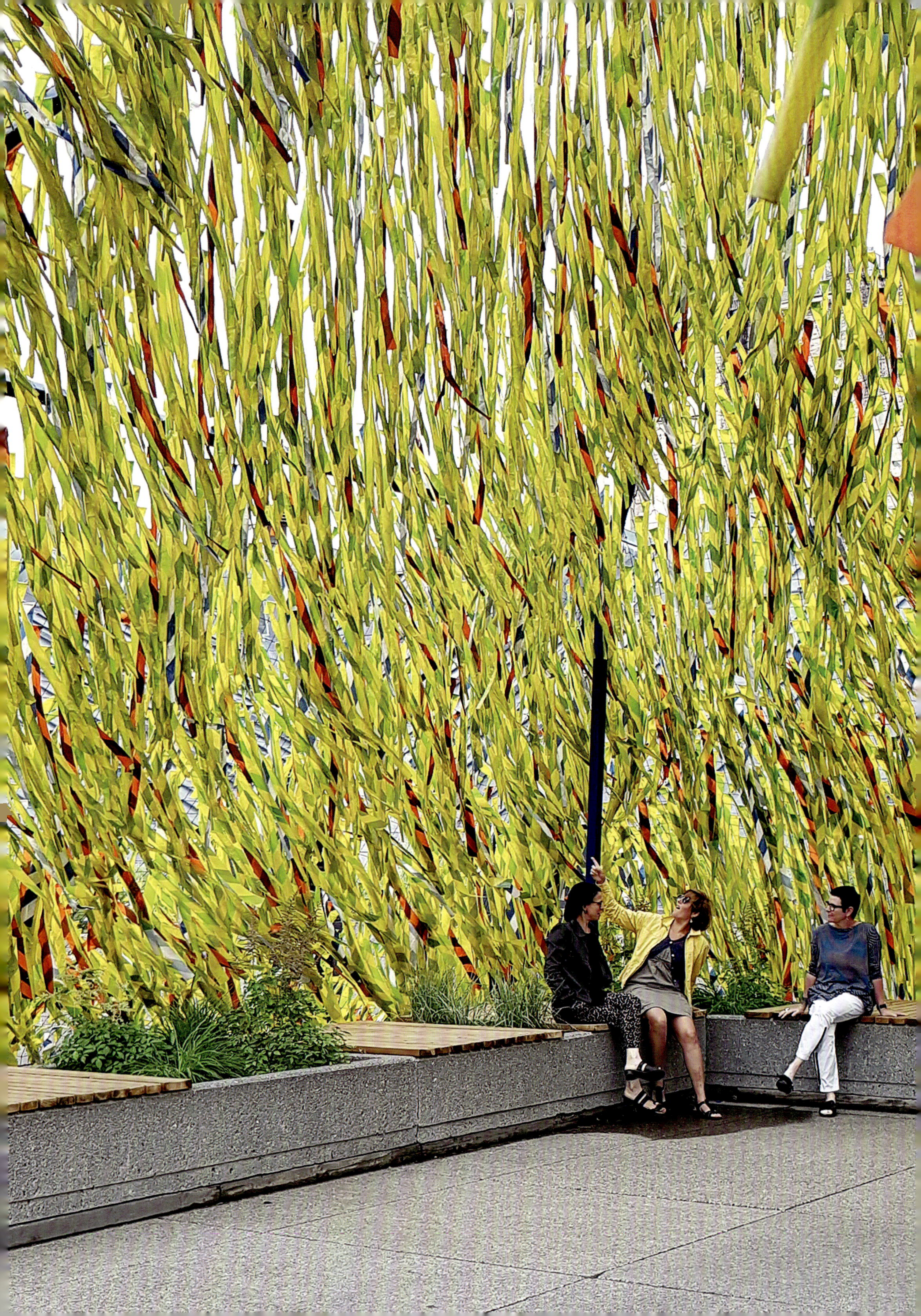

"We are interested in the way that our projects can be physical prompts for engagement in public spaces. To this end, we refer to our projects as 'social infrastructures.' Through playful and colorful experiences, we hope that they can encourage people who might not know one another and who may come from very different backgrounds culturally, economically or racially, to share a moment of connection."

Coryn Kempster and Julia Jamrozik

—
Artists
Designers
Educators
—

Coryn Kempster and Julia Jamrozik are Canadian designers, artists, and educators who have collaborated since 2003. Together, they endeavor to create spaces, objects, and situations that interrupt the ordinary in critically engaging and playful ways. Their multi-disciplinary practice operates at a variety of scales, from temporary installations to permanent public artworks and architectural projects.

Art as Social Infrastructures: Building Connection through Play

Coryn and Julia met when they pursued their Bachelor's degrees at the University of Toronto. They attended classes together, became friends, and worked together on group installations. After graduation, Coryn went to the Massachusetts Institute of Technology to earn his Master's degree in architecture, while Julia studied at the University of British Columbia for her Master's degree in architecture.

After working for some architectural design studios, Coryn and Julia decided to work together as a duo. "We are quite aligned in our thinking overall, but we rarely agree to begin with. Our projects evolve through conversations and often disagreements. When one of us has a strong opinion, things get particularly productive because we have to find arguments to support our positions," Julia mentions. Their collective aim is to make their work approachable and accessible. Even though there are themes that govern the work, they hope people can enjoy their experience rather than being forced to ponder the underlying concepts.
"We hope people will feel compelled to spend time in the installation, experiencing how the space transforms from a quiet and still place to a space full of sounds and movements when the wind rustles the barrier tape," Julia explains the work *Line Garden*. "People may start to speak and interact with strangers, starting simple conversations and enjoying each other's company."

They take inspiration from everyday materials, off-the-shelf products, color, and color combinations. Additionally, the history of art and design is also a major source of inspiration for them, especially the world of play and the design of play spaces. "The 1950s, 60s, and 70s were full of intense, creative yet unabashedly abstract ways of creating play spaces in the urban fabric. Architects like Aldo van Eyck or collectives such as Group Ludic worked tirelessly to bring playful infrastructures into the city," says Julia.

For their best-known work, *Line Garden* series, color is a prominent element. Initially, the color combinations were based on the tapes available on the market, for example, the first version of *Line Garden* in 2014 was made from a German tape with diagonal stripes formed by two different tape stocks fused together (yellow and black, yellow and red, yellow and blue). For *Vertical Line Garden* in 2017, they used scraps of barrier tape from previous years—literally recycling the left-over material. "We did not have enough, so we were augmenting it with a few new color combinations of yellow with various pinks (by then, we had developed a relationship with a manufacturer who was willing to mix custom colors for us)," says Julia. In 2018, they had an opportunity to work for the first time on the rooftop of the Musée de la Civilisation in Quebec City, Canada, and brought *Roof Line Garden II* to life. Unlike their previous artworks, they were asked to use the colors of the Union Jack (the UK's national flag) to respond to the British-themed exhibition on show in the musuem. "We obliged the museum with red, white, and blue tape, and took the liberty to add light blue and pink tape." Coryn adds, "then we asked the manufacturer to mix inks to match the colors of the tapes and print each color of ink on each color of tape. The final results became 25 combinations of tape colors and inks, which, for us, represented a more nuanced response to the client's prompt."

Apart from practical operation in art and design, Coryn and Julia engage in academic research and focus on the role of play in the built environment and alternative methods of documentation as a form of historic preservation. Julia is an assistant professor, and Coryn is an adjunct assistant professor in the Department of Architecture at the University at Buffalo SUNY. In 2018 the Architectural League of New York honored their work with the Architectural League Prize for Young Architects and Designers.

Roof Line Garden II

Barricade tape is a ubiquitous, man-made material, typically used to delineate a perimeter and keep people out, but in *Roof Line Garden II*, it invites people in, to inhabit an immersive environment. Installed for the International Garden Festival presented by the Reford Gardens, it occupies the rooftop terrace of the Musée de la Civilisation. Visible from the street, the installation reinterprets the roofline of the museum, referencing the roofs of Old Québec City. Thousands of strands of tape are suspended from a triangulated metal framework with a stretched net as armature, creating a canopy of colorful lines.

Photography: **Johanne Lacoste (photo on page 114), Marc-Antoine Hallé (photo on page 116), May Tang (photo on page 117)**
Material: **Barricade tape, net, steel structure**
Location: **Québec City, Canada**

Vertical Line Garden

Working with patterns, order, color, and density, this garden is a play on formal traditional gardens with contemporary ready-made means and hyper unnatural materials. As a both graphic and playful space, it encourages interaction without being prescriptive about use. While adults enjoy the comfort of the loungers and take pleasure in the moment of repose that the garden provides, youngsters use the tape as a maze to run through, frolic in, and explore. The installation creates a fluid space which responds to its environmental conditions. Depending on the weather, the space is kinetic and very open, or it can be quiet and forms a permeable but closed space.

Photography: **Coryn Kempster** | Material: **Barricade tape, net, wood structure, custom loungers** | Location: **Grand-Métis, Québec, Canada**

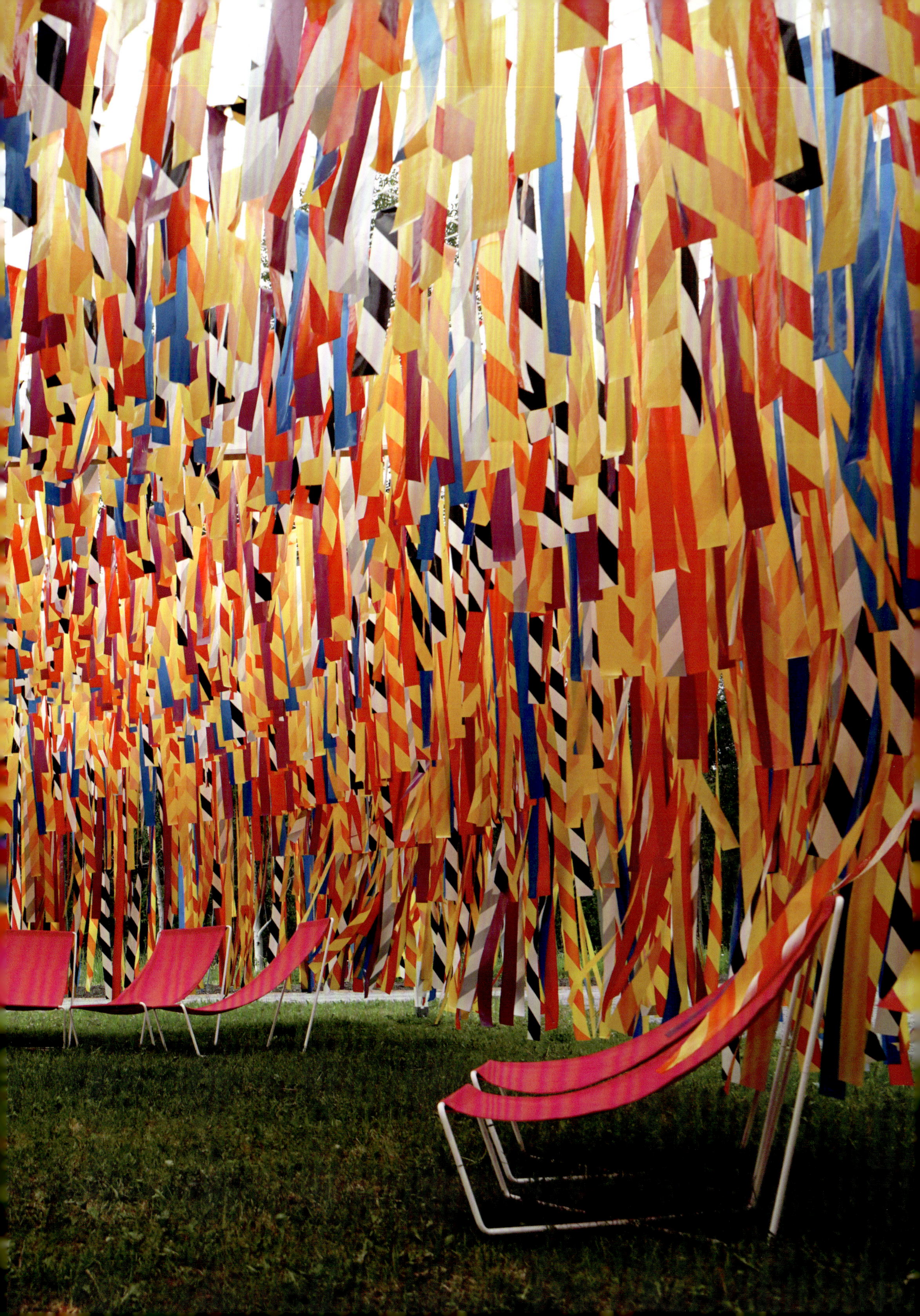

Breakwater

Dolosse are reinforced concrete elements interlocked to form breakwaters protecting shorelines from erosion. The project salvages four of these seven-ton elements originally fabricated for a United States Army Corps of Engineers project on Lake Erie and decontextualizes them. With the infrastructural scale and utilitarian nature, the sculptural shape of the dolosse is suitable for human-scaled uses. Using the form of the elements in different orientations and blurring the lines between playground and sculpture, *Breakwater* leads to a productive ambiguity that allows the public to interpret and occupy the installation in their own way, including sitting, climbing, sliding, lounging, and playing hide-and-seek.

Photography: **Coryn Kempster** | Material: **Concrete dolos, polyurea coating, EPDM rubber** | Location: **Jamestown, New York, USA**

· 121 ·

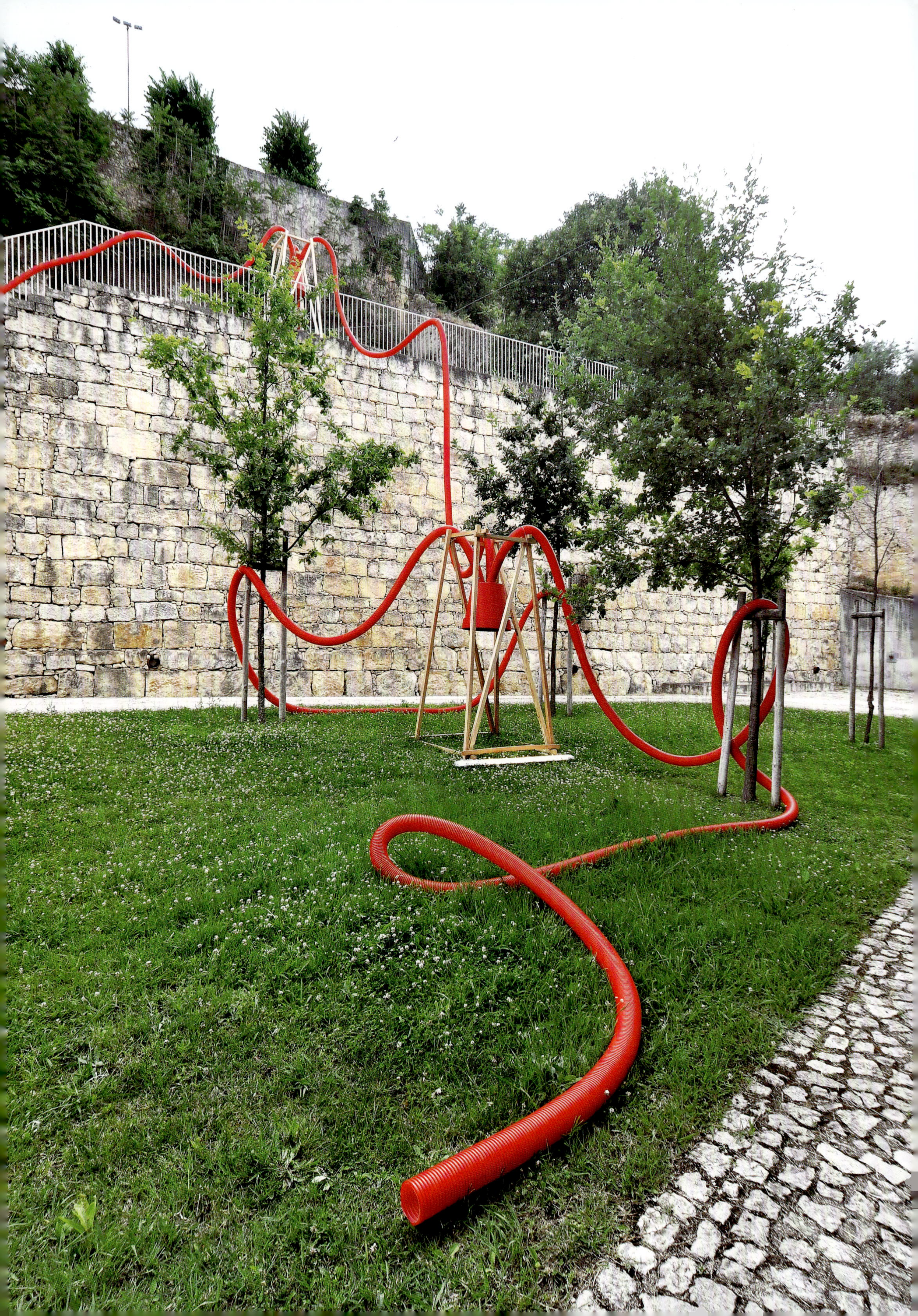

"In our daily routine, sometimes we may look at things from the same perspective. We are inclined to the vision habit, and our senses can get a bit dull. Then, maybe with a twist, you can rediscover a common thing by seeing it from a different light. These moments of surprise are important to our work, and that is also why sometimes our projects are playful and fun."

Moradavaga

—

Designers
Architects

—

Based in Kaltern/Caldaro (Italy) and Porto (Portugal), Moradavaga (a contraction of the Portuguese words for "vague address") is a collective born from the collaboration of architects Manfred Eccli from Italy and Pedro Cavaco Leitão from Portugal. Intersecting architecture, art, and design, their works function as "dormant tools" in waiting status, requiring the user's engagement to activate them.

Experience the World Anew:
Art Installations for Fun and Surprise

Manfred Eccli and Pedro Cavaco Leitão started working together in the name of Moradavaga in 2006 around the themes of vacant spaces, derelict buildings, and the activation of the public realm, devising performative objects and active interventions, such as social workshops, ideas competitions, and architectural installations. Both Manfred and Pedro studied architecture and worked as architects after graduation. The way they met each other was an interesting story. In 2004, Pedro lived in Portugal, while Manfred in Austria. Surprisingly, their girlfriends at that time were twin sisters. Therefore, they met and became friends. With a similar background and shared interest in abandoned spaces and derelict buildings, they shared the common desire to experiment with urban interventions. And of course, as individuals, they both have their different points of view on some topics, but as they said, the differences help unlock new ideas when they are brainstorming and make the design process meaningful. "Probably our upbringings and memories from childhood also affect our sensation for certain moments, like, for example, the moments of surprise or playful interactivity. During the process of doing each work, we hope to find these moments and be free to try and experiment," Manfred and Pedro says.

Their collaboration started in late 2006 in the northern Portuguese city, Porto, centering on the temporary reuse of abandoned buildings, empty and neglected public spaces. In Portuguese, "moradavaga" means "vague address." How they ended up with this name was also an intriguing story. It all began with an organization that they had involved. Manfred

Origlia!

Origlia! is an interactive installation first presented at the festival Terminal in Udine, Italy, in 2017. Inspired by old telephone booths, Moradavaga endeavored to create a new communication space with *Origlia!*. Like old wire phones, it allows people to chat with groups without consuming too many "tokens." The installation was displayed also at the exhibition "The Game" at the Kunsthalle West in Lana, Italy, at the Palazzo Ducale in Massa-Carrara, Italy, and in the city of Coimbra, Portugal.

Photography: **Moradavaga**
Material: **Wood, corrugated tubes, plastic buckets**
Location: **Udine, Italy; Lana, Italy; Massa-Carrara, Italy; Coimbra, Portugal**

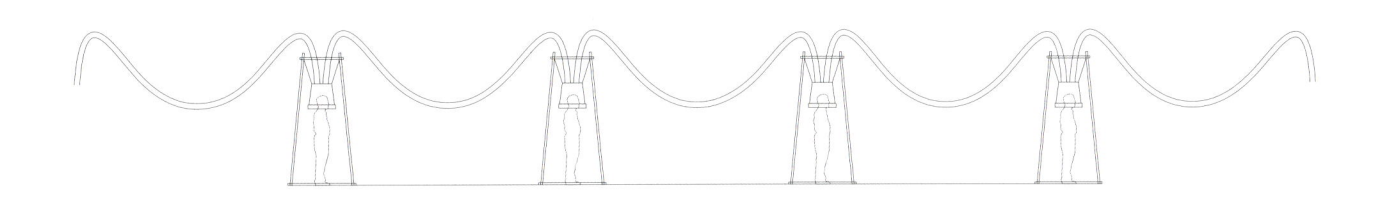

and Pedro launched an open call for proposals and asked the participants to present their ideas of temporary "activation" for any area they chose within the city of Porto. They tried to think of a name that could illustrate their initiative better, and eventually, they settled on the contraction of two words: "vague" and "address," which referred to an undefined space or place.

Over these years, the outcomes of their projects vary in concepts and formats, since they are more or less subject to their personal interests and changing contexts. But overall, they focus on a fundamental leitmotiv, and that is, seize the present and the fleeting moment. "For that, we create objects, spaces, or situations that have practical functions, which go beyond a purely contemplative dimension. We like to regard our projects as 'performative objects;' only when the work interact with the audience and evoke a moment of surprise will we call it a completed work." Manfred and Pedro continue, "In our daily routine, sometimes we may look at things from the same perspective. We are inclined to the vision habit, and our senses can get a bit dull. Then, maybe with a twist, you can rediscover a common thing by seeing it from a different light. These moments of surprise are important to our work, and that is also why sometimes our projects are playful and fun."

Moradavaga's varied and eclectic body of work has gained international recognition over the years, as evidenced by its participation in events promoted by renowned institutions and organizations. Among their work, *Origlia!* is a project that has been travelling to different cities. It was first installed for the festival Terminal in Udine, Italy, in 2017. Then it became part of the collective touring exhibition called "The Game" held in Lana and Massa-Carrara, Italy. The more recent visit was made in Coimbra, Portugal, as part of a festival for sound called "Dar a Ouvir." "It is very light work in terms of logistics and production, making it easy to travel around and attract different kinds of organization and cultural events," explains Manfred and Pedro.

Kami in the Whispering Forest

Moradavaga's installation *Kami in the Whispering Forest* is an interactive audiovisual installation for the Christmas Market in Neumarkt/Egna, Italy. The playful approach of the installation invited visitors to approach the topic of "connection and communication" at different levels. The work was based on the classic motif of the chimney/fireplace frequently found in Christmas tales, with the red hut named "Kami" being the starting point of the work. By entering "Kami," visitors would hear a question raised by an audio station, "Where do I find Christmas?" The work reminded the audience of the central living shelter during the cold seasons, and Moradavaga imagined it as a core space of encounter and exchange.

Photography: **Arno Ebner** | Material: **Corrugated tubes, LED lights, wood, speakers, spruce trees** |
Location: **Neumarkt/Egna, Italy**

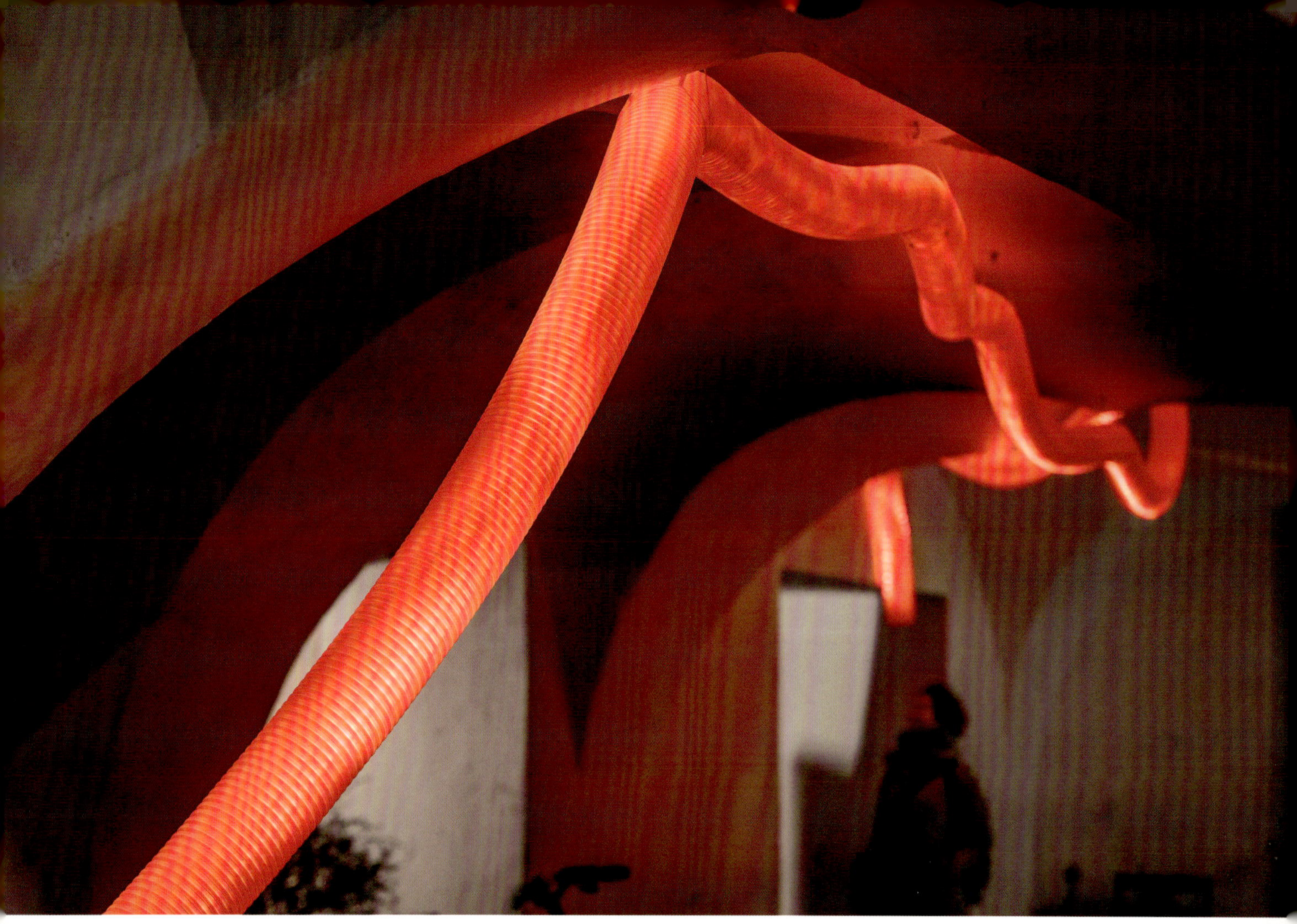

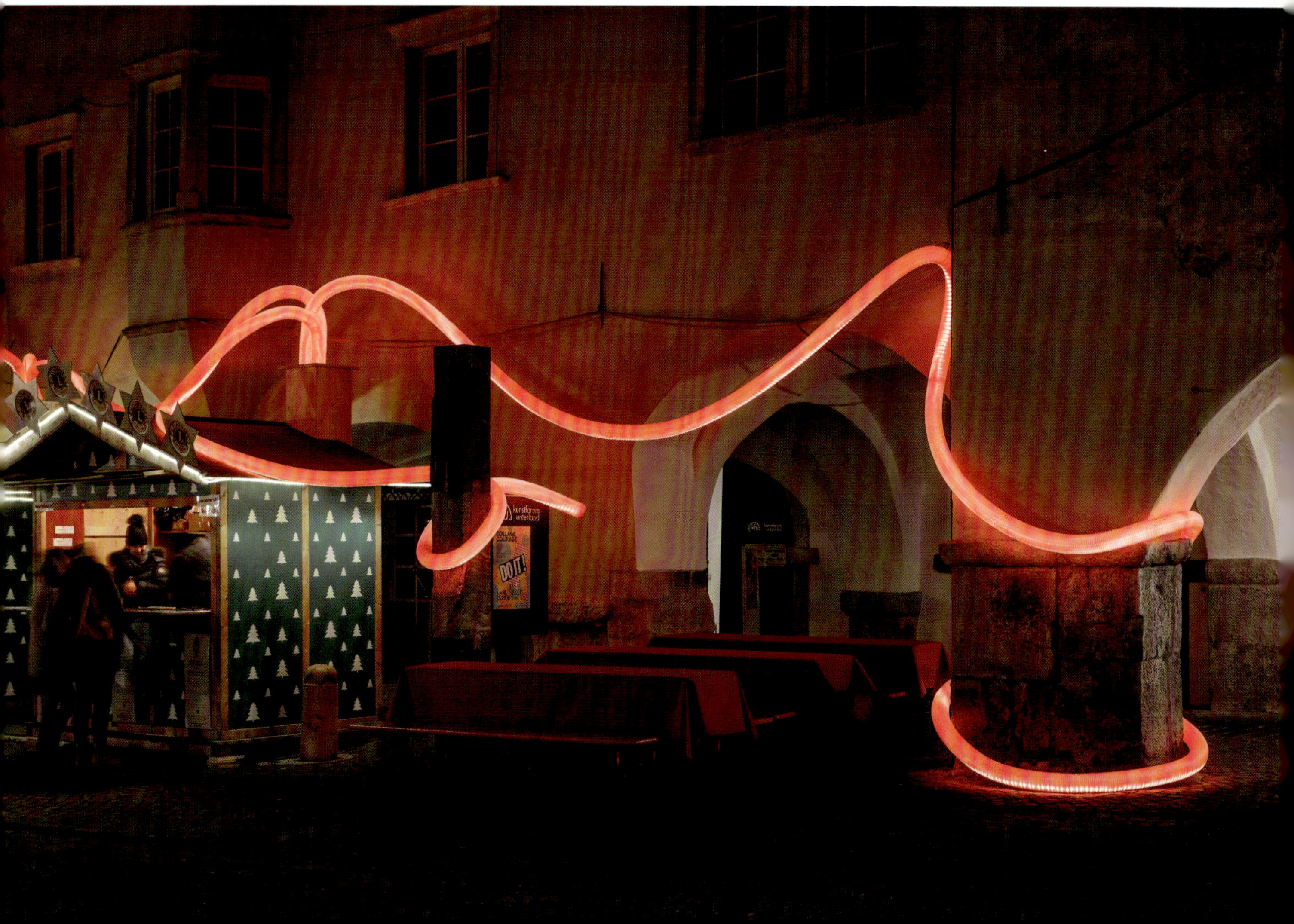
DO IT!

Kraki

Inspired by the theme of the 2017 Taipei Public Arts Festival, "Story of a River," Moradavaga devised an interactive acoustic installation with a strong visual impact that could resonate with the aquatic memories of the old course of the Keelung River playfully and imaginatively. *Kraki* was based on the descriptions found since the late 13th century about legendary sea creatures named "kraken," creatures that probably inspired Herman Melville and Jules Verne on some of their most notable writings, like *Moby Dick* and *Twenty Thousand Leagues Under the Sea*. *Kraki* came from the depths of the ocean, up the imaginary river course, and served as a lively communicative tool for passers-by of all ages at the Meilun Park in Taipei, Taiwan.

Photography: **Moradavaga** | Material: **Corrugated tubes, gypsum board ceiling/wall u-shaped profile, plastic buckets** | Location: **Taiwan, China**

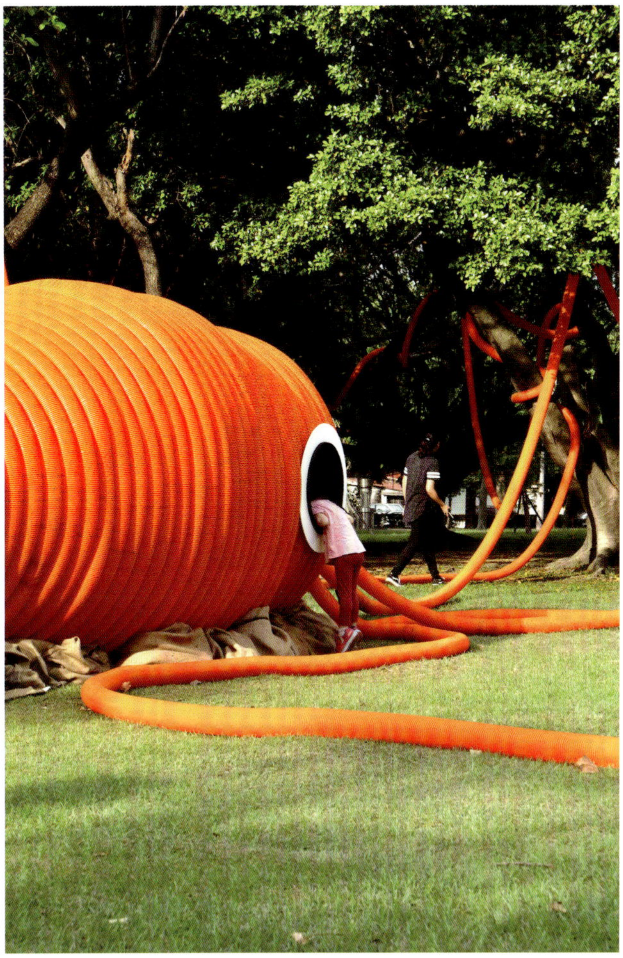
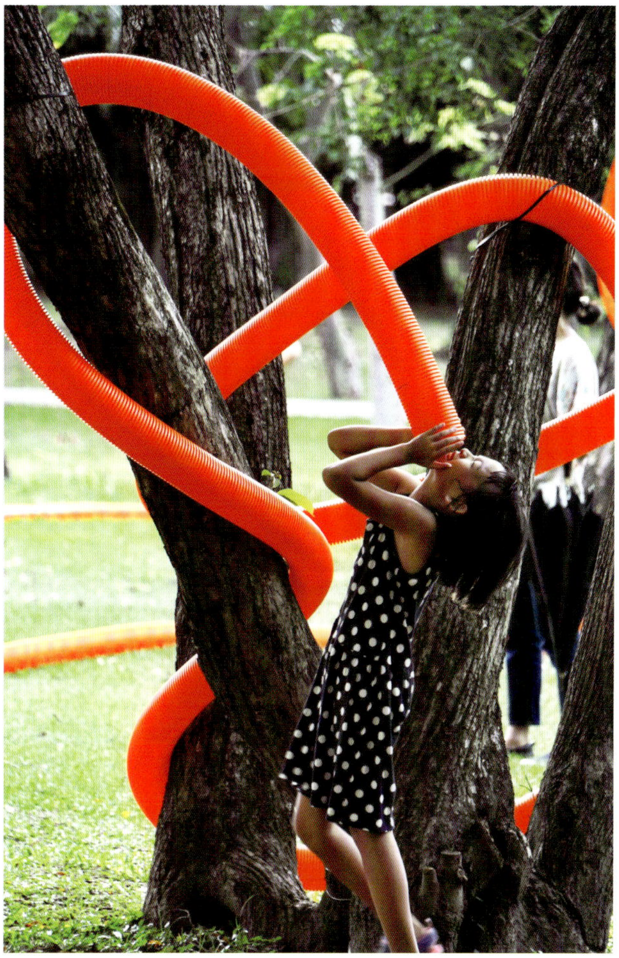
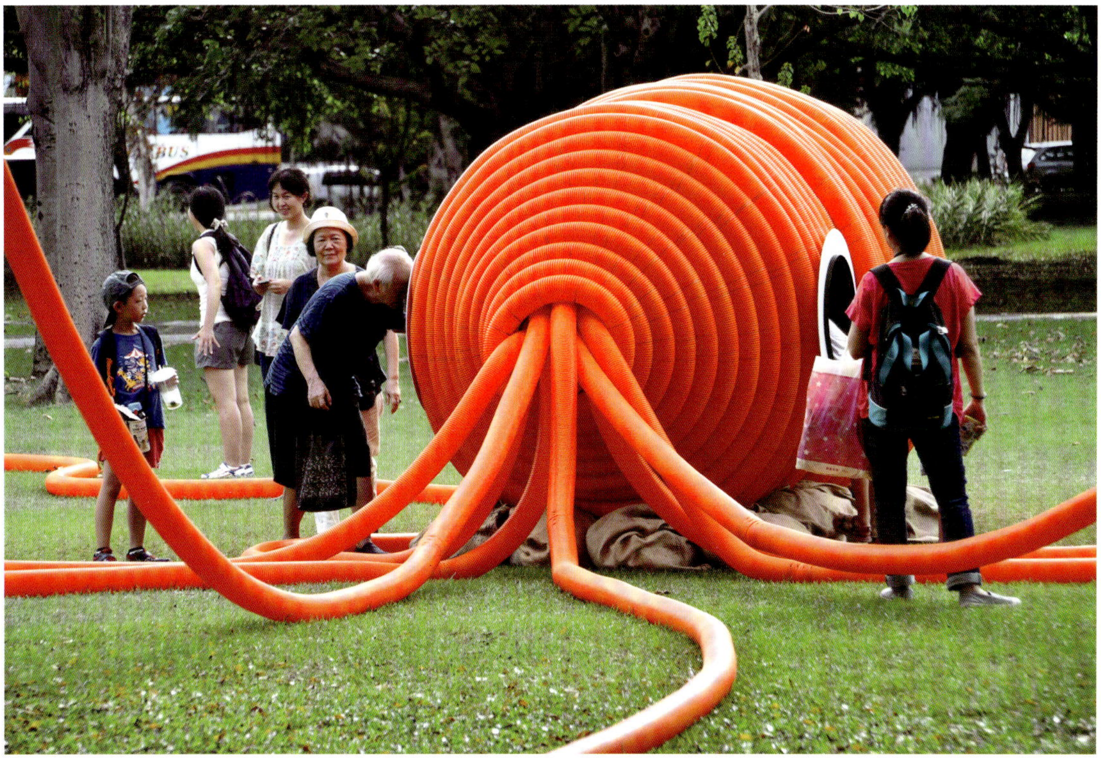

Flip-it

Commissioned by festival Imaginarius, Moradavaga created a site-specific piece to mark the local football club's centennial. Drawing inspiration from old placards and information boards used in sports, Moradavaga made an interactive analogical pixel screen that can be used to display graphical messages like typography, patterns, or simple icons on the main façade of the stadium. The screen measures 11 meters in length and 2.8 meters in height and is composed of 2500 pieces of square pixels in ten centimeters. It is divided into 100 columns to indicate the 100th anniversary of the club with 25 pieces in each column. The pixels are fabricated as custom-made plastic boxes with two sides in two colors, white and blue, echoing the club's identity. This installation acts as a new tool of communication between the club, the fans, and the city as everyone can leave a message on the screen.

Photography: **Moradavaga** | Material: **Injected ABS plastic double colored pixels, metal frame, metal tubes** | Location: **Santa Maria da Feira, Portugal**

THE WORLD IS YOURS.

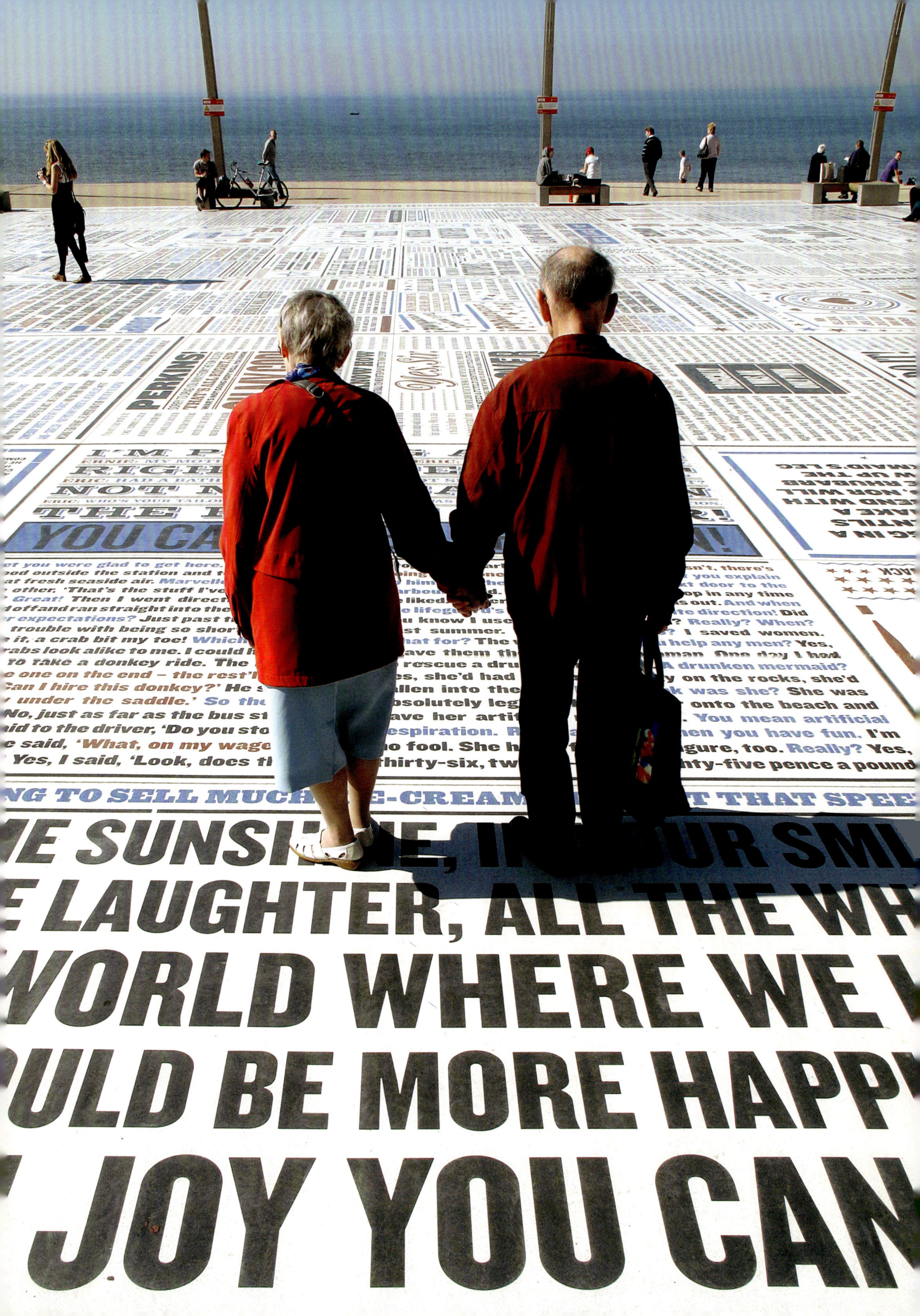
PERKINS!
LAUGHTER, ALL THE
WORLD WHERE WE
BE MORE
JOY YOU

"I think, given my limitations, that words can have power and can be a mystery. To use and tailor the particular text to place allows language to do many things: to recount, share a desire, protest, praise, etc. What is used may be a poetic or artistic expression—Umberto Eco shows that even a list of words can have a potency with his The Infinity of Lists. It is the basis of our Trading Words in the former London Docks. Typography is an important detail too. Typography is the clothes that naked content gets dressed up in!"

Gordon Young and Why Not Associates

—
Artist
Designer
—

Gordon Young is a British visual artist who focuses on creating art for the public domain. His work ranges from sculptures to typographic pavements for places as diverse as village squares, sea fronts to schools and government headquarters. Why Not Associates is a British multi-disciplinary design studio formed by Andy Altmann with his fellow graduates Howard Greenhalgh and David Ellis. Portrait photo by Lee Mawdsley.

Go Beyond Words:
Typographic Tribute to Public Space

Gordon Young was born in Carlisle, a city that borders Scotland in 1952. As a child, he had problems with language and was diagnosed with dyslexia, but luckily, he was gifted with a good sense of art and sport. He went to the local College of Art, which was a gateway to further his learning at Coventry Polytechnic (today's Coventry University) and the Royal College of Art. Perhaps due to childhood dyslexia experience, it enables him to emphasize text and typography while still imbibing creations with a vitality that goes beyond words.

Andy Altmann, founder of Why Not Associates, was born in Warrington in the northwest of England in 1962. Both his parents were from working-class backgrounds and spent their childhood during the Second World War. His mother was an infant teacher, and his father, an architect and talented watercolor painter who loved to read about art and artists and had a small studio stacked with books, paints, and paper. "They both influenced me in many ways, and they certainly influenced my work. I was surrounded by the books that my mum used to help children read and the teaching aids she made by hand. Many of the learning-to-read books of that era used the font Gill Sans. We have used this font on numerous projects, and it is still my favorite font today," says Andy.

Andy founded Why Not Associates with fellow graduates David Ellis and Howard Greenhalgh when he left the Royal College of Art in 1987. "We had no real plan at that moment to set up a design studio; we were just working as individuals who came together to design a magazine." Andy continues, "However, we started to land more projects together, and it became obvious that we needed to form a company and find a studio space." The cornerstone that holds all their projects together is a love and understanding of typography.

Gordon and Andy met at an opening party to the Hull Festival in 1991. At that time, Andy and his team were designing all the branding for the Hull festival, and Gordon was installing his *Fish Pavement* around the city as part of the festival. At the opening party, the director of the festival introduced them to each other, and they became friends. They discovered that they had certain similar points of reference, attitudes, and empathy for what they each were doing. "At first, I don't think we thought about working together; we were just mates. However, in 1996, Gordon asked if we could help him with designing a set of granite steps that he had been commissioned to produce in Scotland, and the collaboration grew from there," recalls Andy. "We can bring different elements, knowledge, understandings, and skills to the collaboration. The artworks are confections of diverse elements. I think the crucial underpinning of working together is respect and empathy," explains Gordon.

Their most ambitious work to date is *The Comedy Carpet*, a 2200-square-meter granite typographic pavement made up of jokes, songs, catchphrases of more than 1000 comedians and comedy writers in British comedy. No one is credited on the actual carpet, so the audience needs to be familiar with the joke or catchphrase to truly understand. It was commissioned by Blackpool Council as part of the multi-million-pound regeneration of the seafront. Gordon viewed the work as a celebration of a shared tradition. "It very soon displayed aspects that were not planned—it became a memorial sometimes (e.g., flowers appeared at a death of a much-loved comedian) or functioned as an educational place, a meeting point for protest groups, a dance floor for charity events, an aid with Alzheimer groups, a photographic backdrop—all kinds of functions which we never thought about," Gordon says delightfully. "Only the skateboarders I am unsympathetic to—they have plentiful alternatives—but narcissism trumps them…" jokes Gordon. In addition to *The Comedy Carpet*, they have collaborated on many other projects, such as *Trading Words*, *The Flock of Words*, and more, grabbing people's attention and getting positive responses.

The Comedy Carpet

Commissioned by Blackpool Council and funded by the Commission for Architecture and the Built Environment (CABE), *The Comedy Carpet* is a celebration of comedy on an extraordinary scale. The carpet gives a visual form to jokes, songs, and catchphrases of more than 1000 comedians and comedy writers dating from the early days of variety to the present. Sited in front of Blackpool Tower, the 2200-square-meter work of art contains over 160,000 granite letters embedded into concrete, pushing the boundaries of public art and typography to their limits. A remarkable homage to those who have made the nation laugh, it is also a stage for popular entertainment that celebrates entertainment itself.

Photography: **Why Not Associates (photos on page 132, 134), Josh Young (photo on page 135), Angela Catlin (photo on page 136–137)** | Material: **Concrete, granite** | Location: **Blackpool, England**

The Comedy Carpet. Photo by Angela Catlin.

NICK NACKY NICK NACK NICKY NACKY NOO!
A LOT OF PEOPLE SAY: DO YOU BELIEVE IN REINCARNATION? I DON'T SEE THE POINT IN COMING BACK AS A TIN OF MILK.
I WANT TO DIE LIKE MY FATHER PEACEFULLY IN HIS SLEEP NOT SCREAMING AND TERRIFIED LIKE HIS PASSENGERS.
A MINIATURE VILLAGE IN BOURNEMOUTH CAUGHT FIRE AND THE FLAMES COULD BE SEEN THREE FEET AWAY
LET'S DO IT!
SMEAR AN AVOCADO
WHERE'S ME SHIRT?
WHAT A WONDERFUL DAY IT IS FOR RUNNING DOWN THE ROAD, STICKING A GREEN CUCUMBER THROUGH THE LETTER BOXES AND SHOUTING, 'THE MARTIANS ARE COMING!'
ALWAYS LOOK ON THE BRIGHT SIDE OF LIFE!
THIS IS AN EX-PARROT
GOOD EVENING AND IN A PACKED SHOW TONIGHT
DAISY, DAISY,
BEER
YOUR SWEATER JUST GOES IN AND OUT
THE VET'S NEXT DOOR
SILLY YOU
IT CERTAINLY IS!
PANTS!

DIAMONDS

TIN

TORTOISESHELLS
CREAM OF TARTAR

SLATE PENCILS

SPONGES
SQUILLS
STARCH

ORANGE BUDS
ORANGE FLOWER WATER

QUILLS

CUMBLIES

TALLOW

SOUNDING-BOARDS

ELEPHANTS' TEETH

STATIONERY
QUICKSILVER
BRISTLES

OSTRICH FEATHERS
OTTO OF ROSES

LUCIFER

PHILLIPSON'S
PIANOFORTE
ROOT

CHARIOTS, 4-WHEEL CHAISES
CHAISES, 2-WHEEL CARRIAGES

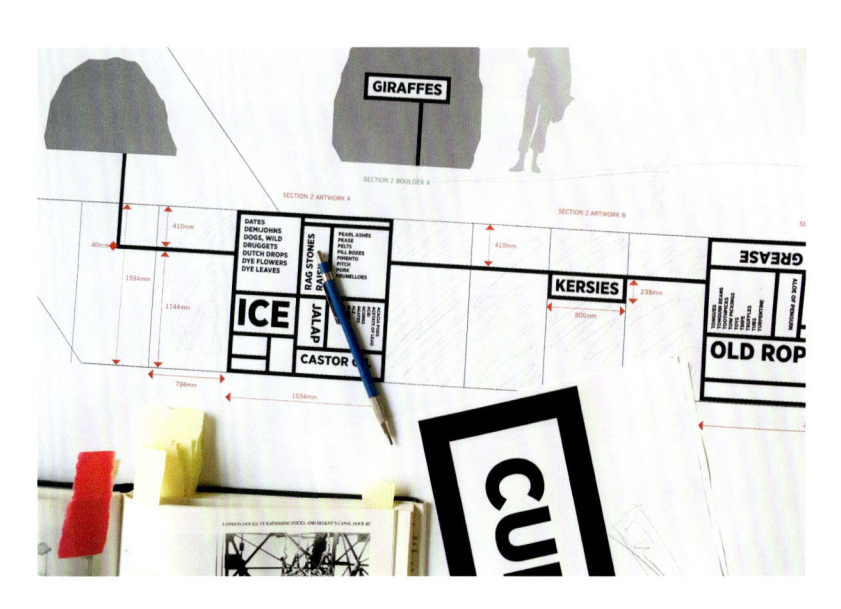

Trading Words

Trading Words is a typographic pavement trail at the London Docks in Wapping, East London. The artwork is situated at Gauging Square, an area which comprises of shops, bars, and restaurants and is just a part of the 7.5 acres of new public space at London Dock. The trail's text explores the historical ledgers of the imports and exports at the docks during its time in operation from 1805 to 1968. Items cited in the artwork include elephants' teeth, quills, bear's grease, sounding-boards, goats' beards, dragon's blood, to name a few.

Photography: **Lee Mawdsley** | Material: **Concrete, granite** | Location: **London, UK**

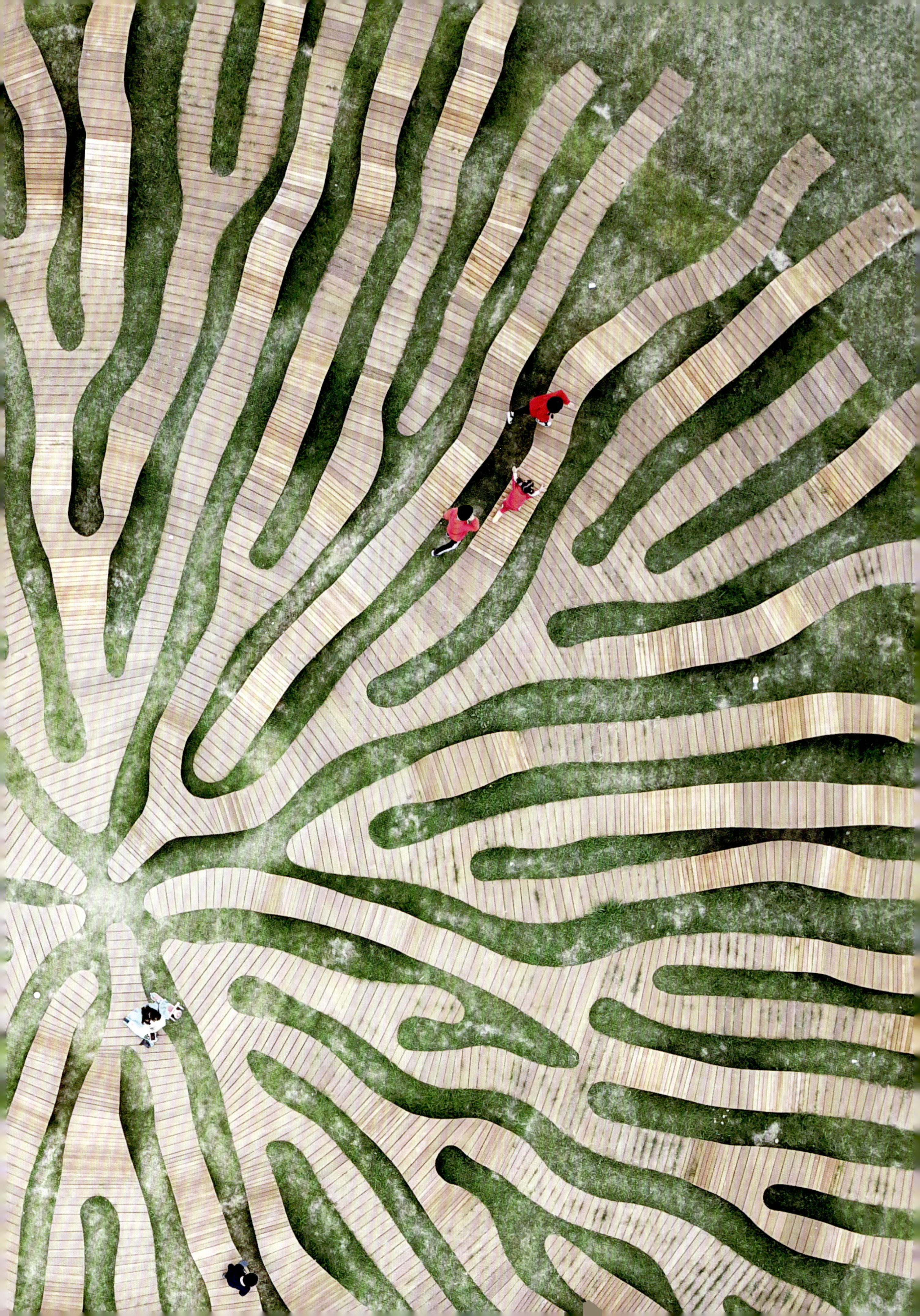

"I want to make people stop their daily routines and experience great refreshment through my work, even in a short moment. People pass by public space every day, sometimes mindlessly. A good project in public spaces help people perceive the space and awaken people's interest in the spatial value."

Yong Ju Lee

—

Architect

—

Yong Ju Lee is a registered architect in the US and Seoul public architect. After graduating from Columbia University (2009), he has worked as a founding partner of New York-based E/B Office. Now he is the principal of Seoul-based firm, Yong Ju Lee Architecture, and an assistant professor at Seoul National University of Science and Technology.

Refreshment in Urban Spaces: The Collision of Art and Science

Yong Ju Lee grew up in Daedeok Science Town in South Korea, where clusters many research and development institutes. The town sites in sub-urban with small houses, low-story buildings surrounded by green hills and rice fields. "The reaction against this quiet life possibly made me pursue something visually stimulating or radical," Yong Ju says. In his childhood, Yong Ju enjoyed watching films and explored his vision and curiosity in sci-fiction. Even now, he often draws inspiration from many imaginary creatures and spaces as well as narratives in movies and novels, such as David Cronenberg's worlds, especially *Videodrome* (1983), and futuristic inventions like Daniel Simon's Light Cycle from *Tron: Legacy* (2010) produced by Walt Disney Pictures.

Yong Ju received a Bachelor's degree in architectural engineering from Yonsei University in 2006. In 2006, he moved to the US to pursue his Master's degree in architecture and received it at the Columbia University Graduate School of Architecture Planning and Preservation (GSAPP) in 2009. He has worked at the architecture and design firms in the US and Korea, including Asymptote and most recently Handel Architects. He has taught graduate design studio and tech elective class at Montana State University and served as a guest critic at Columbia University and the New York School of Interior Design.

His work keenly focuses on the geometric experiment, complex parametrics, and architectural tectonics in terms of new vocabularies of pattern and tessellation based on information. For instance, his latest project, *Root Bench*, designed by a computer algorithm, presents dynamicity from three-dimensional geometry. The metal frame with concrete footing supports the overall form as the main structure with a wooden deck covered it. To articulate the spreading-out branch intensively, Yong Ju applied the reaction-diffusion system to the design process. This mathematical model describes the change in space and time of the concentration of one or more chemical substances: local chemical reactions in which the substances are transformed into each other, and diffusion which causes the substances to spread out over a surface in space. Through the algorithm from the system, the overall radial form is generated with the foreground (installation) merging into its background (grass). With its complete shape of a circle, *Root Bench* is fused into the grass and blurs the boundary between artificial installation and the natural environment. It also functions perfectly as furniture with three different heights: child chair (250 mm), adult chair (450 mm), and table (75 mm).

With his attractive designs for buildings, pavilions, and public installations, Yong Ju wants to make people stop their daily routines and experience great refreshment through his work, even in a short moment. "People pass by public space every day, sometimes mindlessly. A good project in public spaces help people perceive the space and awaken people's interest in the spatial value," explains Yong Ju.

Over the years, Yong Ju has won numerous design awards, lectured and exhibited nationally and internationally, including the Teton County Library's public art competition (winner, realized in 2013) and recently Young Architects Program 2014 finalist for the National Museum of Modern and Contemporary Art, Korea.

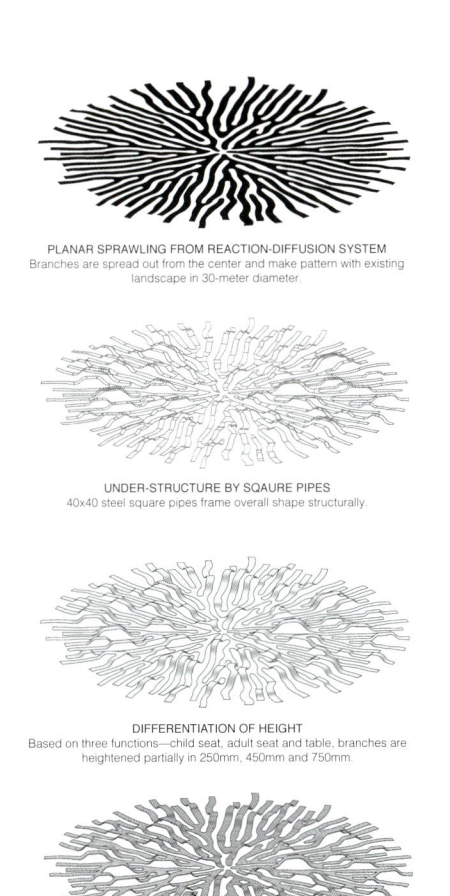

PLANAR SPRAWLING FROM REACTION-DIFFUSION SYSTEM
Branches are spread out from the center and make pattern with existing landscape in 30-meter diameter.

UNDER-STRUCTURE BY SQAURE PIPES
40x40 steel square pipes frame overall shape structurally.

DIFFERENTIATION OF HEIGHT
Based on three functions—child seat, adult seat and table, branches are heightened partially in 250mm, 450mm and 750mm.

WOODEN DECK INSTALLATION ON TOP
120x30 hardwood deck covers steel structure and makes functional space.

Root Bench

Root Bench is the reinterpretation of the winning proposal in the Hangang Art Competition in Hangang Park. It is circle-shaped public furniture with a diameter of 30 meters, installed in the grass, which shows the dynamic shape of root spreading throughout the park. It provides visual stimulus creating a sharp contrast to the background of a spacious outdoor park. People can take a rest with it while sitting and leaning on a different height.

Photography: **Yong Ju Lee Architecture** | Material: **Metal, concrete, wood** | Location: **Seoul, South Korea**

Wing Tower

Korea's traditional folktale, *A Fairy and A Woodcutter*, has been passed down for generations in multiple versions, of which the narrative basis is a story about the encounter and separation between a woodcutter and a fairy, straddling between the heavenly and earthly worlds. Presented at the Sulwha Cultural Exhibition, *Wing Tower* is an installation visualizing a dramatic moment when the fairy left for the heaven fluttering her feathers. This project features a computer-generated dynamic image of a rotating tunnel, representing the image as a medium of bridging the heaven and earth. As the cylindrical tube moves up, it opens up, breaking into triangles. The rising and splitting space represents the sad visage of the fairy and the despair of the woodcutter.

Photography: **Jong Wook Koh, Yong Ju Lee Architecture** | Material: **Painted metal plate** | Location: **Seoul, South Korea**

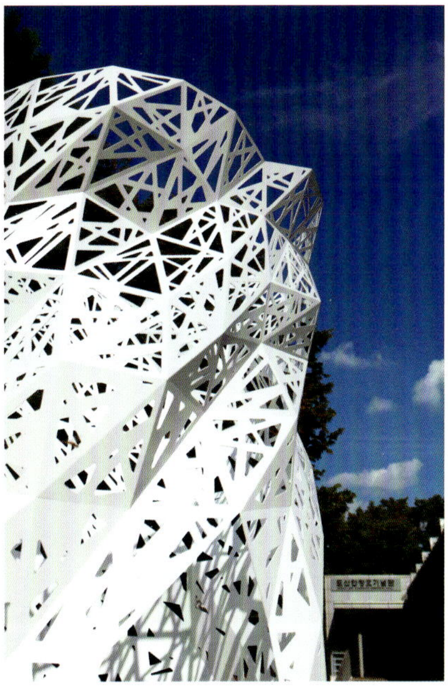

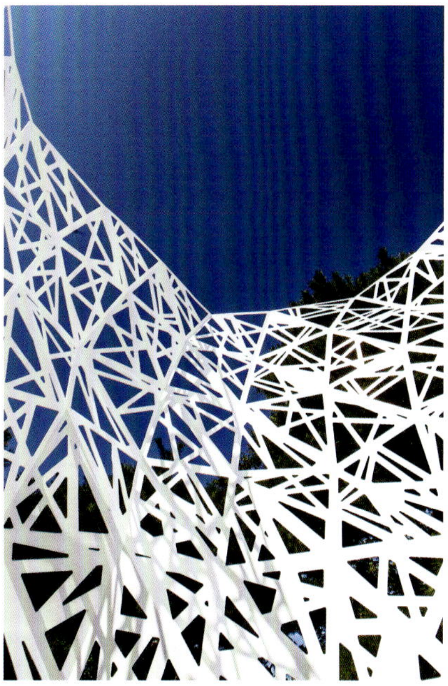

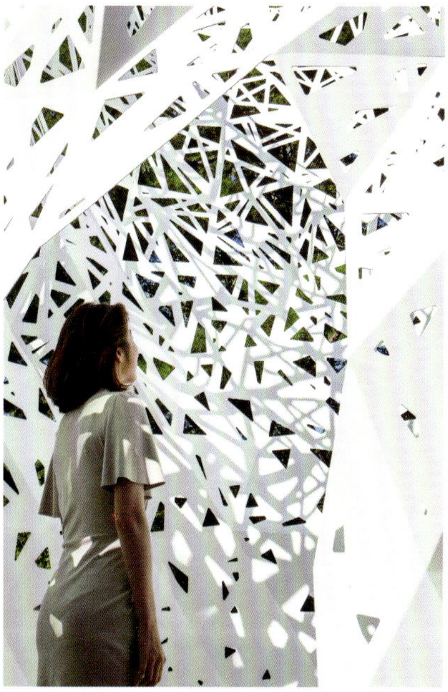

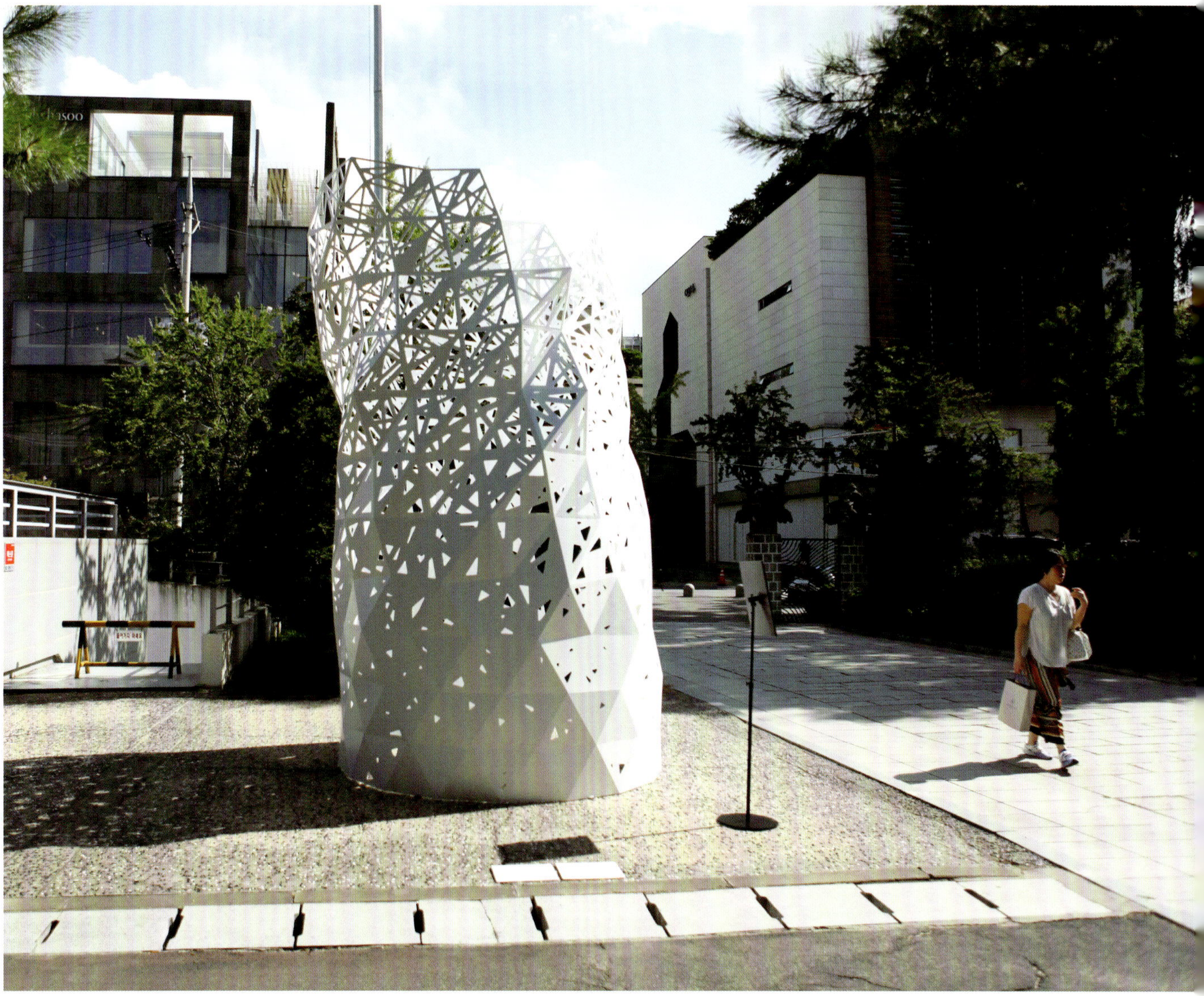

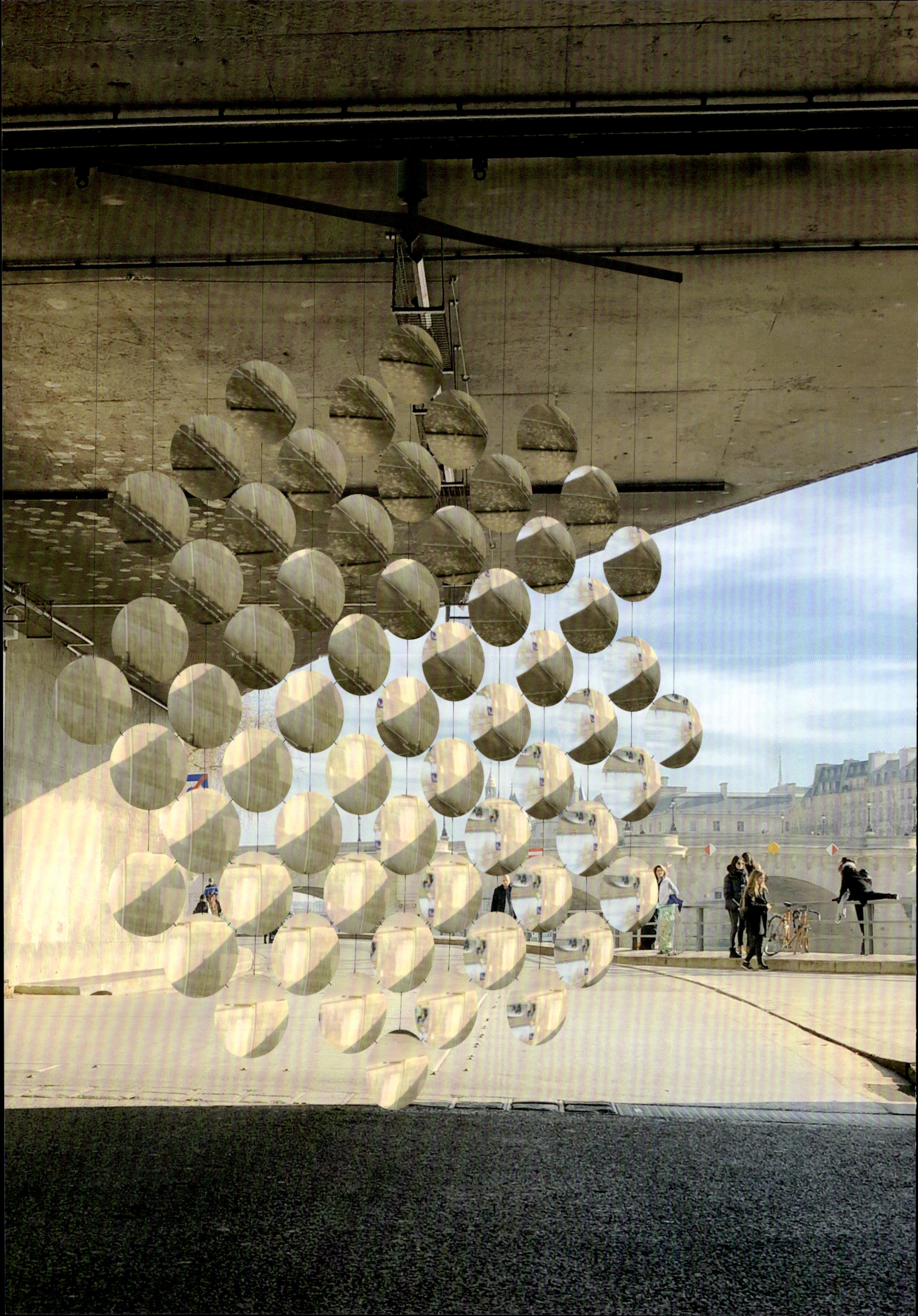

"I like to arouse wonder comparable to move the audience and myself. Also, I aim for creating work that can trigger people's curiosity—if I succeed—I am fulfilled. Work in motion has the advantage of achieving this goal since it allows the audience to view from different angles. It is more dynamic and perhaps more integrated into urban life. But it can also disturb the traditional urban pattern and provoke new ideas and perspectives. Good public work should play well with its environment and seems surprising."

Vincent Leroy

—

Artist

—

Vincent Leroy, a French artist, focuses on contemporary art in an international context and creates sculptures in movement mixing poetry and technology. His work navigates between poetry, technology, and freedom of spirit. Portrait photo by Andrea Aubert.

Poetic Game in Motion:
Play with Vision and Light

Vincent Leroy was born in Avranches, a small town in northwest France, in 1968. As a child, he crafted many objects on his parent's farm in Normandy, France. From a sailing boat to a glider with an eight-meter wingspan, this ten-year-old boy explored his curiosity and creativity through various games. The farm became his creative laboratory stocked with numerous ideas. From a young age, Vincent stretched his imagination in objects in motion, and this interest followed him into adulthood. It was in his 20s, in Paris, that he started his artistic career. "It is a very natural choice. I think what I do today is exactly what I have done as a child. I don't have to force or gear myself to a particular path," says Vincent.

He is renowned for his reflective and kinetic installations, which navigate between poetry, technology, and freedom of spirit. In his view, movement is everywhere. "Movement is like a fourth dimension." Vincent adds, "Movement is life." He can never imagine if he creates art without bringing in movement. Light and reflection embody the concept of movement in a more implied, poetic way. Therefore, Vincent tries to integrate them into his research and play with them, not only in a visual way, but an experiential way by engaging and connecting the mind, body, and soul.

Creating a kinetic installation is much more complicated than a static one, let alone a specific form of motion. There are many factors that an artist needs to take into account: durability, security, and technical constraints. "The most difficult is to overcome the technical constraints and bring the idea, the intention to life. We must forget the rigid technical system, get out of a rut, and realize the poetry, the idea. We must remain sensitive and creative despite the big constraints," Vincent explains. Whenever Vincent starts a project, he will approach the place, investigate it, and clarify the intended audience and the local culture beforehand. It is his vision to create work that can break convention and banality of a place, breaking down the traditional urban pattern, which is often known as an aggregation of buildings, sidewalks, traffic, trees, urban infrastructure, etc. "I like to arouse wonder comparable to move the audience and myself." Vincent continues, "Also, I aim for creating work that can trigger people's curiosity—if I succeed—I am fulfilled. Work in motion has the advantage of achieving this goal since it allows the audience to view from different angles. It is more dynamic and perhaps more integrated into urban life. But it can also disturb the traditional urban pattern and provoke new ideas and perspectives. Good public work should play well with its environment and seems surprising."

Vincent draws inspiration from everywhere and everything, from masters like Picasso, Alexander Calder, and Jean-Michel Basquiat to exciting things in the universe, different cultures, or even way of thinking. He never confines himself to the realm of art; instead, he buries himself to various activities like photography, electronic music, and so on. "The idea of having some expertise, of being a 'specialist,' scares me somehow. I think the involvement in various practices is very beneficial to one's mind. And I like the idea of keeping a beginner's mind, leaving room for openness and curiosity," Vincent concludes.

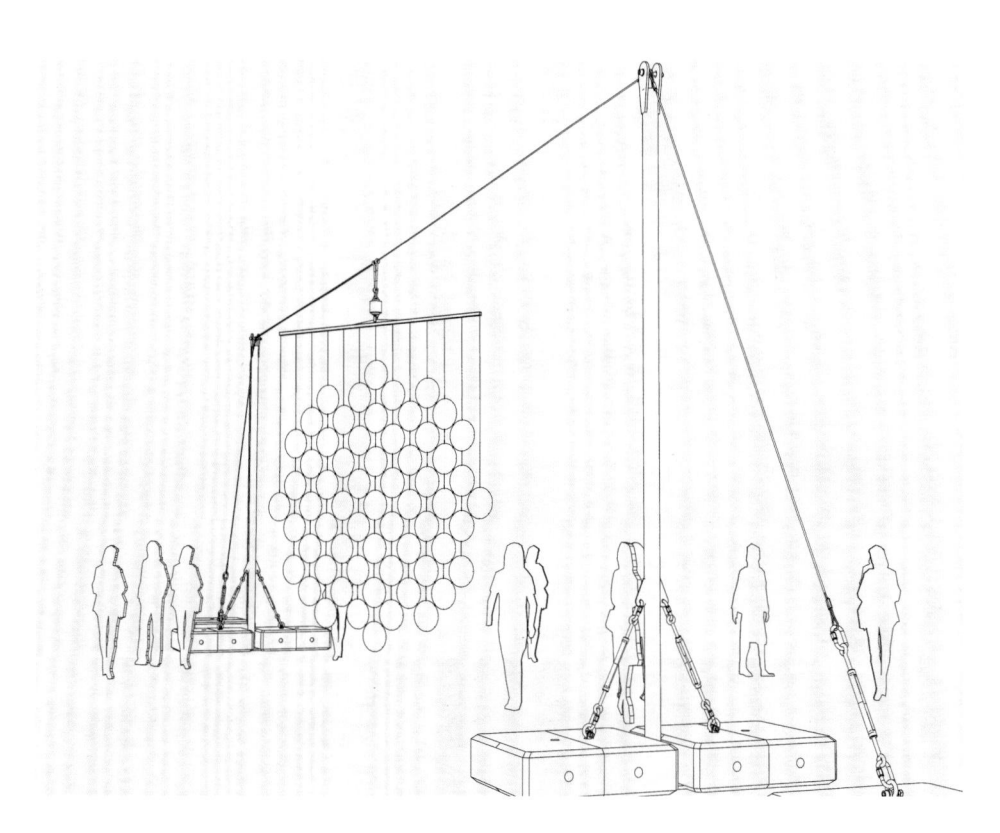

Slow Lens

Slow Lens is a project proposal outlining a network of curved, translucent lenses hanging in the air and distorting the viewer's perspective. Like a suspended magnifying glass curtain, it rotates and offers multiplied visions of the environment to the viewer. It breaks down the architecture by invoking a new assembly. The vision seems to become disturbed and unreal; a focus on a detail becomes captivating. It is a subtle mix of low technology and poetry that detaches the audience from the real world.

Photography: **Vincent Leroy** | Material: **Lens, stainless steel, engine, stainless cable** | Location: **Paris, France**

Slow Lens. Photo by Vincent Leroy.

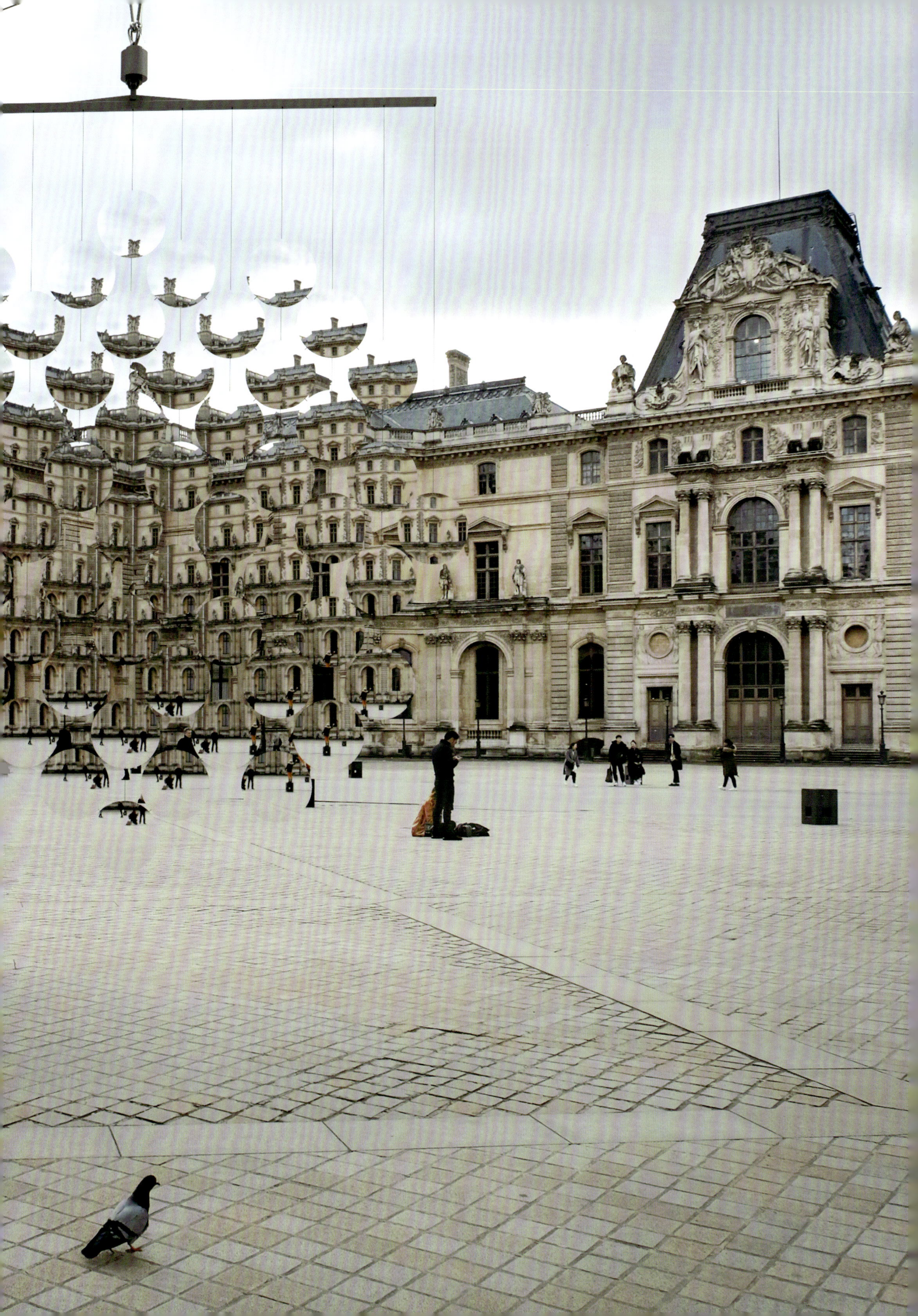

The Pebble

The Pebble, a project proposal, occupies the space with an incredible aesthetical experience. This gigantic elliptical mirror floats with utmost grace, softness, and voluptuousness. It is a sensory experience more than a visual one. With the mirror effect, the ground moves slowly, and the horizon disappears. Vincent slows down time and displays his magical mechanism, using the same technology for his halo: inflatable with steel cables in slow rotation.

Photography: **Vincent Leroy** | Material: **Inflatable, engine, stainless cable** | Location: **Paris, France**

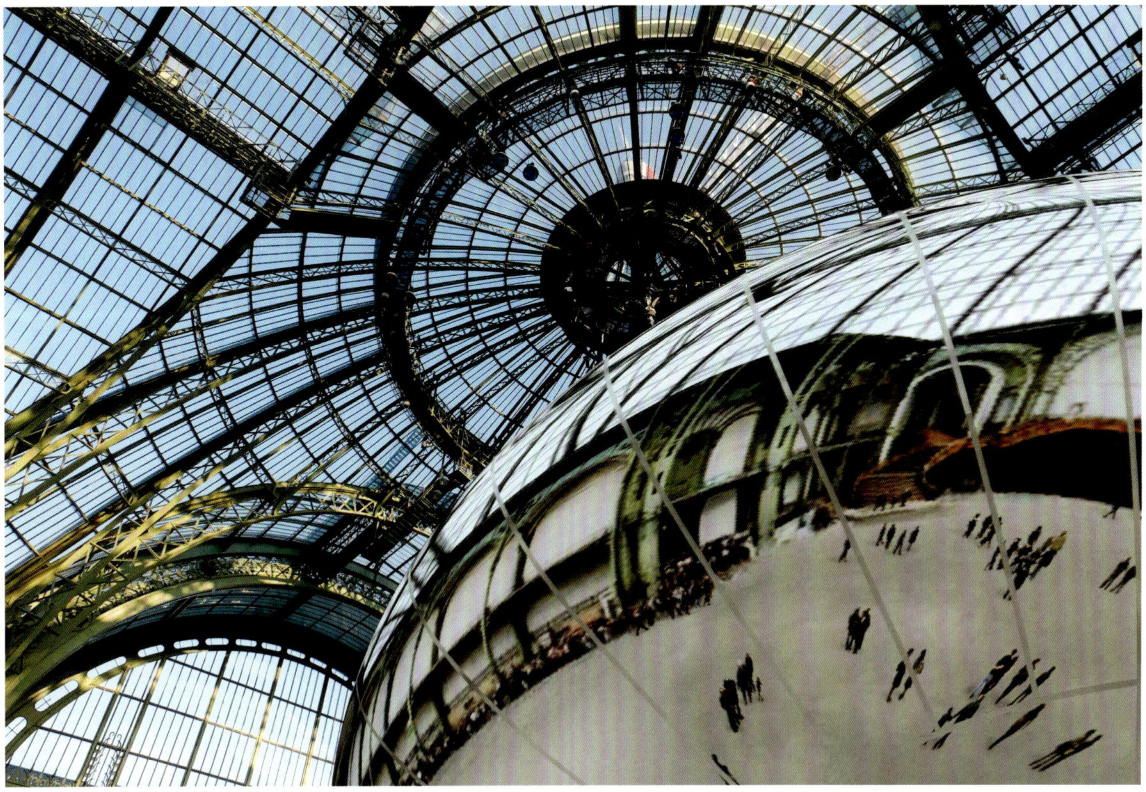

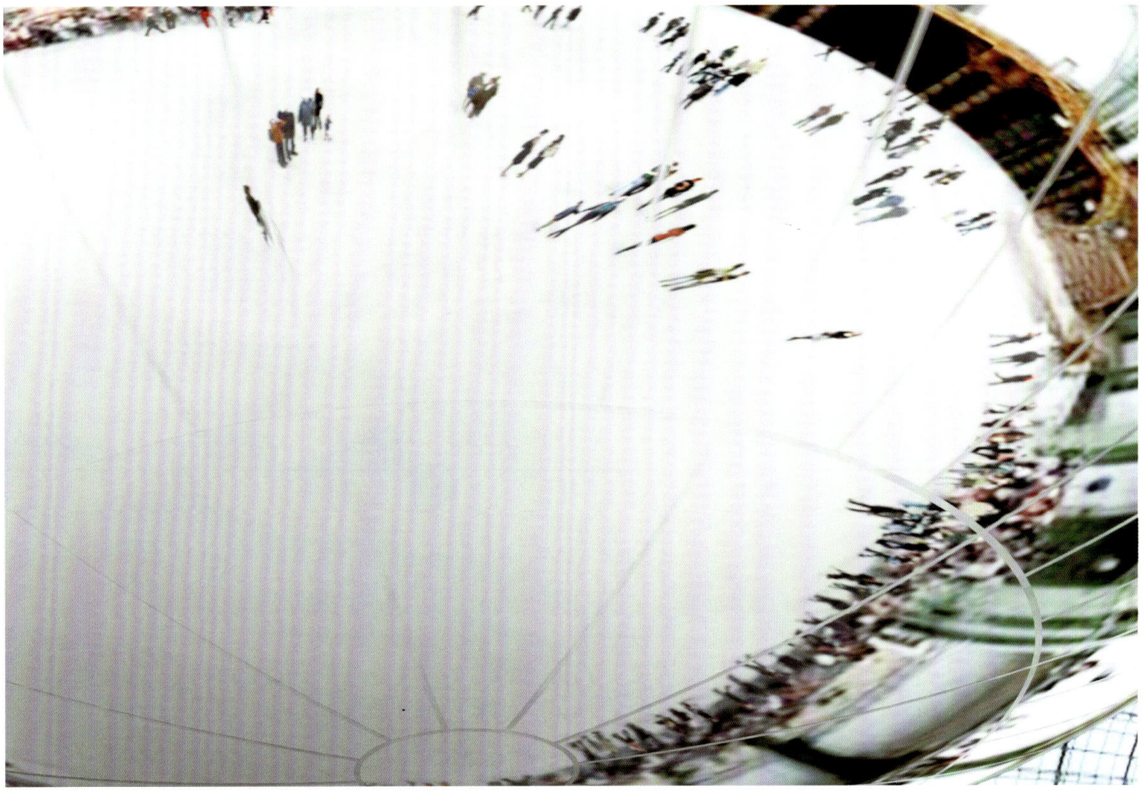

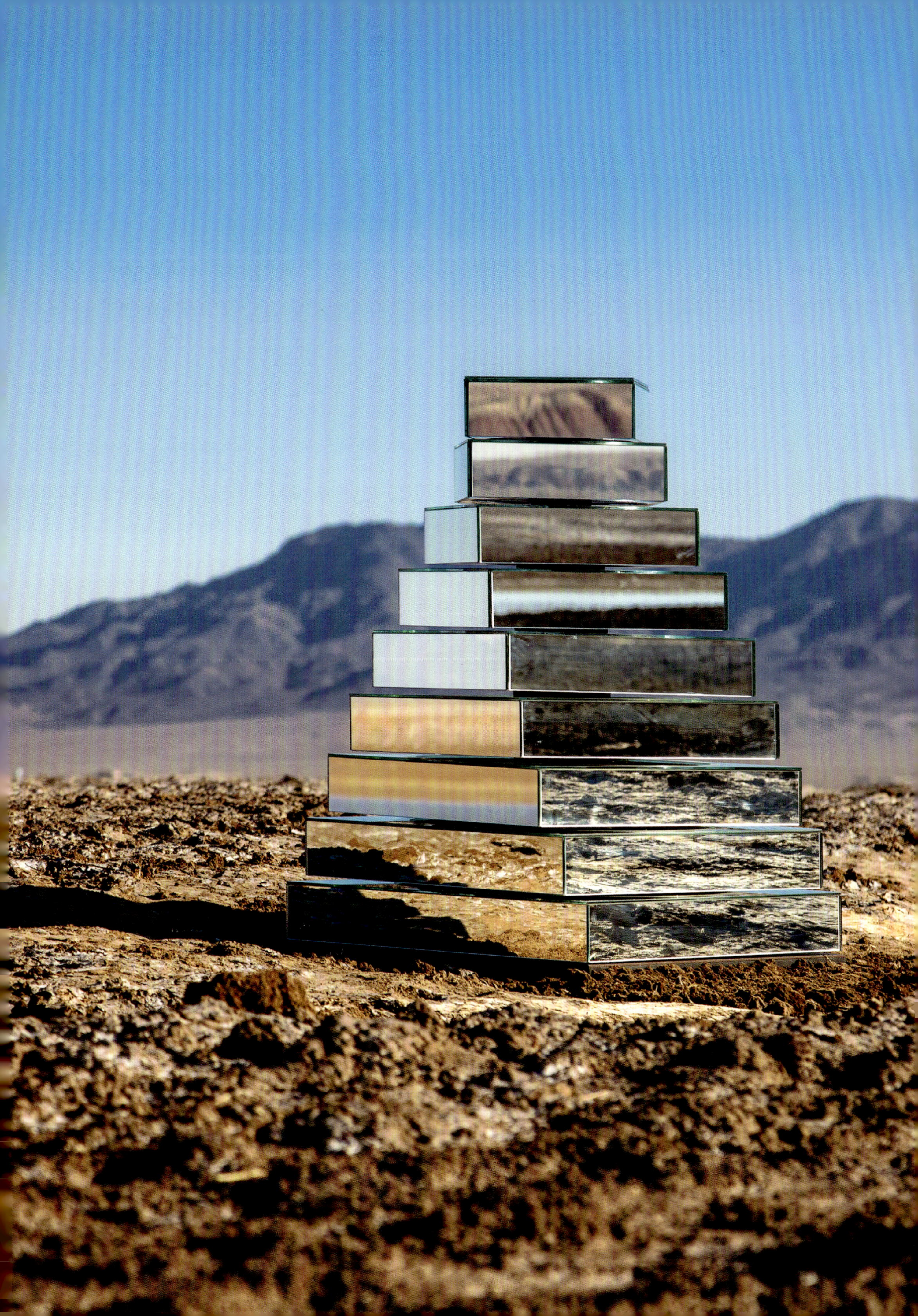

"I want to draw the audience's attention to nature, to look at the sky, and bring light to them. As we see a flood of selfies on social media, people are really interested in taking selfies; thus, when they came across my work, they enjoyed taking photos of themselves, with the sky. I think a good piece of public work will make people stop for a few seconds on their busy day and make them think."

Shirin Abedinirad

—
Artist
Designer
—

Shirin Abedinirad was born in 1986, in Tabriz, Iran. In 2002, she began her artistic activities with painting. She studied graphic design and fashion design at Dr. Shariaty Technical College in Tehran, where she shifted the focus of her research to conceptual art and how it overlaps with fashion design. Portrait photo by Mehdi Teimory.

Land of Purity:
Inviting Nature into Cities

When Shirin Abedinirad was a child, her parents' first ambition for her was to become an artist. They sent her paintings to international contests and took her to parks where painting contests were held for kids. "I remember a book in which all the pages were graph paper with some shapes on it, and I could draw shapes on those graph paper. Now, as I recall, I realize that my geometric way of thinking is coming from those days," Shirin says.

Shirin studied graphic design in high school and spent two years at Dr. Shariaty Technical College in Tehran, where she got a bachelor's degree in fashion and textile design. Later, she got a one-year scholarship from Fabrica (Communication Reserach Center of United Colors of Benetton) based in Treviso, Italy; between March 2014 to March 2015, she was at Fabrica as an artist working on various projects. It was there that she created *Heaven on Earth*. During her time in Italy, Shirin worked at Fabrica's Editorial Department and published an original book *Conceptual Art & Fashion Design in the 21st Century* published by Nazar Publication.

Around this time, Shirin started engaging in performance art pieces around Iran, confronting issues of gender, sexuality, and human compassion. She has also put on public shows in Spain, Turkey, and India. When Shirin studied under the acclaimed Iranian artist and film director Abbas Kiarostami, she became aware of the power of nature and made her first land art installation. After exhibiting her work in festivals, she became more interested in public art. "In public art, you can have the interaction with kids, adults, and people who probably do not know much about conceptual art," explains Shirin.

Reflective materials are often used in Shirin's work. For her, reflections are magic. "By using mirrors, I don't add any element to nature or cities." Shirin adds, "I just change its composition and create illusions. I believe if I show the same installation inside of the gallery, people will not like them as much as they do outdoors because I am using the beauty of nature; without its beauty, my work is not complete." For instance, in *Babel Tower*, Shirin can change the place of the mountains merely by moving the mirrors, which is a kind of magic for her. She believes that if *Babel Tower* is installed in a city location, it will react with different city patterns, and humans will be having a dialogue with the city and nature in front of the installation.

As an artist with Iranian rooting, Shirin is much inspired by Iran's architecture and Islamic geometry. The mirrors in the interior design of mosques are apparent evidence. Also, she draws inspiration from Iranian poets like Rumi and Khayyam, whose work has influenced her a lot in terms of the ways of thinking. The concept of mirrors was also drawn from Rumi's poems, in which mirrors often embody the imagery of the purity of the soul. And lastly, nature has always been a constant source of inspiration for Shirin. When it comes to nature, people tend to imagine the scenario of forest and green fields, but to Shirin, what happens to her mind is desert—barren and remote place—which is more aligned with her vision of purity.

Babel Tower

Inspired by the story of Babel, *Babel Tower* is an interactive installation that re-contextualizes the spiritual architecture of the Babel Tower with modern materials, creating a union between ancient history and the present world; it is combining the past, present and offering a union for future. The top view of the installation that reflects the sky symbolizes the aim of Babel Tower: connecting the earth and heaven. The mirrors serve as a reflective vessel for light, an integral feature of paradise and an essential mystical concept in Persian culture.

Photography: **Shirin Abedinirad** | Material: **Mirrors, sensors, gears, and Arduino processor** | Location: **Tehran, Iran**

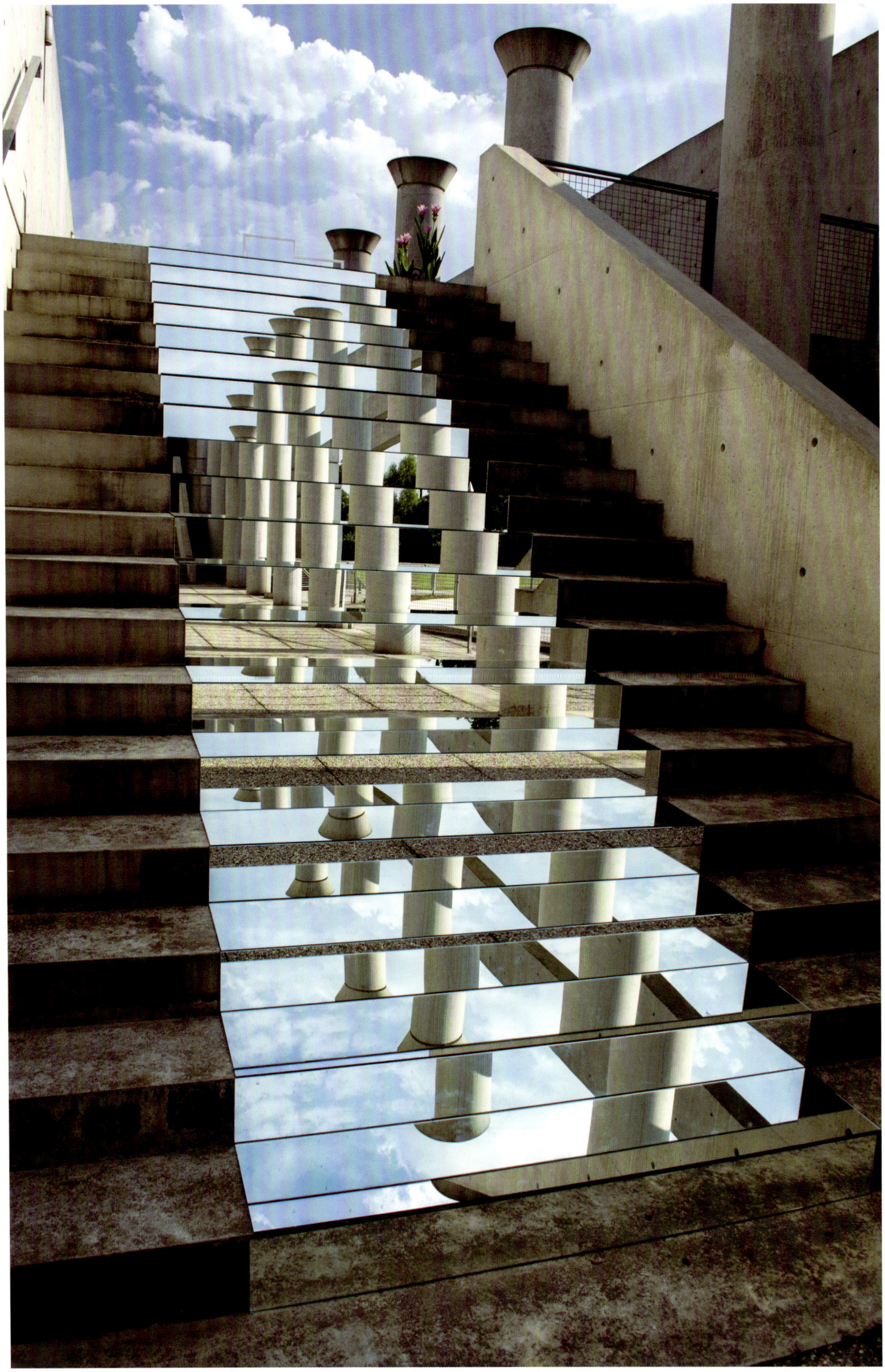

Heaven on Earth

One of the first uses of mirrors in architecture was in Persepolis, Persia, at the Tachara Palace. Glossy black stones were polished till their surface was reflective so as to expand the palace's size and beauty. Two thousand years later, Shirin returns to the concept of doubling space and light with *Heaven on Earth*. The basic geometric shapes and symmetrical composition of the mirrors angling up the cement stairs are borrowed from Islamic art, where symmetry is considered the highest form of beauty. When the audiences stand at the top of the stairs and looks down, they come face to face with an optical illusion that increases their light, and therefore their spirituality of the space.

Photography: **Shirin Abedinirad** | Material: **Mirrors** | Location: **Treviso, Italy**

Revision

"You use a glass mirror to see your face; you use works of art to see your soul," wrote George Bernard Shaw in his set of plays *Back to Methuselah* in 1918. Drawing inspiration from the plays, Shirin Abedinirad's monumental assemblage of mirrored retro television sets in the shape of a Ziggurat interrogates similar themes of reflection, revelation, illusion, and truth. Situated on the grassy isthmus at the mouth of the Erskine River, *Revision* is a site-specific land art project that mirrors all its surroundings. When the space is empty, the mirrored TV screens reflect nature as it transforms itself from night to day. The ocean, sky, and birdlife of the area become the only subjects on the screens. When the isthmus is populated, it reflects the movements of people—joggers, walkers, children, dogs, lovers, and loners who visit the site each day. Shirin comments, "This project invites audiences to watch nature in a new frame."

Photography: **Shirin Abedinirad** | Material: **Retro televisions, wooden structure, mirror silver vinyl** | Location: **Lorne, Australia**

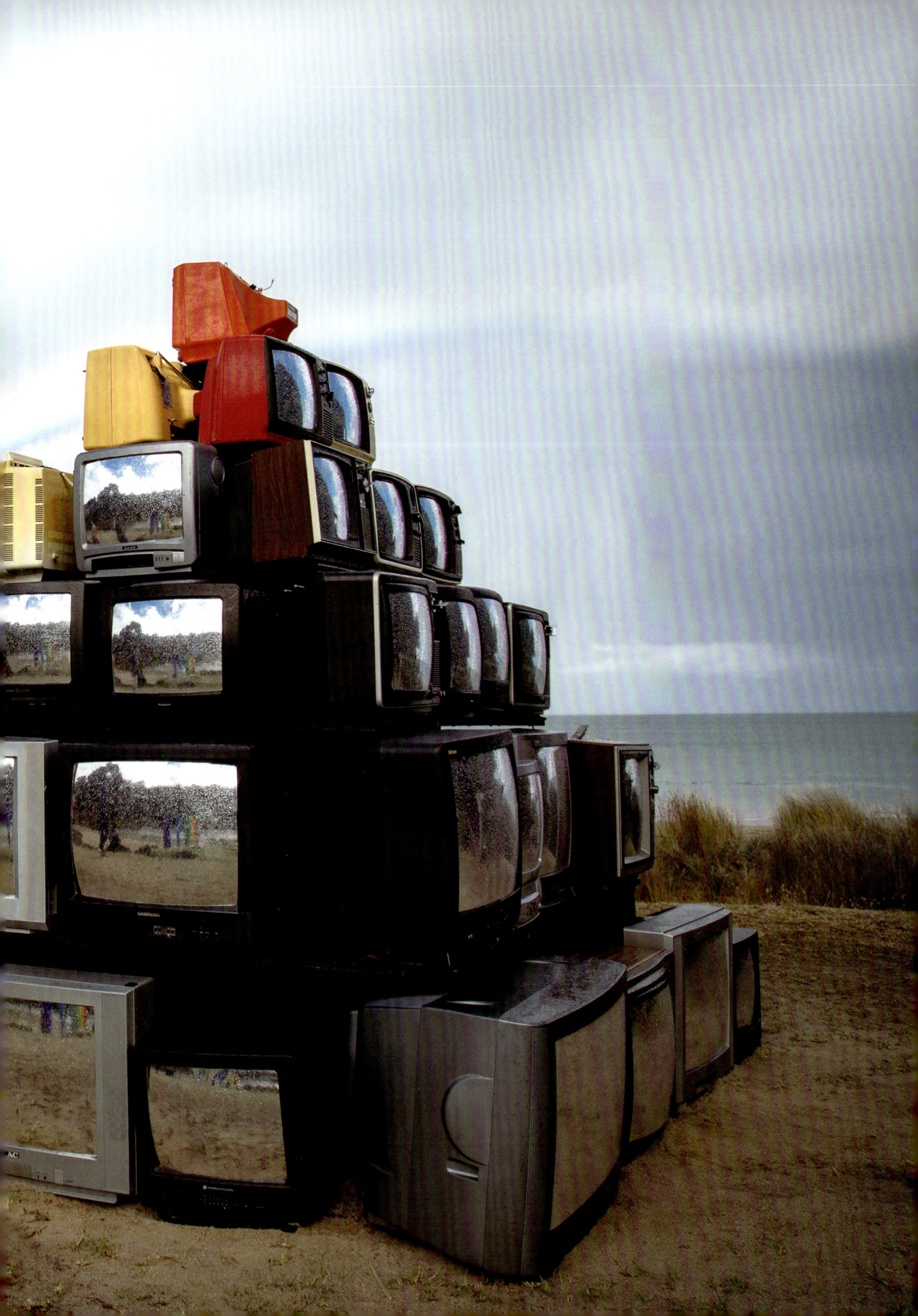

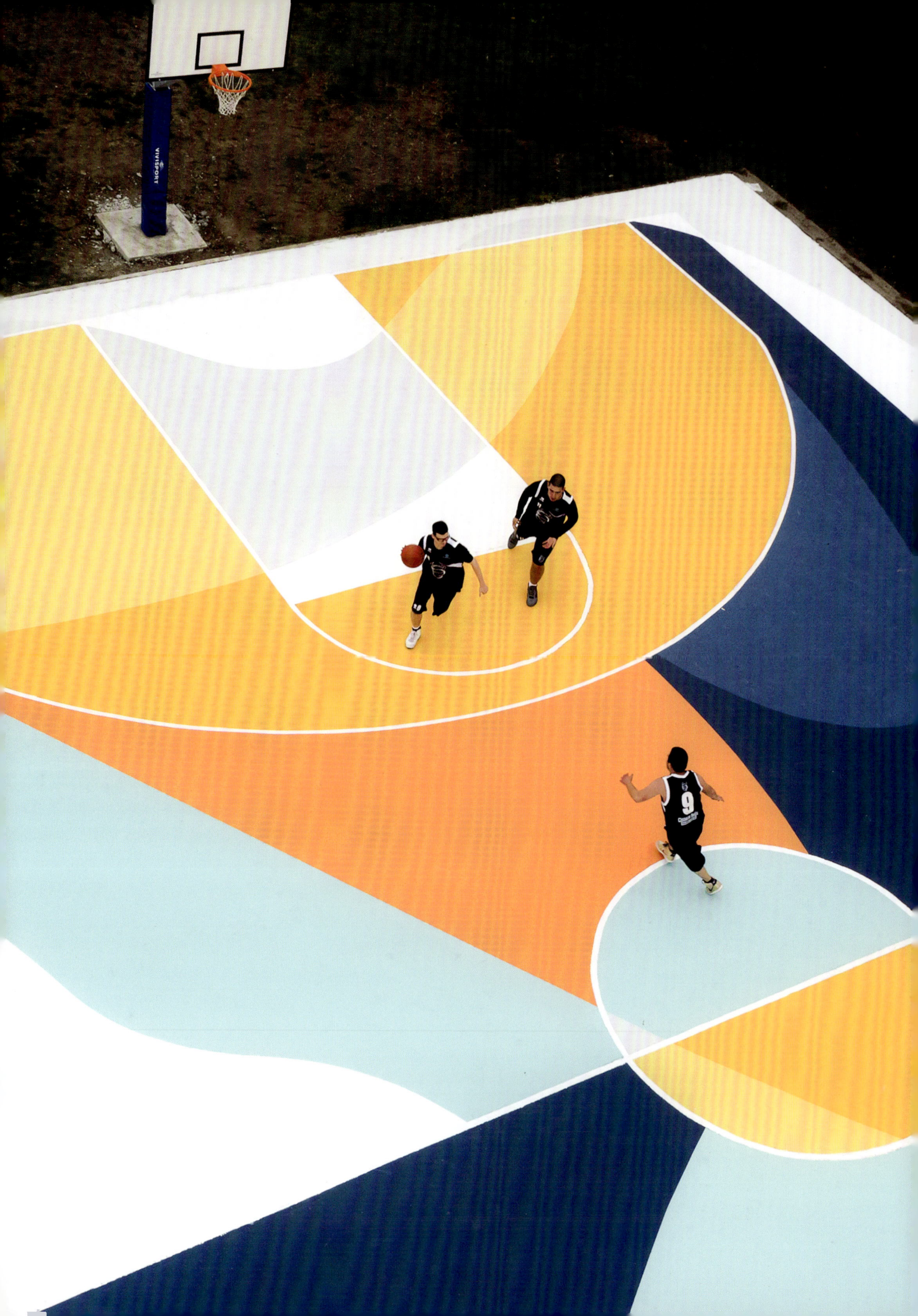
VIVISPORT
9

"Several of our projects are made within sports facilities and recreational areas, where the audience can experience various activities. Through a variable painted surface, we experiment with the new forms and expressive possibilities of mural art—from wall-mural to ground painting—and intervene in different environments designed for collective activity. The breakdown of geometric elements is a quest for synthesis that expresses positive and vibrant vibes to a flexible space, inviting an open dialogue with the architectures, the flow of people, and urban environments."

Gummy Gue

Artists

Born in Catania, Italy, in 1986, Gummy Gue is an artistic duo formed by twin brothers Marco Mangione and Andrea Mangione, who work mainly in public spaces. They came to the graffiti writing environment in the early 2000s. Since then, they have been investigating and experimenting with the expressive possibilities of urban contemporary art.

Shapes and Colors:
A Dialogue with Urban Environment

Marco Mangione and Andrea Mangione are two Italian brothers and street artists known as Gummy Gue. Growing up in a family with an artistic background, they had a shared passion for drawing. They were motivated to attend art school and later the academy of fine arts in Catania, Italy. As monozygotic twins, it was natural for them to unite and form a duo. In the early 2000s, they stepped into the world of graffiti since Marco showed a great interest in this form of creation.

Initially, they created graffiti under the name of Gue, which was derived from a code name of Marco given by his playmates. Later, as they developed, paired with a clearer vision, they added Gummy in front of their existent name to highlight the soft and playful character of the shapes applied to the compositional schemes. "We try to bring together different ideas and points of view towards a common vision, a single direction to find a stylistic coherence," explains Marco and Andrea.

After doing graffiti work for years, they noticed that not everything that appeared on the street art scene was to their liking, some of which were merely aggressive overlapping of paints. Marco and Andrea tried to identify their voices as artists, and they finally fell upon abstract yet accurate solutions to urban interventions, with which they search for a dialogue with the surrounding environment. "What fuels the desire and motivation to do this type of urban interventions is the awareness of creating something that remains in a place in the city—something that puts us in relation to the city and lets us feel like part of it," Marco and Andrea said. To achieve their aspiration, they try to remove all forms of improvisation that they have done many times in graffiti art and center on the ideation behind each piece of work. Marco and Andrea believe that through working with abstract, geometric, colorful shapes, they can give an exactitude to their work, putting the right balance between the rationality of a project and the emotions it may arouse. "The trace you left on the wall at night continues to speak for you in the following days, with its ability to capture people's eyes or even become part of their daily life."

Their latest work, *Orbital*, made in Breda, the Netherlands, grasped the public's attention soon after its birth. It is a large mural art painted all over the floor of a football field. They spent months on this project in the winter season. Breda is a small town and reported as a place with a high crime rate and severe contamination. Therefore, when approaching this project, Marco and Andrea held a precise aim in mind: to give new life to this area. In Gummy Gue's projects, there is always the desire to find a meeting point with the structural reality where they operate, and this project is no exception. They developed the project through the search for proportional relationships between the irregular shape of the concrete perimeter and the field's area, and finally brought to life a dynamic of shapes in colors surrounding the rims of the field, breathing new life to the playground and giving a refreshed gathering place for the community. "Several of our projects are made within sports facilities and recreational areas, where the audience can experience various activities. Through a variable painted surface, we experiment with the new forms and expressive possibilities of mural art—from wall-mural to ground painting—and intervene in different environments designed for collective activity. The breakdown of geometric elements is a quest for synthesis that expresses positive and vibrant vibes to a flexible space, inviting an open dialogue with the architectures, the flow of people, and urban environments," Marco and Andrea comment.

Playground

Playground is part of Rigenerazione Urbana, a project for the renovation of Carlo Carrà park, in collaboration with the Municipality of Alessandria, Italy. The idea was to explore the possibility of using shapes and colors to keep the function of the playground while breaking people's conventional perception of the space. The choice of colors was inspired by a direct reference to the world of sport. Gummy Gue collected the frequently used color samples in basketball courts, combined them while adding variants. The curves of the graphic pattern generated a compositional rhythm, amplifying the notion of movement and leaving a visual echo to the matches held on the playground.

Photography: **Ugo Galassi** | Material: **Multi-layered acrylic resin system in water dispersion** | Location: **Alessandria, Italy**

Interview with Gummy Gue

Where do you get inspiration?

Before approaching each work, we undergo a careful analysis of the place, to find out a relationship that will determine the character of the project. During this stage, we try to understand the visual codes used in the area or space and thus, creating a dynamic cohesion. The optimum choice of colors and shapes converges towards the representation of a flexible space in an open dialogue with the architecture and environment.

Do you use computer-aided tools to get the desired palette for a specific project?

The work begins on paper, through preparatory sketches, which are then imported to the computer and processed. We consider the computer an essential tool for every creative process of our work, even if paper and pencil remain a good way to express ourselves better and more freely. Using the computer, we do a lot of color tests, looking for the right palette for the project we are working on; we do the same for the shapes we draw on a sheet of paper until we reach a balance that satisfies us. Usually, the design process is longer than the realization itself.

How do you think your work affect the audience?

Several of our projects are made within sports facilities and recreational areas, where the audience can experience various activities. Through a variable painted surface, we experiment with the new forms and expressive possibilities of mural art—from wall-mural to ground painting—and intervene in different environments designed for collective activity. The breakdown of geometric elements is a quest for synthesis that expresses positive and vibrant vibes to a flexible space, inviting an open dialogue with the architectures, the flow of people, and urban environments.

Skatepark

The project is part of Subsidenze, an annual event dedicated to public art in the northern city of Italy, Ravenna. The skatepark is nestled in a newly refurbished urban area, close to the historical center of Ravenna, the Darsena Popup, a recreational and sports complex built along the banks of the river, designed and realized by Officina Meme. Through the use of abstract codes, the intervention covers the entire skatepark, offering the possibility of sensory and perceptual involvement to those who cross the surface. Soft shapes and curved lines suggest the idea of movement generated by skaters and bikers on ramps; colors seek to highlight the surface's three-dimensionality.

Photography: **BD Studio** | Material: **Two-component epoxy resin** | Location: **Ravenna, Italy**

Orbital

The project is curated by Blind Walls Gallery and supported by the Municipality of Breda, the Netherlands. It consists of a horizontal painting on the surface of the playground in Odilia van Salmstraat, in the Gerardus Macella neighborhood in Breda, which surrounds the football cage dedicated to Dutch former football player Hein van Gastel.

Photography: **Edwin Wiekens, Justin van der Moezel** | Material: **Multi-layered acrylic resin system in water dispersion** | Location: **Breda, the Netherlands**

How would you define good work for public spaces?	Good work in public spaces should feed the culture of encounter and contribute to the emotional participation of the community. Intervening in public spaces means, above all, entering the social fabric and structure of the city. Therefore, public art deals with the regional and urban context in the broadest sense of the term.
Are there any artists whom you admire?	The artists we admire are the ones who helped us develop, find a way/a key to access the languages of art. We admire artists such as Henri Matisse, Hans Arp, Joan Miró, Sol LeWitt, Fortunato Depero, and many others from urban art such as 108, MOMO, Eltono, as well as designers like Alessandro Mendini and Ettore Sottsass. We like many different things; we want to approach everything that can help us find a forward path.
Any advice for newcomers in this field?	One piece of advice that we feel we can give to newcomers is not to lose sight of the sincerity and enthusiasm for their work. You may learn how to compare yourself with other artists by avoiding a fruitless emulation, but try to obtain incentives to reach authenticity. We recommend you to learn how to choose between the things you feel closest to your own sensibility, and also, we wish you know how to discover the beauty behind those things and find a good way to express it to the audience.

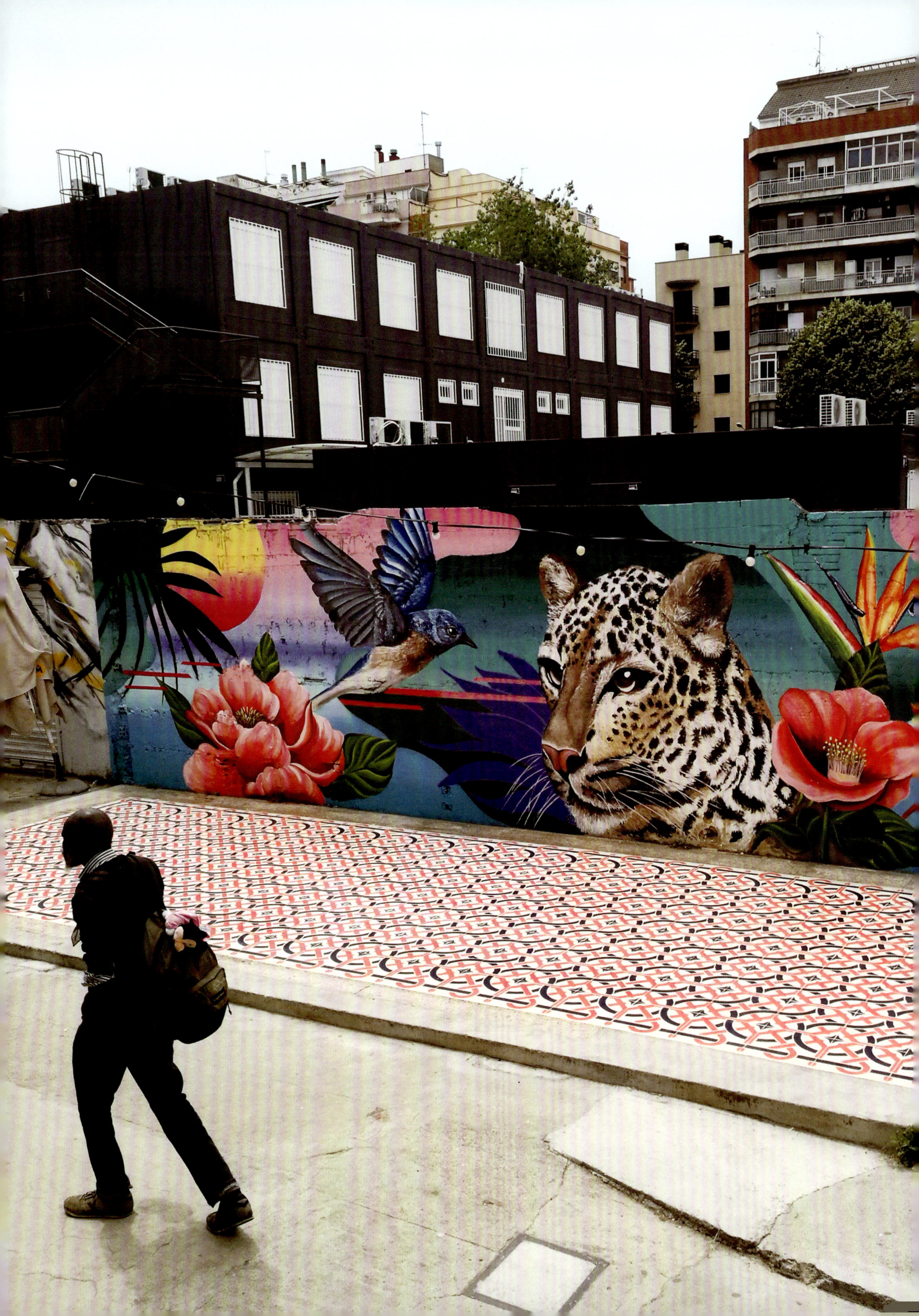

"I think the mosaic floors are appealing to people who stand upon because they make a public space cozy. For example, in Shenzhen, China, I painted tiles in two public spaces— one was to mark a safe pedestrian zone in a parking lot, and the other to signify a sidewalk. Before I did the interventions, few people walked on the two zones, but after my projects were finished, people seemed to love them and stepped on my work, which I found very interesting."

Javier de Riba

Artist

Javier de Riba is a Barcelona-based artist and founding partner of the Reskate Studio. Among his most notable works are *Varnish*, a collection of wood pieces painted with varnish, and *Floors*, a series of painted tiles interventions on the floors of abandoned buildings and public spaces.

Urban Kaleidoscope: Enliven the Floors with Hand-painted Mosaics

Barcelona-based artist Javier de Riba studied graphic design and turned out to be artistically inclined. In recent years, he leans more towards art because he finds that graphic design promotes an image in a more commercial way; yet he wants to use images as a tool to improve society.

In the previous years, he started painting murals in public spaces with María López, co-founder of Reskate Studio, while the idea of painting floors came to his mind too. "The idea seemed to be interesting, and I decided to develop it on my own in abandoned places," says Javier. After a while, he began to find a way out and understand what he was doing. "I find it very interesting to provide order and color to the chaotic and grey places," Javier continues to explain, "and for me, the space is as important as my intervention." This idea eventually became the cornerstone of his ongoing project, *Floors*. The name of *Floors* comes not only from the concept of using floors as a canvas but also from a Catalan word "flor," which means "flower."

As an artist growing up in Catalan Countries, Javier has a close link to patterns, simple geometric designs that spread like carpets and tiles. It was by no means accidental that Javier chose mosaic patterns as his artistic language. "In

Catalan Countries, many houses have hydraulic concrete pavements titled with geometric and floral patterns. I have lived with them all my life, and when I see those tiles, I feel like at home," Javier recalls. Javier wants to raise people's awareness of the abandoned or less-crowded spaces by turning the floors of these spaces as canvas carpeted with beautifully handcrafted geometric, colorful patterns, enlivening the areas. "It moves me to think that one day these floors harbored experiences," he explains, "and helped form a part of someone's daily life." Passionate about patterns, Javier believes that each tile is identical, but the repetition generates new forms, born out of how each of the tiles joins and intersects.

For the *Floors* project, the most time-consuming part lies in the planning, looking for a location, and taking measurements of the area because he has to assure the accuracy of the stencils. He positions the stencils on the floors and sprays paint on until each piece tiles up and forms a blooming pattern. "Sometimes I paint on several days and nights. Each day one layer (one color), but other times, I finish the same day or night, depending on the project dimension," says Javier.

Besides, Javier has been teaching in various workshops. To Javier, working in this way allows him to paint on a larger surface and reach a broader range of audiences. "It makes participants have a direct bond with the intervention. I think it is very important that people feel that their city and streets actually belong to them," Javier says.

Nau Bostik

Nau Bostik was produced during a floor painting workshop held in Barcelona for the urban art center B-MURALS at La Nau Bostik.

Photography: **Fer Alcalá Losa** | Material: **Water-based paint, varnish** | Location: **Barcelona, Spain**

Interview with Javier de Riba

Do you have a philosophy that drives your work?

I like to draw the public's attention to forgotten corners. I go for pleasant and easily understandable aesthetics and create works of art in unappealing locations. In doing this, I try to shed light on how many spaces are fallen in disuse. I find it shameful that there are so many empty spaces while on the other hand, many people are out there without a home. Some homeowners leave their houses deteriorated rather than take them as a living space.

Patterns are predominant features in your work. What do you like about patterns?

In Catalan Countries, many houses have hydraulic concrete pavements titled with geometric and floral patterns. I have lived with them all my life, and when I see those tiles, I feel like at home. They invite the inhabitants and visitors in and make them feel the space. When designing a specific pattern, I always try to create a flower at the intersection of the four tiles. In the Catalan language, "flor" means "flowers." I find it interesting to see how the repetition of the same tile creates new forms and rhythms.

Where do you get inspiration for the patterns?

In the beginning, I took a reference to classic patterns and made some changes. Later, I started to create my own designs. For each pattern, I get inspiration from the place I decided to paint. I want to point out that in my designs, there are some recurring shapes: squares, crosses, and eight-angled stars.

How long does it take to finish a project in general?	The process of designing the pattern is complicated. I am quite picky and give a lot of importance to weights and distances between the elements and color combinations. The time spent on the painting process depends on the dimension of the space. I can finish a small intervention in one day. But for an intervention that is supposed to last for long, I will do preparatory work and figure out later maintenance. In this case, it usually takes me three days to complete. The trickiest part is to prepare the grids because they need to be precise and feasible.
How do you think your work affects the audience?	I think the mosaic floors are appealing to people who stand upon because they make a public space cozy. For example, in Shenzhen, China, I painted tiles in two public spaces—one was to mark a safe pedestrian zone in a parking lot, and the other to signify a sidewalk. Before I did the interventions, few people walked on the two zones, but after my projects were finished, people seemed to love them and stepped on my work, which I found very interesting.
Are there any artists whom you admire?	I admire the work of Escif and Aryz. Escif expresses an artistic language that is really powerful. And I like how Aryz works with colors and how he tests new styles for public spaces.

Pont

Pont transformed a place of passage into a living space. The recent years saw an alarming immigration tide. Refugees, displaced, and exiled people have been forced to live in non-residential environments. Javier tried to convey a view that when people lost their homes, each place can be a home. The painting was done with the students from the Escola d'Art i Disseny d'Amposta (ESARDI) in Catalonia.

Photography: **Javier de Riba** | Material: **Water-based paint, varnish** | Location: **Amposta, Catalonia**

Interblocs

Since the 1990s, the residents of Sant Salvador quarter in Tarragona have demanded that the council should take care of the blocks of their apartments. The zone where *Interblocs* sited was formed by about thirty blocks that were built in the 1960s and were getting deteriorated. But due to the inadequate income of the neighborhood, maintenance of this zone was almost impossible. Javier refreshed the area with an eight-angled stars pattern with the help from Polígon Cultural and El teller de llum.

Photography: **María López** | Material: **Spray paint, varnish** | Location: **Tarragona, Catalonia**

Sidewalk

Produced by the Fringe Art Center, *Sidewalk* was the result of a floor painting workshop held in Shenzhen, China. The purpose of the 78-meter painted floor was to mark on the floor the sidewalk where pedestrians can walk safely in a parking lot.

Photography: **Javier de Riba**
Material: **Water-based paint, varnish**
Location: **Shenzhen, China**

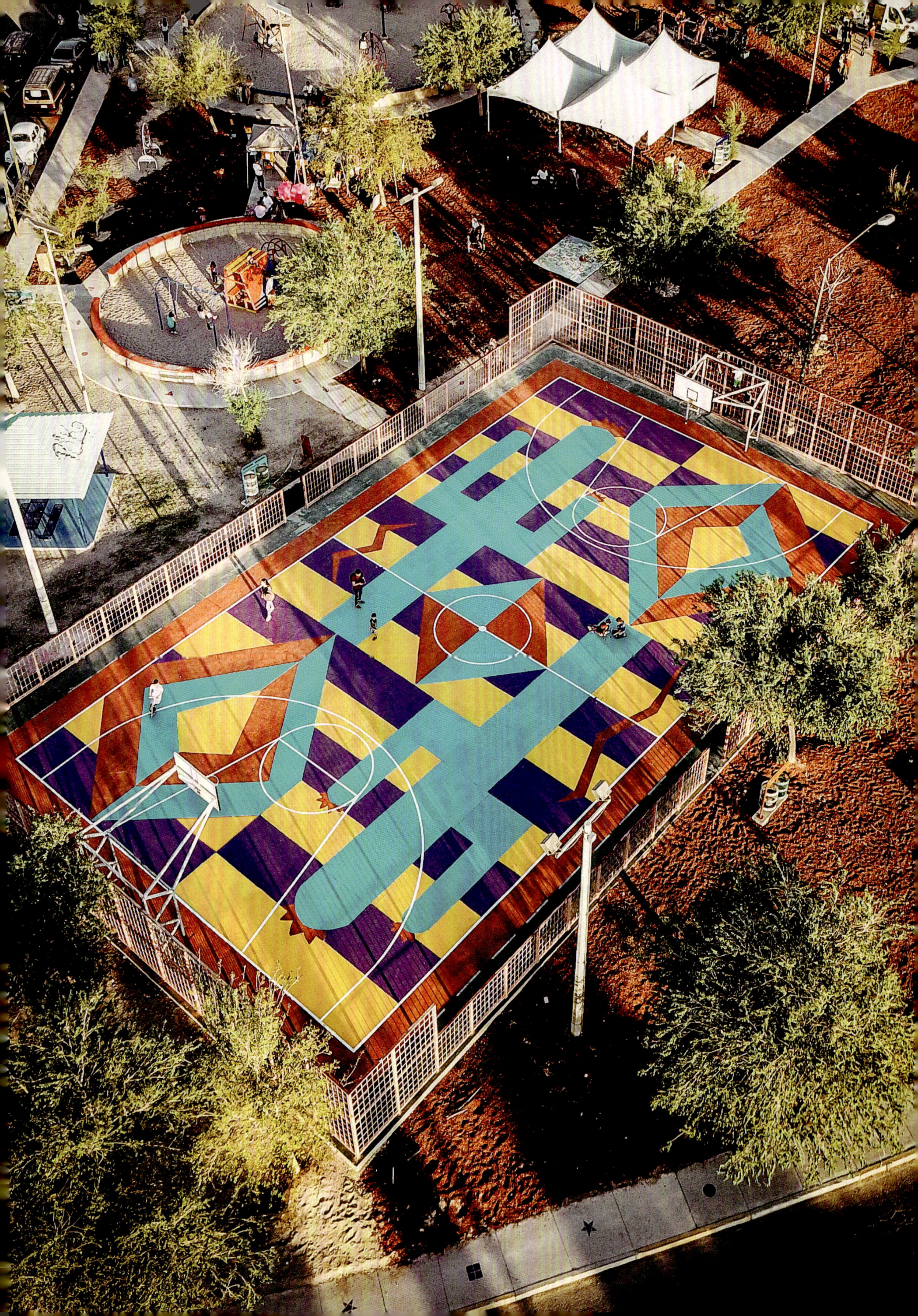

"It is fascinating to observe how through art, color, and community-based concepts, a new identity of the neighborhood begins to be polished, and the public spaces become landmarks of encounter and coexistence again. We believe that public spaces should be the postcards of the present days. Therefore, they are not perpetual but must be in constant evolution or transformation. When the community is involved in the transformation process, the process itself becomes a success story. We live in a complicated urban context and for a public space to be considered as 'good,' we need citizens to be their leading promoters."

Nómada Lab

Artists

Nómada Lab is a group of experimental agents on the northern border of Mexico, in the city of Juárez. Nómada Lab develops projects, strategies, and interventions of urban and sociocultural character through the hybridization of architecture, urban planning, and citizen participation. Portrait photo by Christian Marck.

Community in Multicolor: Urban Interventions with Citizen Participation

Miguel Mendoza and Evangelina Cordero are the co-founders of Nómada Lab. They were both born and are currently based in Juárez, Mexico, a city on the border with El Paso, Texas, in the United States. From an early age, they began to experience border identity and urban dynamics of living in a bi-national community. "Since we have memory, the Juárez-El Paso border has nourished us with its multiculturalism in all aspects, from food, music, language, clothing, traditions, to art itself. We are both children of the 1990s and remember the first urban art outbreaks in the community through graffiti on train cars and near the border," Miguel says.

They came from different backgrounds and met each other in 2013. Miguel was an architect, while Evangelina a dentist, but they both have a shared passion for art and ambition to improve their community. A year later, they founded Nómada Lab, a creative laboratory with an objective to generate urban and cultural projects and interventions that promote the recovery of public spaces. In Spanish, "nómada" means "nomad;" the reason why they chose this term is that Juárez has an extensive urban morphology containing various communities. "Something about being 'urban nomads' gave us the stimulus to intervene in our city," Miguel explains. They hold a common view that art and design can be used as tools of socio-cultural transformation. "Our philosophy is based on promoting the common good and citizen participation through projects, dynamics, and interventions that encourage the inhabitants to become actors and champions of their community," as Miguel mentions.

Inspired by urban interventions that are carried out in Latin American countries such as Colombia, Chile, and Brazil,

Nómada Lab values citizen participation in their projects and urban interventions. They are also greatly influenced by movements such as Bauhaus, Chicano, and Southwest art in terms of the way of conceptualizing. "Many times, the communities are the ones who invite us to intervene in their spaces." Miguel adds, "We, then, act as cultural managers and urban facilitators, and they participate from the initial concept and proposal to the final stage and work on-site." Following this work mechanic, they believe that it can help consolidate community ownership from the pre-intervention process and achieve the real need of the inhabitants.

When they work for small-scale communities, such as neighborhoods and local parks, the effect generated by a participatory urban intervention is immediate and measurable, since from the beginning, all the voices and ideas of the people who occupy, or once occupied those public spaces, are contemplated. When it comes to interventions of a larger urban scale, they must undergo a process of socialization and transparency so that citizens go hand in hand with these projects. For example, when they approach the historic center of Juárez known for its socio-cultural diversity, they need to take into the multiple public and private interests before intervening in a space. "It is fascinating to observe how through art, color, and community-based concepts, a new identity of the neighborhood begins to be polished, and the public spaces become landmarks of encounter and coexistence again." Miguel continues, "We believe that public spaces should be the postcards of the present days. Therefore, they are not perpetual but must be in constant evolution or transformation. When the community is involved in the transformation process, the process itself becomes a success story. We live in a complicated urban context and for a public space to be considered as 'good,' we need citizens to be their leading promoters."

Basketcolor: Praderas del Sur Community

Basketcolor series emerges as an urban and cultural strategy with the objective of using street art and participatory design as recovery tools for sports facilities located in vulnerable public spaces of Juárez, Mexico. Also, *Basketcolor* acts as a mirror of the neighborhood identity. The community of Praderas del Sur is located in the southern periphery of the city, and like many of the urban dispersion sectors, it faces urban, social, and cultural deficits.

Photography: **Miguel Mendoza** | Material: **Traffic paint, oil-based paint** | Location: **Juárez, Mexico**

Basketcolor: Paquimé Community

It is designed for the community of Paquimé, located in the southeastern periphery of Juárez, and like many of the urban dispersion sectors, the region faces urban, social, and cultural deficits.

Photography: **Miguel Mendoza** | Material: **Traffic paint, oil-based paint** | Location: **Juárez, Mexico**

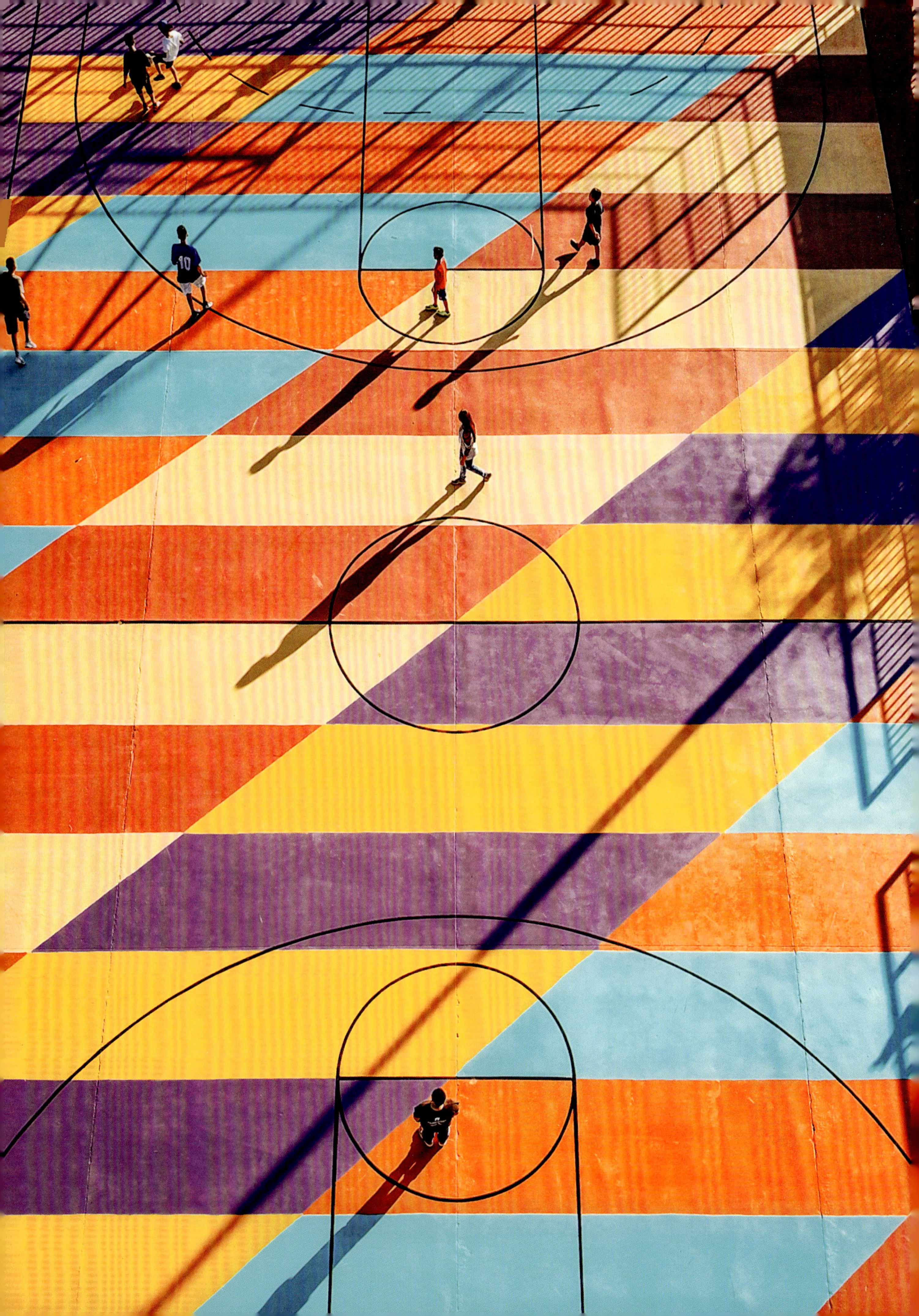

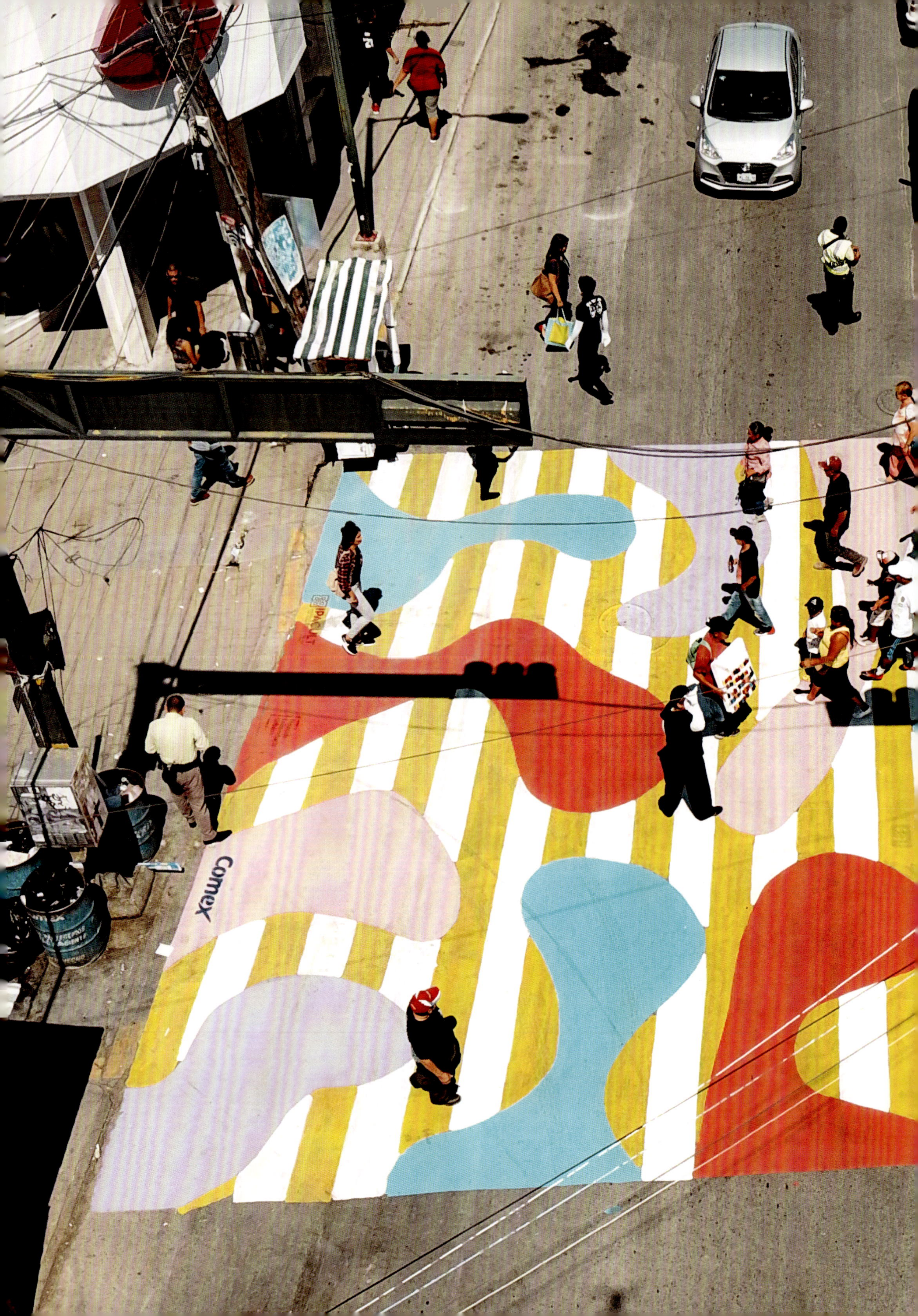
Comex

Peatones Primero: Centro Histórico

Peatones Primero (Pedestrians First) series is an intervention of tactical urbanism to make visible the importance of pedestrian mobility in the historic center of Juárez. This dynamic is only one step to influence medium-long-term urban actions that favor the reformulation of public policies, which directly benefit citizens. With this project, Nómada Lab dreams of a city on a human scale and hope that these practices bring people closer and closer to the city, step by step.

Photography: **Miguel Mendoza** | Material: **Traffic paint, water-based latex paint** | Location: **Juárez, Mexico**

Building Wrap at 34th Street and 8th Avenue in NYC

A giant squiggly building wrap at the 34th Street and 8th Avenue in New York City. Produced by Art Production Fund and Vornado.

Photography: **MOMO** | Material: **Printed Vinyl, construction hoarding mesh** | Location: **New York City, New York, USA**

"All the artwork I have ever been involved with has curiosity mixed up with it. Discovering things, even basic things, can be a beautiful experience for the artist and audience, literally like opening your eyes. Thus, having some intellectual dimension, even just a playful one, within a good aesthetic is like beauty and brains, the most attractive."

MOMO

Artist

MOMO is the pseudonym of American artist David Blas, who began his experimental outdoor work in the late 1990s, working with homemade tools and borrowed public spaces. Portrait photo by Callie Marshall.

Exploring Post-graffiti Murals: Gradients with Concentric Circles

MOMO is an American artist originally from San Francisco, best known for his post-graffiti murals, featuring large gradients, concentric circles made with rope. He is currently based in New Orleans, Louisiana. MOMO began his experimental outdoor work in the late 1990s by working with homemade tools in public spaces. Since 2009, he has been expanding his focus to include a substantial studio practice, like painting on canvases or making sculptures. MOMO always work out the designs and techniques for his murals in advance in his studio, including the custom tools that he needs during the process. "There is more control indoors, to develop ideas, but then to bring this to people I need to find a way to put it on the road," MOMO said.

Over ten years of free-ranging projects, centered around adapted masonry techniques, strategies based on collage, computer code, and seriality, came to form the basis of MOMO's visual language. This language finds its expression in paint, on commissioned walls and studio work from 2009 to the present day. "All the artwork I have ever been involved with has curiosity mixed up with it. Discovering things, even basic things, can be a beautiful experience for the artist and audience, literally like opening your eyes. Thus, having some intellectual dimension, even just a playful one, within a good aesthetic is like beauty and brains, the most attractive."

MOMO's notable mural commissions include those from Facebook, Pepsi, the NFL, the World Trade Center, John Hancock Tower, Art Production Fund in New York City, European Capital of Culture, New York City Department of Transportation (NYC DOT), and Yohji Yamamoto's Y-3. However, for MOMO, self-organized walls in Jamaica, Sicily, and Arizona (2013, 2016, 2018), painted at the artist's expense, have been important in demonstrating innovative techniques for a genera audience free of the usual commercial concerns. In 2016, Maya Hayuk, MOMO, Swoon, and Faile inaugurated the new Millennium Iconoclast Museum of Art in Brussels, with installations on five floors. Solo shows in the following year 2017 were held at Delimbo Gallery in Sevilla and Alice Gallery in Belgium, with an experimental group show of Mark Flood, Revok, Paul Kremer, and MOMO at Library Street Collective in Detroit.

In 2018, MOMO and Australian creative agency Creative Road were selected as the winning team from over 100 entries to deliver "The Tower Project" for the Home of the Arts, Gold Coast Arts Center along the Gold Coast. MOMO, together with Sydney-based artists Georgia Hill and Elliott Routledge, painted large-scale murals in his signature style on the three walls of the center. "This region is gorgeous," MOMO added, "as I adjusted to the sights and summer, I felt I had to make small adjustments in the mural, to be even sunnier and bolder, to try to match what I have seen."

Mural for Open Source (Market Street, Philadelphia)

The project was organized by Pedro Alonzo and Philadelphia Mural Arts, located on Market Street, Philadelphia, Pennsylvania.

Photography: **MOMO** | Material: **Paint** | Location: **Philadelphia, Pennsylvania, USA**

Mural for Open Source (Franklin Street, Fishtown Philadelphia)

The project was organized by Pedro Alonzo and Philadelphia Mural Arts, located on Franklin Street, Fishtown Philadelphia, Pennsylvania.

Photography: **MOMO** | Material: **Paint** | Location: **Philadelphia, Pennsylvania, USA**

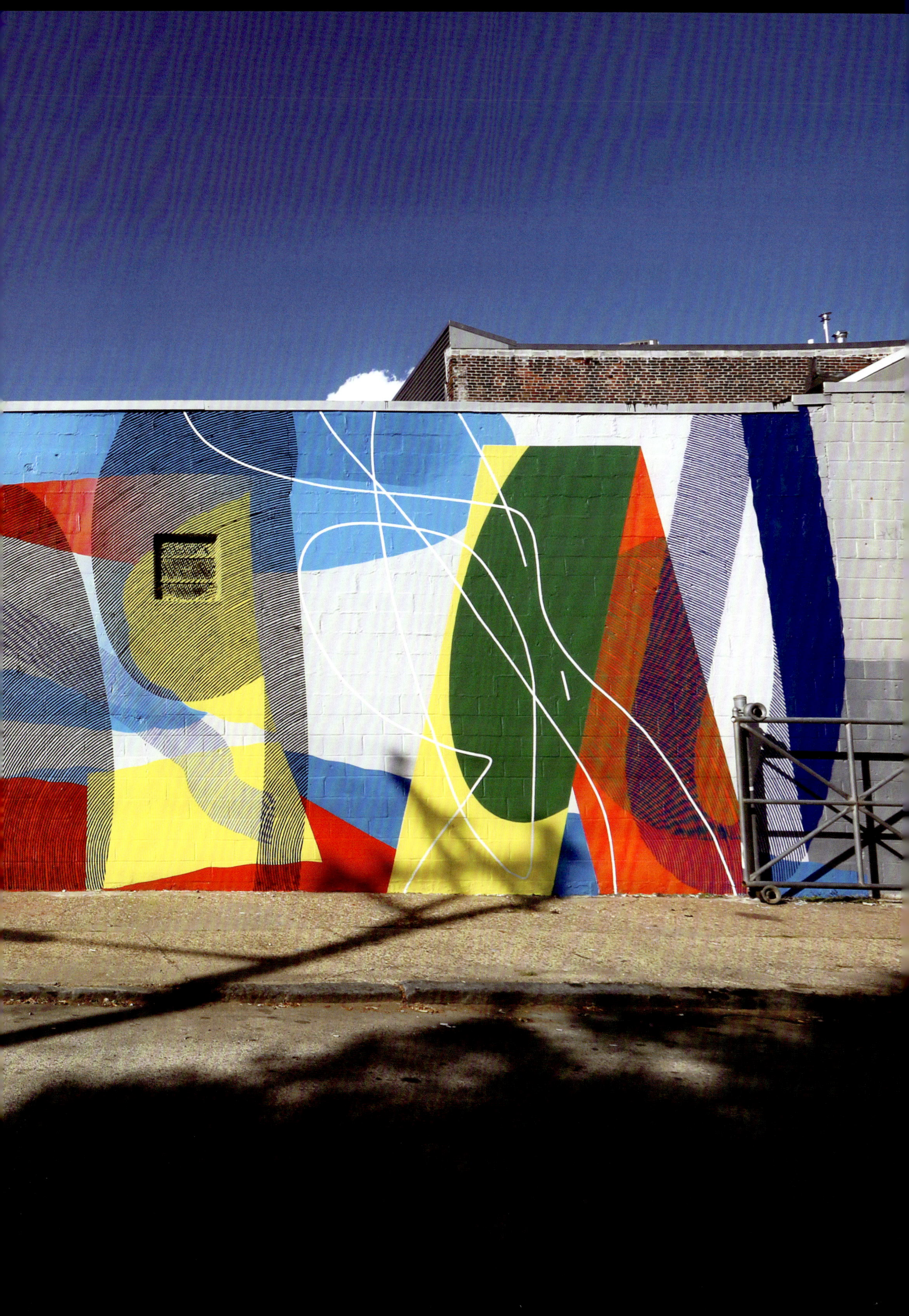

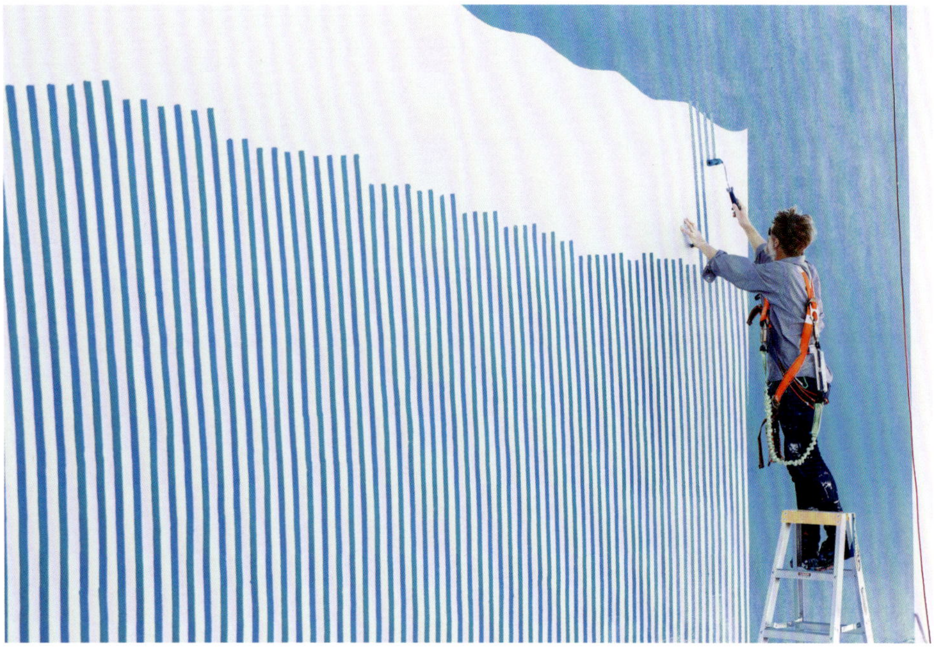

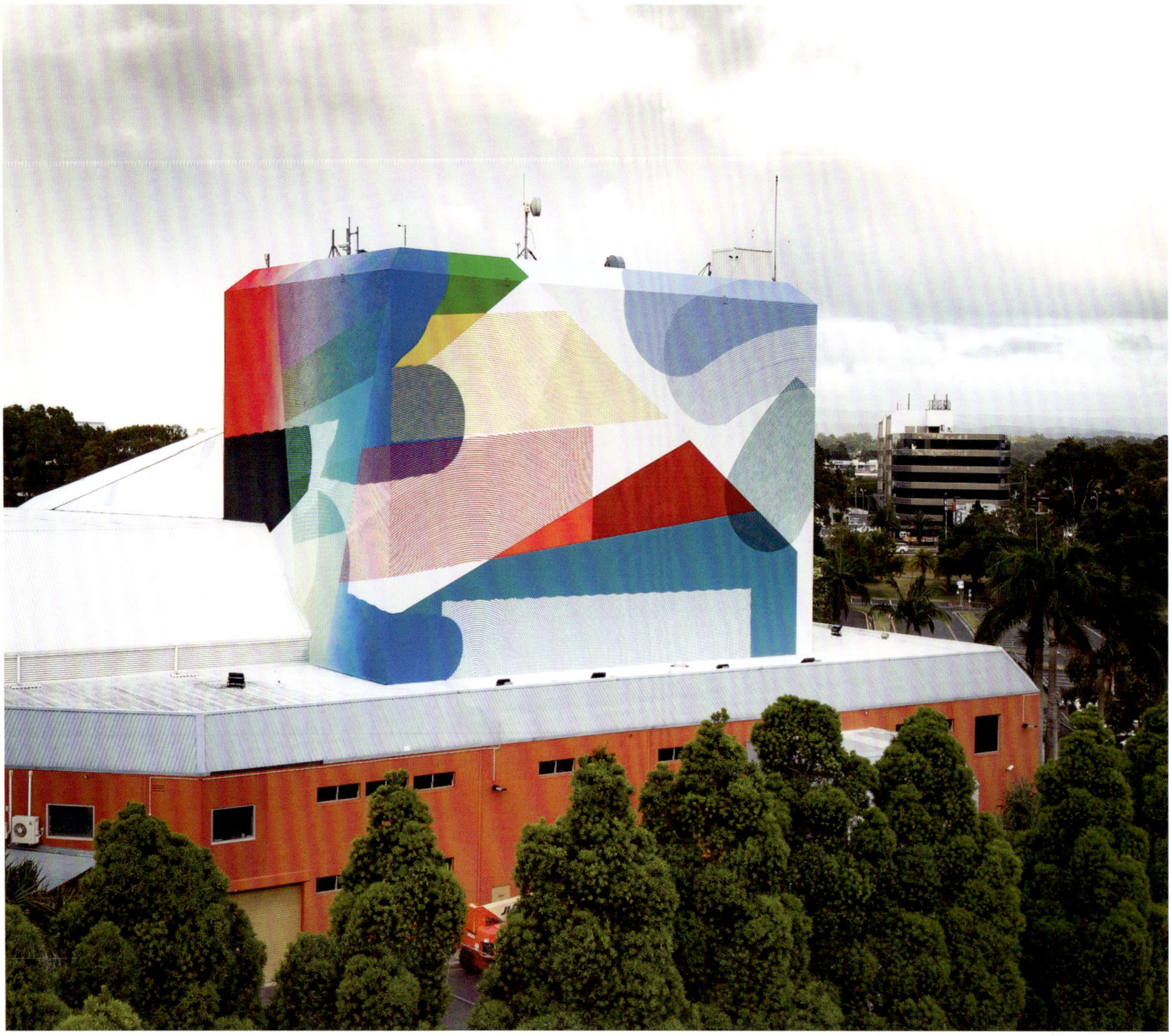

Mural for Home of the Arts, Gold Coast Arts Center

MOMO collaborated with Sydney-based artists Georgia Hill and Elliott Routledge to install the large three-sided mural for Gold Coast Arts Center in Queensland, Australia.

Photography: **Selina Miles** | Material: **Paint** | Location: **Gold Coast, Queensland, Australia**

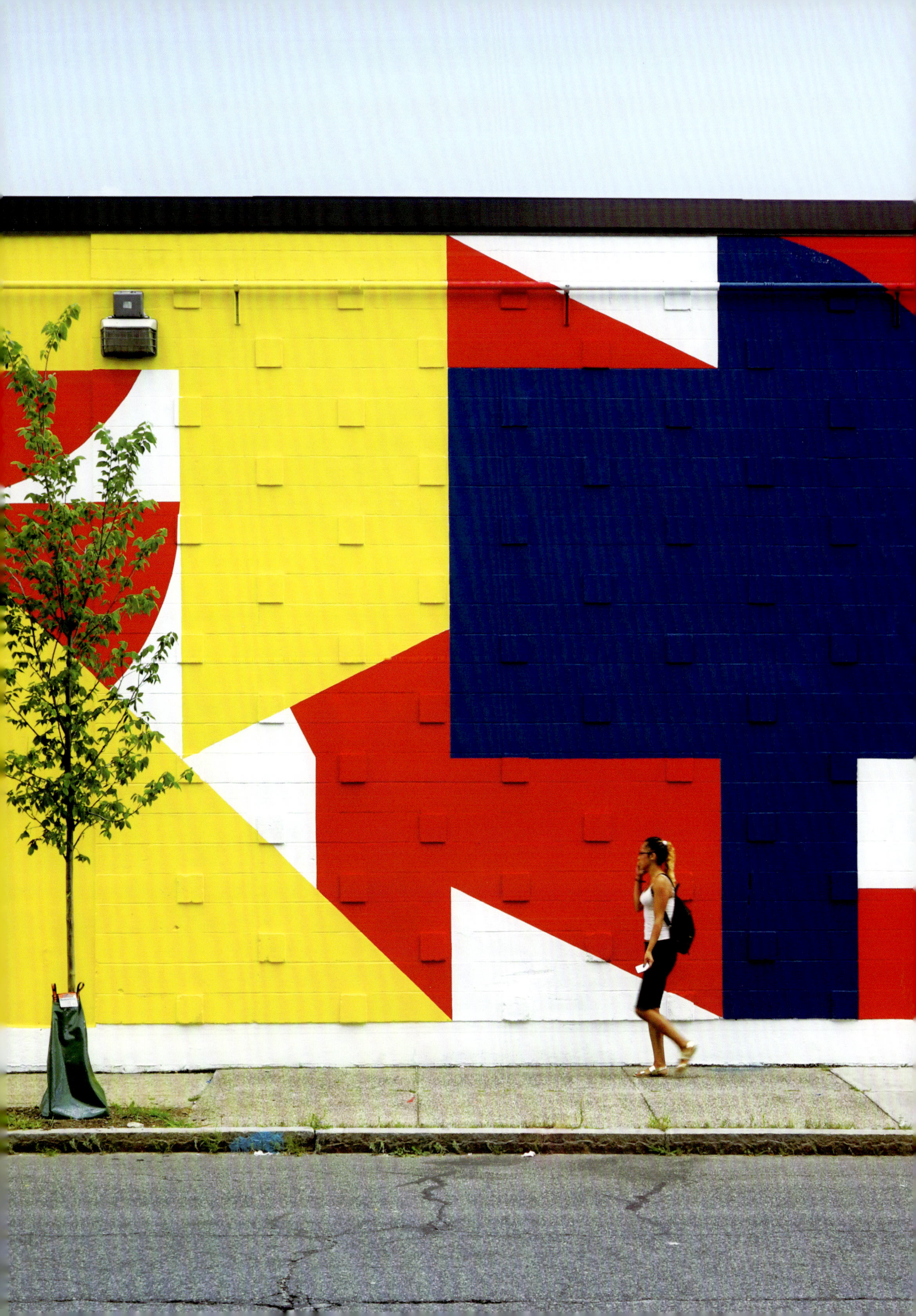

"When you work in the public spaces, you are not in your studio. A building is not a blank paper. After the work is done, the artist leaves, and two things remain: the artwork and the people living with it. I find it essential to create a link between them, and this is why it is important for me to integrate my pieces with the existing elements, and when possible, involve residents."

Eltono

Artist

French artist Eltono, born in 1975, worked in Madrid for the last decade, then in Beijing for four years and now lives in southern France. Flâneur, stubborn walker, and chronic observer, for years, Eltono has used public spaces as support, studio, and inspiration source.

French Artist on the Road: Integrate Art with Architecture and Environment

Eltono considers himself a flâneur, stubborn walker, and chronic observer. He discovered his interest in mural art when traveling on the commuter train from the suburbs to Paris. Around 1989, he started painting on train tracks and highways in his neighborhood. In 1999, he had an opportunity to participate in the Erasmus student exchange program and went to study in Madrid. Since then, he has stayed in Madrid for 11 years and achieved fame there. "I always found the experience of getting to know a culture and learn a language very exciting," explains Eltono, "and after 11 years in Madrid, I wanted to live a new experience like the one I had when I first moved to Madrid." Therefore, he made a decision to move to Beijing, China, in 2010 with his wife, who he had met in Madrid. They stayed in Beijing until 2014, and now, Eltono lives in southern France.

When living in Madrid, he started painting abstract symbols with tape and acrylic paint using the name "Eltono." The name was originally derived from a name he used in Paris, "Otone," but his friends often called his name backward as "Tono." "Some of the most famous graffiti writers in Spain were using names like 'El Vino' or 'La Mano,' so when I moved to Spain, I decided to add the 'El' and make my name 'Eltono'," Eltono recalls.

Before starting a new project, Eltono always looks around to find relevant colors in the surroundings. He reviews the architecture, takes a lot of measurements, and looks for repeating proportions. Also, he does a study of the main lines and looks for adequate patterns. His sensitivity to what is happening around him and his knowledge of the nature of the street—its whims and its unpredictability—are his main tools when generating works. He always considers a building like a work of art. "And with respect for the artist who drew it, I have to take into account what he did before painting on it." Eltono adds, "I like to say that instead of painting on the wall, I paint with the wall."

For Eltono, every painting is a challenge as he is painting in the public space. "When you work in the public spaces, you are not in your studio. A building is not a blank paper. After the work is done, the artist leaves, and two things remain: the artwork and the people living with it. I find it essential to create a link between them, and this is why it is important for me to integrate my pieces with the existing elements, and when possible, involve residents," Eltono comments. For example, in November 2017, Eltono was invited by his good friend and artist Nano4814 to paint in São Vicente village in Cape Verde. Eltono discovered the house of Auzenda and José Lopes, the house on which Eltono painted *Composition on Building n.°22 (Familia Lopes)*. "When I saw the geometry of the building and the location—the last house in the village before the mountains—it was clear to me that this was where I wanted to paint," says Eltono. He introduced himself to the Lopes family and started sketching for a couple of days under a tree in front of their house. During these days, Eltono interacted with them and watched their daily life. Finally, he chose the colors based on the surroundings and tried to find a balance between the already existing landscape and the task at hand. "The composition was created using geometric elements found around the house and other shapes that I chose so I could play with the building in a way that would not disrupt the overall balance," Eltono explains. He painted the house in four days with the help of Patrick, the son of Lopes, and several volunteer students from a nearby city.

Over the years, Eltono has worked in the street of more than ninety cities and has shown his works in many world-renowned galleries and museums, including the Tate Modern, the Somerset House, Fundacion Miro, and Artium Museum.

Modo n.°27

Generative and collaborative mural painting situated on Tremont Street, Lynn, Massachusetts, for Beyond Walls Festival, executed with nine participants from RAW Art Works, a youth arts organization.

Photography: **Eltono** | Material: **Latex paint** | Location: **Lynn, Massachusetts, USA**

Modo n.°24

Generative painting on La Courrouze Water Tower for Teenage Kicks Biennal.

Photography: **Titouan Massé** | Material: **Latex paint** | Location: **Rennes, France**

Composition on Building n.°24 (CSC, Clou-Bouchet)

Composition on Building n.º24 CSC, Clou-Bouchet, Niort, France. Project curated by Winterlong Gallery and produced by Ville de Niort.

Photography: **Eltono** | Material: **Latex paint** | Location: **Niort, France**

Composition on Building n.°22 (Família Lopes)
Mural painting for the house of Auzenda and José Lopes in São Vicente village in Cape Verde.

Photography: **Eltono** | Material: **Latex paint** | Location: **São Vicente, Cape Verde**

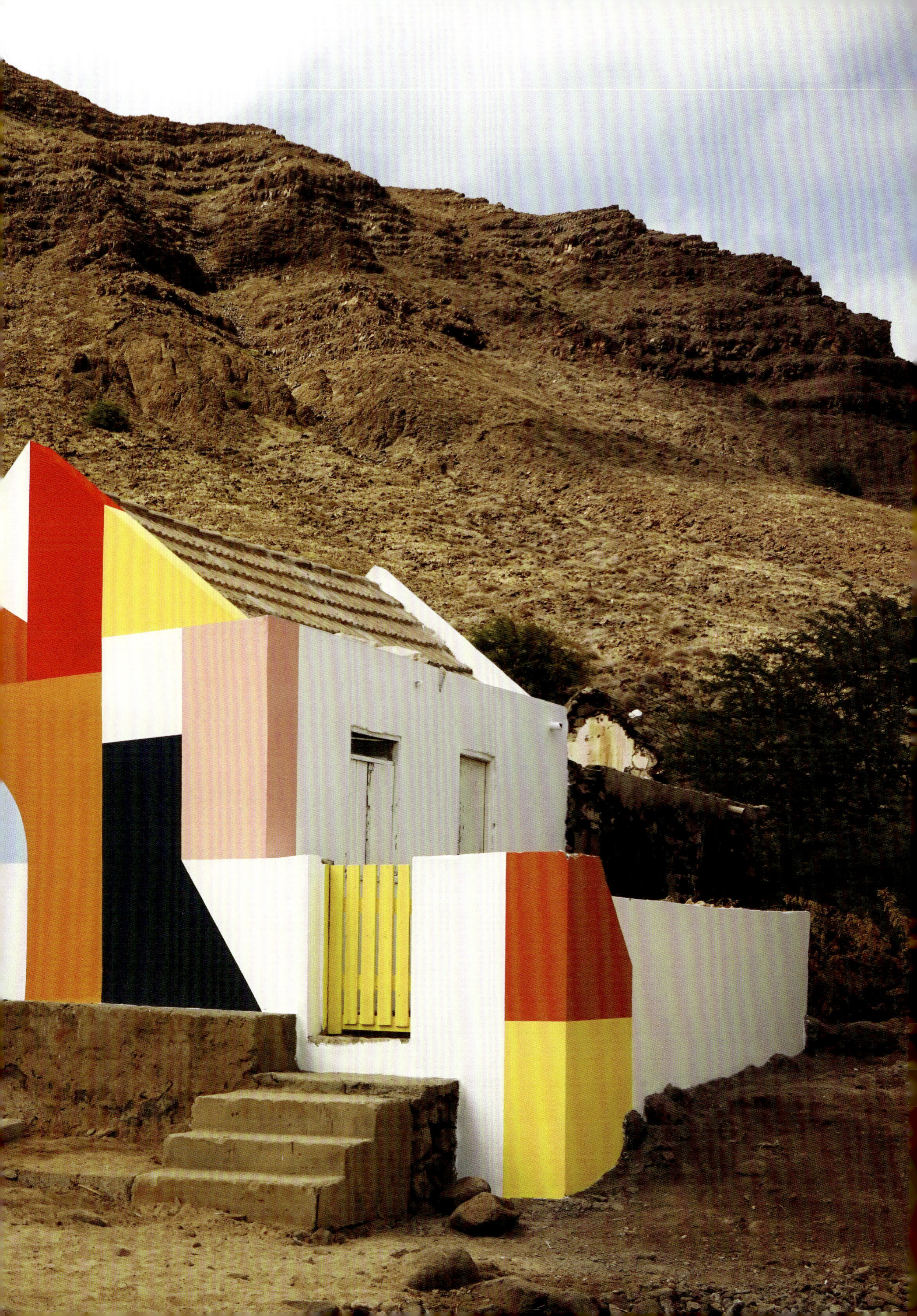

POP LIFE

HAPPY + HEALTHY
PEOPLE + PLACES

"I love public art. It's so important in the city to bring a little bit of joy and make people smile. That's what I've always tried to do. Ultimately, I want to make people's everyday life a little happier with my work."

Camille Walala

Artist
Designer

French artist and designer Camille Walala graduated in textile design from the University of Brighton. In 2009, she established her namesake brand, Walala Studio, in East London and continues to live and work there today. Her practice has taken her all over the world to transform homes and workspaces with her signature tribal-pop style. Portrait photo by J. Lewis.

Vitality and Glamor: Bold Colors Bring New Life to the City

French-born artist and designer Camille Walala first arrived in London in 1997 and fell in love with the city instantly for the diversity and freedom that it offered. After finishing her study in textile design in 2009, Camille founded Walala Studio, specializing in art direction, interior design, and large-scale public commissions.

Growing up in the south of France, Camille was surrounded by colors in everyday life. Their house was a vibrant place where Camille could find many colors. When Camille moved to the city, she realized that there was a vast lack of colors in the constant surrounds. Camille says: "Color can affect your mood so strongly; it is so uplifting! I believe there should be more color everywhere to make people happy!" Camille loves collecting color swatch cards from DIY stores and keeps hundreds of cards. She creates many combinations with these cards and keeps them in her color archive. Thus, whenever she starts a new project, she will look through her colors library to find a good match for the work at hand. Also, she loves to walk along the streets and take pictures of color combinations to store inspiration.

Besides eye-catching, bright colors, Camille's works of art are known for the playful, graphic patterns inspired by the Memphis Movement, the African Ndebele tribe, and Op Art masters like Victor Vasarely. She has an irrepressible enthusiasm for these styles of artworks that invoke a smile on the faces of the audiences.

Over the years, Camille has created many headline design projects, including *Colorful Crossing* series, *Industry City*, *Pop Life*, *Walala Lounge*, and among others. *Industry City* is the tallest and largest interactive installation that Camille has created so far. Despite the height, Camille spent days staring at the computer screen to find out the best color combinations, paint choice, and pattern—strong yet simple geometry. "I'm thrilled to be producing a design for a 40-meter building—my tallest so far. The design has been inspired by the architecture of the building, particularly the repetition of the windows. The site is bathed in the most beautiful colors at sunset, which has inspired my palette for the project. I'm really excited about this design as I am producing something quite different," explained Camille. Her recent artwork for London Design Festival 2019 also won global praise, in which Camille turned South Molton Street into an open-air living room filled with furniture pieces in geometric shapes, injecting color and playfulness into cityscapes. "I want to push myself by creating another style of public art to make people smile again. This time I have designed public benches, where people can feel at home, surrounded by plants and rugs." Camille continued, "I want to create a place where people can gather, appreciate their surroundings, and enjoy the city. I love the idea of bringing an element of fun to the street, weaving color and joy into a city."

Finding that her style translates powerfully to larger surfaces and installations, Camille is now working with greater scope and at a grander scale than ever before, with an overriding ambition to imbue the world's urban landscapes with eye-popping color and soul-stirring energy.

Pop Life

In September 2017, at Cleveland's Waterloo Arts District, Camille Walala covered an abandoned bank building with a large-scale, transformative, urban mural. Camille transformed the Greek Revival façade of a 1920s bank building into a riot of pattern and color. The building is now an art gallery and yoga studio named Pop Life. A vibrant geometric color mosaic, paired with the stripes of black and white on the columns, adds a dynamic flair to the old building and invites visitors to enter the gallery space, juice bar, and yoga studio within.

Photography: **Walala Studio, Pop Life**
Material: **Paint**
Location: **Cleveland, Ohio, USA**

Better Bankside

Collaborated with Better Bankside and Transport for London, Camille created the second *Colourful Crossing* on Southwark Steet by applying her signature graphic style—bold colors and shapes—to a pedestrian crossing in South London, with the help from a specialist road markings company. "The aim of the *Colourful Crossing* commission is to explore how everyday infrastructures in the city, such as pedestrian crossings, are perceived and can be transformed," said Better Bankside.

Photography: **Walala Studio, Better Bankside** | Material: **Paint** | Location: **London, UK**

Industry City

Commissioned by WantedDesign NYC 2018, an international design show hosting marquee events during NYCxDESIGN, Camille reinvented the façade of a seven-story historic building in Brooklyn's Industry City creative hub. Camille transformed the building's somewhat neglected fascia into a vibrant and decorative statement that did justice to the creativity housed within. The 40-meter-high project is the biggest and largest project that Camille has done so far in New York City.

Photography: **Industry City** | Material: **Paint** | Location: **New York City, New York, USA**

Dream Come True

Camille's exuberant, colorful designs for the five-story Splice Post building bring warmth and vitality to London's Old Street, providing a gift to both the local community and the growing hordes of visitors drawn to the speculative glamour of the East End of London. The massive building has been transformed from a dull black monolith into a supremely colorful, eye-catching work of art.

Photography: **J. Lewis** | Material: **Paint** | Location: **London, UK**

CAMILLE WALALA
SPLICE
GT. EASTERN STREET
Singer Street
Controlled ZONE
Central ZONE

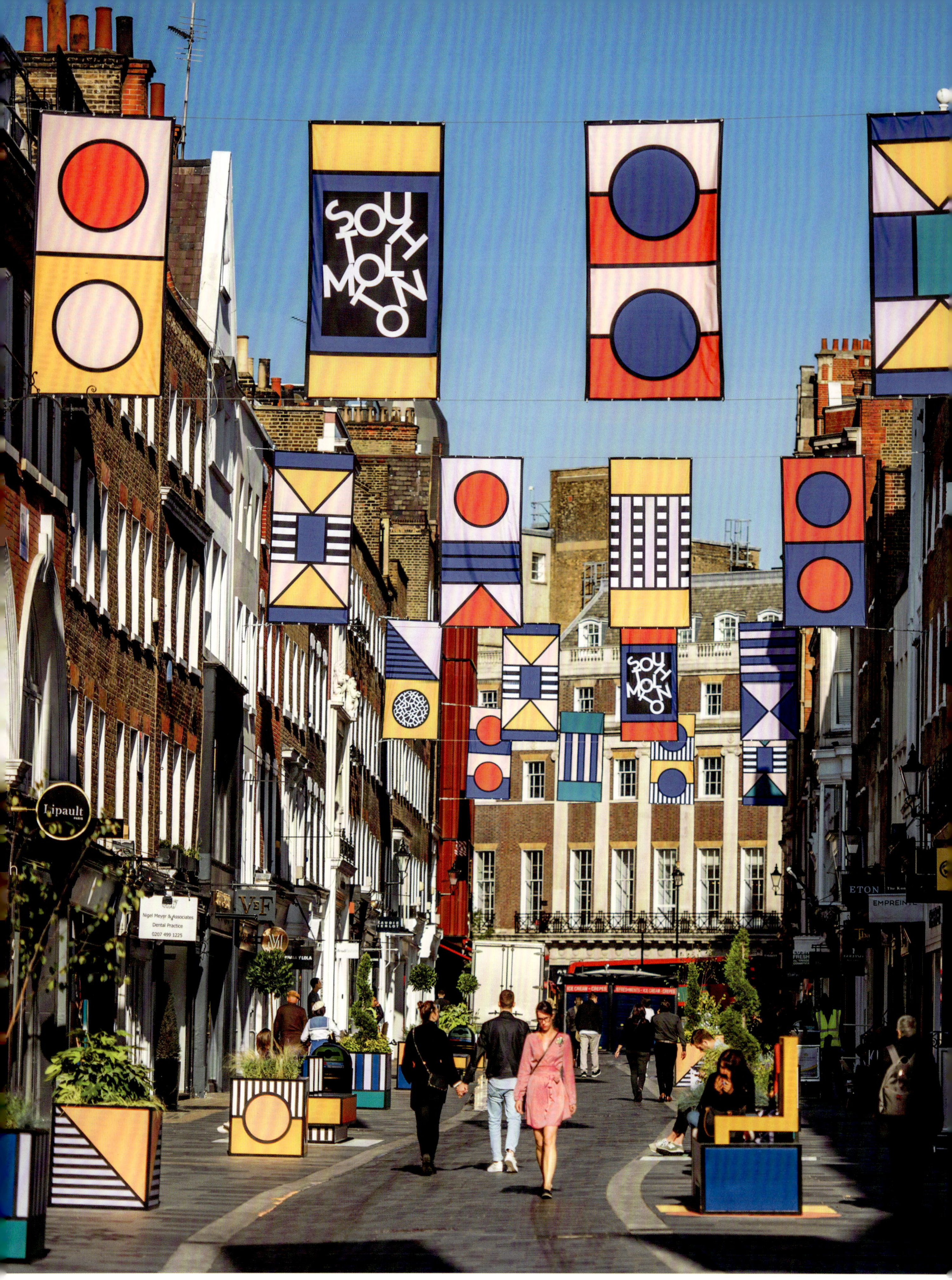
Lipault
ETON

Walala Lounge

Commissioned by Grosvenor Britain & Ireland to energize South Molton Street in Mayfair, Camille Walala transformed the street into an open-air living room for London Design Festival 2019, her second major public installation for the festival. Camille and her studio team, headed by creative producer Julia Jomaa, created a set of ten sculptural benches, accompanied by planters (some freestanding and some integrated into the structure of the benches), and a series of oversized bunting-style flags that can be strung from shopfront to shopfront, completing the conversion of South Molton Street into an immersive corridor of color.

Photography: **Charles Emerson**
Material: **Paint**
Location: **London, UK**

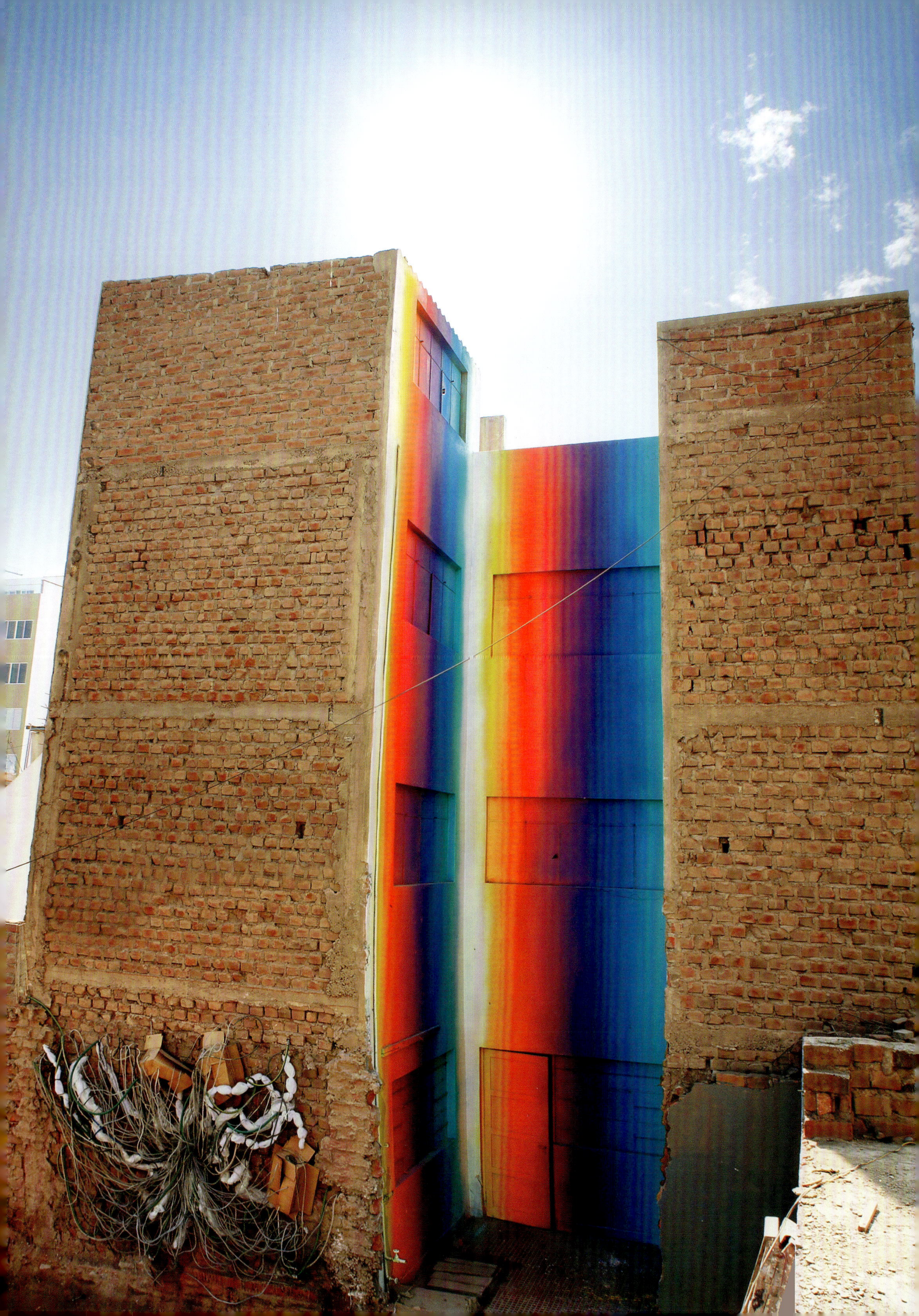

"The gradients are a reminder of the limitations that we have as physical bodies. The chromatic spectrum that is present in many of my artworks is a reference to this fact. It is a beautiful prison from which we cannot break—all colors surround us and accompany us—forming an experience that we call life."

XOMATOK

—
Artist
—

Jesús Camarena Lovera, widely known as XOMATOK, born in 1985, is an artist and art director living and working in Lima, Perú. He has transformed several walls, building façades, and random rock piles with his signature full-spectrum color gradients. Portrait photo by Lavinia Fenton.

Bursts of Color: Tribute to Urban Life

XOMATOK studied advertising design at the National Public Technological Institute of Design and Communication in Perú and worked for several companies and graphic design studios. In parallel, he is passionate about street art. "The possibility of connecting with people through the use of surfaces in public areas, the freedom to express myself freely, and the sharing of visions was basically what motivated me to perform interventions in spaces," says XOMATOK.

Since 2007, XOMATOK has been venturing into urban art, gaining an experience that has led him to intervene in various public and private spaces and achieving recognition within the Peruvian and global urban art scene. His works of art center on the manifestations of colors and the relationship of humans and environment. Best known for his vivid interventions in color pops, XOMATOK sees gradients as a reminder of the limitations that people have as physical

Purificación

This project, based on a personal initiative, was carried out in a family's dwelling building, which was close to being demolished. XOMATOK only used liquid paint and a paint sprayer for this project. He intended to give life to this space by representing the chromatic spectrum in motion as an act of purification of the area.

Photography: **XOMATOK**
Material: **Liquid paint**
Location: **Lima, Perú**

bodies. He explains: "The chromatic spectrum that is present in many of my artworks is a reference to this fact. It is a beautiful prison from which we cannot break—all colors surround us and accompany us—forming an experience that we call life."

Growing up in Perú, XOMATOK sees a significant advance in the art and design environment in this country as many interesting initiatives and projects are popping up. However, restricted by the culture of the country, he also finds that there is a general lack of interest or respect for the profession of artist and designer in public. As an artist himself, XOMATOK is always driven by constant curiosity and adaptability to new environments and times.

In Lima, there are some places forgotten by people and left in ruins. To XOMATOK, these spaces dejected by time are witnesses the urban life. Therefore, he wants to give them revitalization through painting. "Although this can only last for hours or days, it is for me a tribute to life, as ephemeral and beautiful as a rainbow can be," comments XOMATOK. He always keeps in mind that any new element in a public space can affect in many ways, so there is a responsibility for an artist to send a message with the explicit intention of being respectful of people's diverse visions. "I think that a good way to do a job in the public space is simply to contribute something new," XOMATOK continues, "and not just a kind of covert advertising, an artistic proposal that works beyond the ego."

Currently, XOMATOK is represented by the Galería Impakto (Perú). He has participated in several conferences and workshops, such as British Cultural Center in Perú (2017), International Design Festival in Costa Rica (2013), and so on. Also, he has awarded by international artistic platforms like Juxtapoz, Colossal, to name a few. Throughout the years, he has been collaborated with major brands in advertising aesthetics, such as Adidas, Camel, Puma, extending the reach of his art to public platforms in a more massive way.

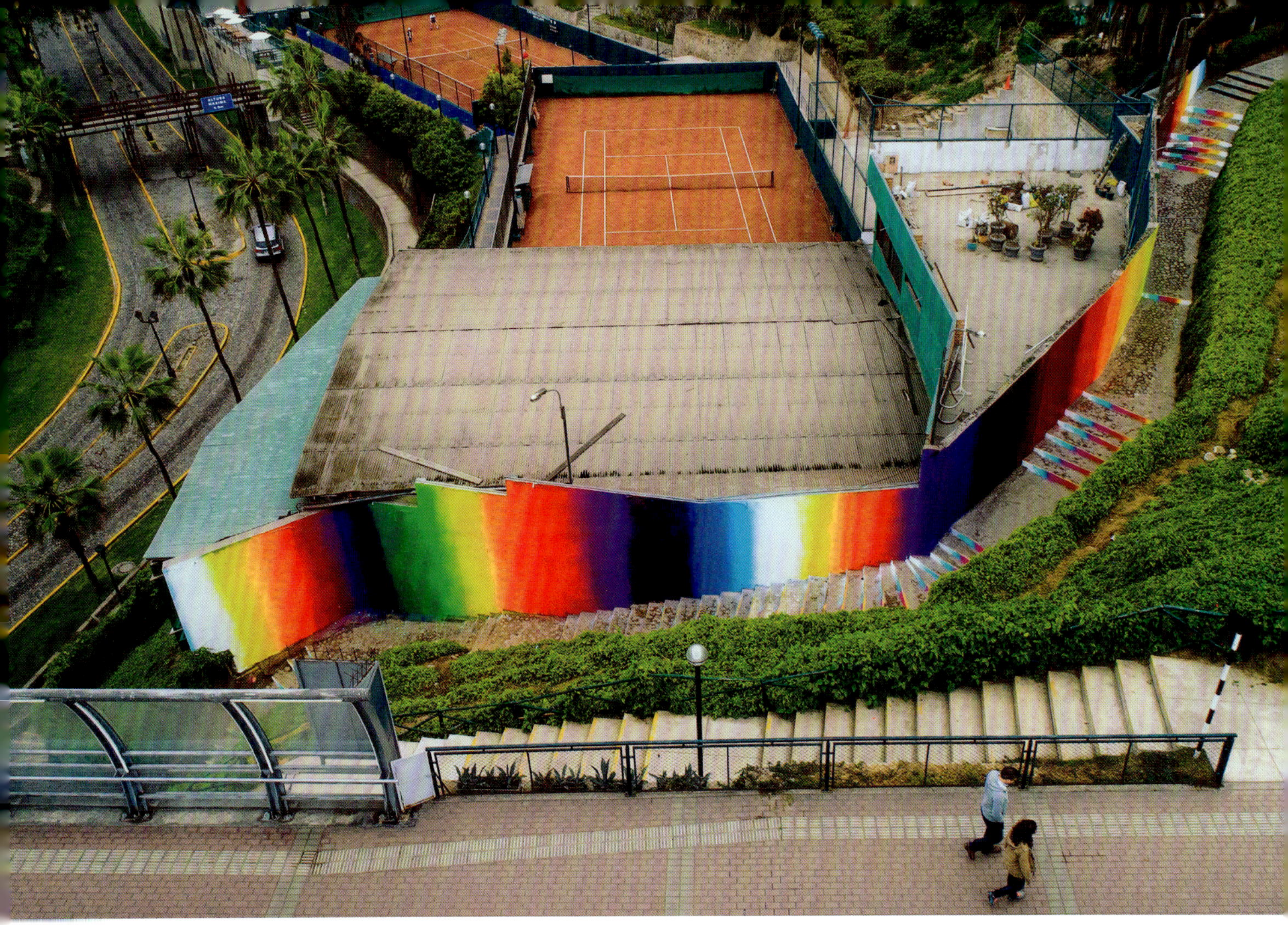

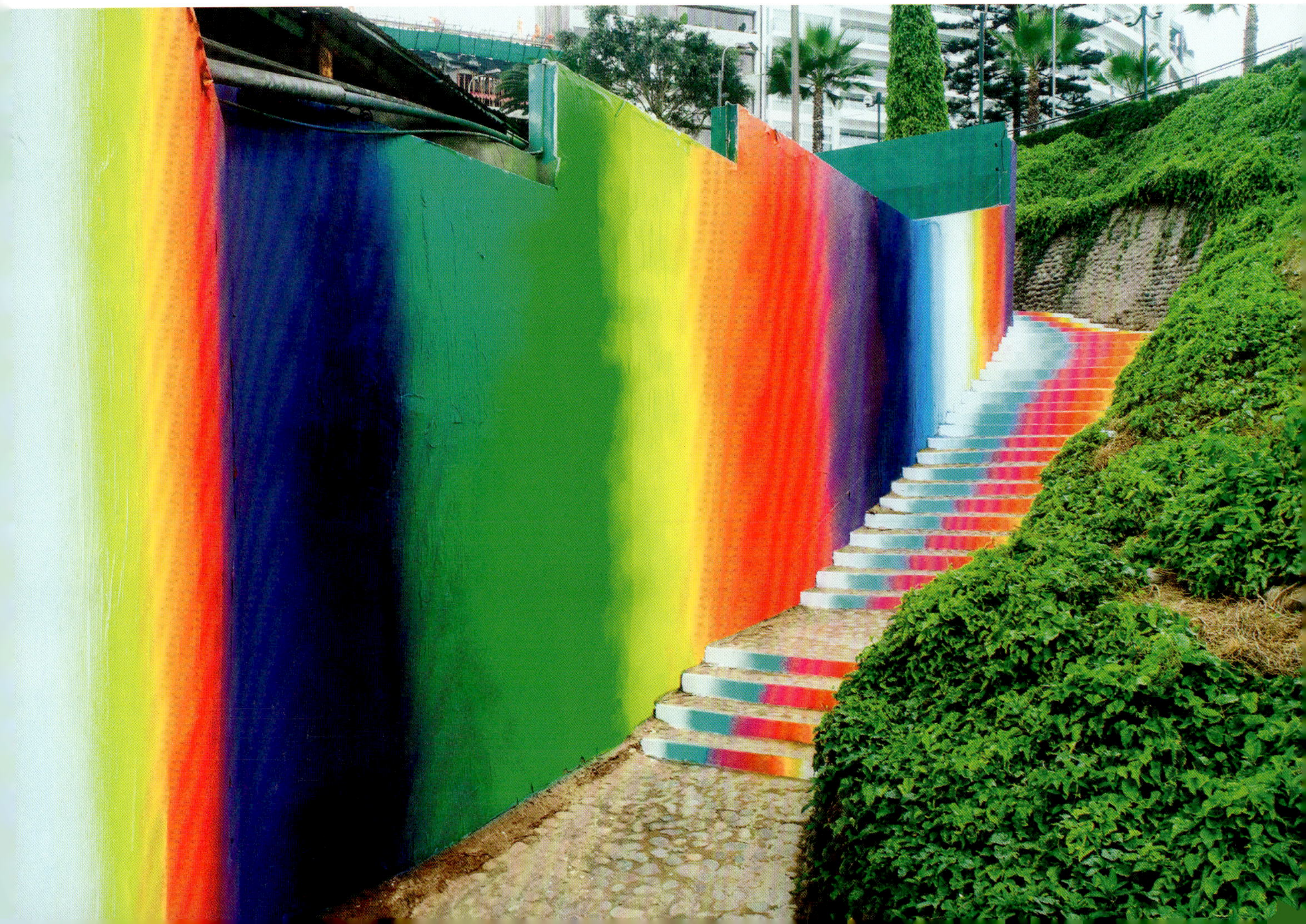

Frontera Cromática

Miraflores is one of the iconic districts of Lima, Perú. In 2018, the city held the Lima Mural festival and invited XOMATOK to perform an intervention in a fluid transit zone that leads to the beaches in the area.

Photography: **Will Flores** | Material: **Liquid paint** | Location: **Lima, Perú**

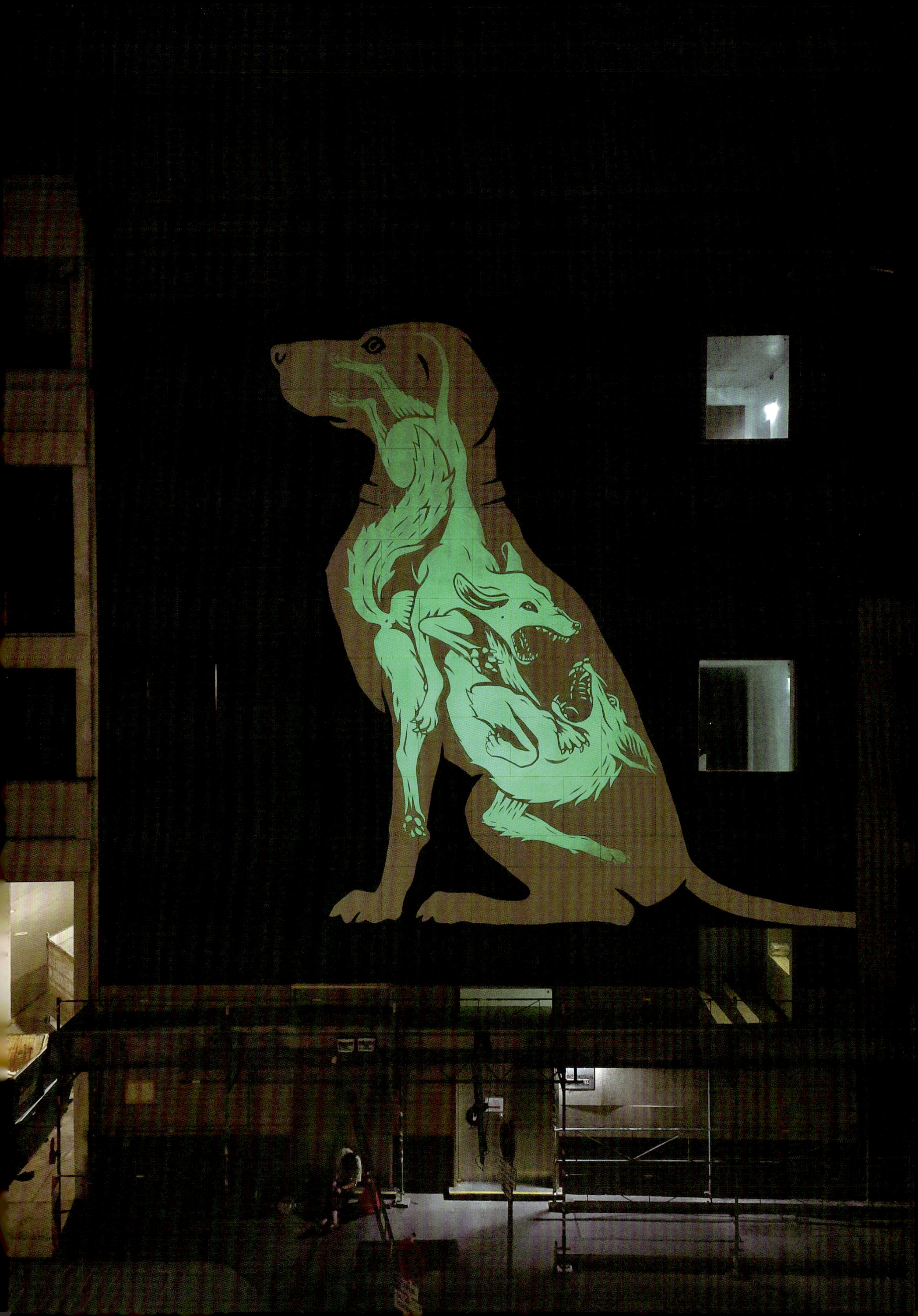

"We find that we have been fortunate to be able to develop our photo-luminescent mural project. It took us time and effort to find our own technique and language and learn how to make the most of this special paint. From the very beginning, we did not want to use this paint in a superficial way merely because it is fun that it glows in the dark. Instead, joining photo-luminescence, concept, interactivity, and light installation in public spaces is something that we enjoy a lot. It is surprising for people."

Reskate Studio

—
Artists
—

Reskate Studio is an artistic collective formed by Spanish visual artists María López (1980) and Javier de Riba (1985). Their studio is located in the Sants district of Barcelona, Spain. Influenced by classic sign-painting, popular culture, and graphic design, their work includes murals, illustrations, exhibitions, and installations.

Murals that Shine:
Illuminate the City at Night

María López grew up in Donostia-San Sebastián, Basque Country. Her father is a retired graphic designer. María remembers that when she was a child, she spent hours in her father's studio, playing with paper, foam board trimmings, Letraset, and pens. Although María showed interest in graphic design from a young age, she chose to study business following her father's suggestion. After working as a secretary for several years, she redirected herself to advertising, graphic design, and typography. Growing up in Barcelona, Javier de Riba entered the world of graphic design more directly, despite his first ambition was to study fine arts.

María and Javier met in Vienna, Austria, in 2009 when they worked as interns at different design studios. María has been admiring the designs in Barcelona, so in the following year, she moved to Barcelona to study typography. In Barcelona, they started a project to collect old skateboards, reshaping and handing them to artists to paint on them. In doing this, they wanted to give a second life to a used, discarded object. That was why they called the project "Reskate," the start of their collaboration. At the time of economic crisis, they lost their day jobs, so to keep a sharp eye on art and design, they kept preparing the boards, repairing them, and curating exhibitions. During this time, they got to know some illustrators and painters who inspired them to paint too. Then in 2011, they organized an exhibition in Asalto, one of the most famous street art and mural festivals in Spain, and from then on, they fell in love with the large-scale mural.

They like to find inspiration from vintage sign-painting and graphic design. Their works of art often showcase a vintage advertising style, which, as they explained, functions as a tool to counteract the saturation of advertisements plastered in public. "It seems that it is acceptable for people that the public space is owned by companies to advertise their products and services. It means a strong visual impact that affects the way we live and offers nothing but empty messages and consumerism. We find it important to redirect the public space into a place where we can express and communicate other values. Beauty, art, and positive or critical messages should have a decisive impact and make the society grow," comments María.

Photo-luminescent murals are one of Reskate Studio's most representative styles. They have spent lots of time and energy to find the technique of painting with photo-luminescent paints and find their voices as visual artists. "We find that we have been fortunate to be able to develop our photo-luminescent mural project." María continues to explain, "From the very beginning, we did not want to use this paint in a superficial way merely because it is fun that it glows in the dark. Instead, joining photo-luminescence, concept, interactivity, and light installation in public spaces is something that we enjoy a lot. It is surprising for people."

As an artistic collective, they question their style in every project, believing firmly that the aesthetics, techniques, and materials used must never be unthinking or gratuitous; on the contrary, they must exist solely as a vessel to convey and amplify the work's underlying message.

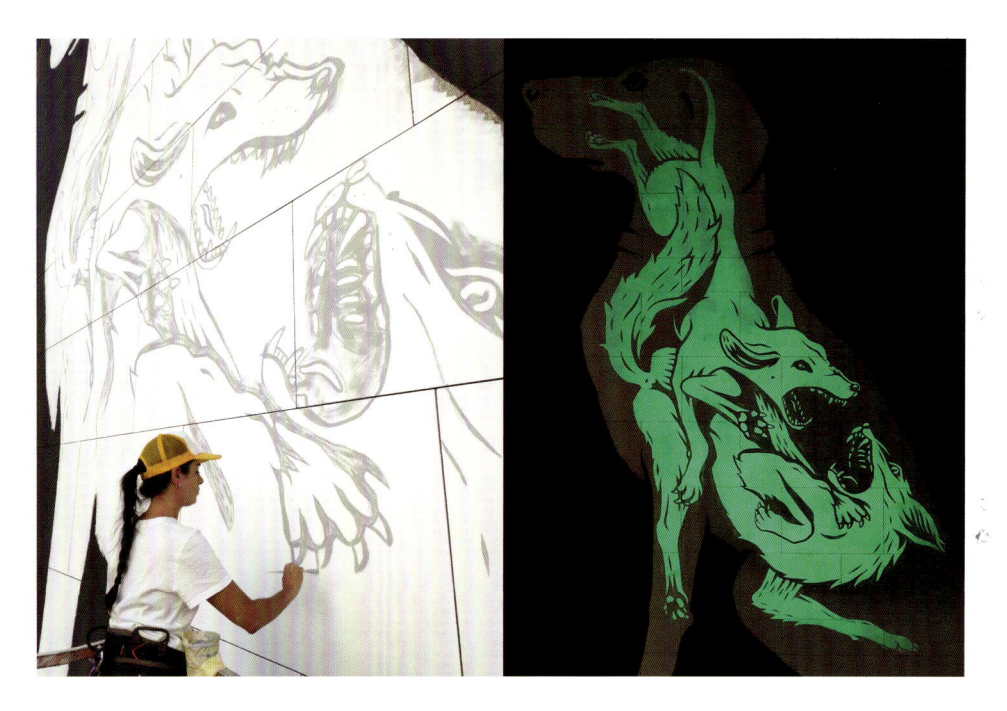

Harreman: Domestication

Harreman: Domestication was painted on the wall of the Wien Museum. The Tyrolean Hound is a breed of dog native to Austrian Tyrol. This kind of hound preys mainly foxes and is habituated to hunting alone.

Photography: **Reskate Studio** | Material: **Acrylic paint, photo-luminescent paint** | Location: **Vienna (Austria)**

Harreman: Connectivity

Harreman: Connectivity is a mural art situated at the Fringe Art Center in Shenzhen, China. With this intervention, Reskate tries to question the role of social networks—a tool that connects yet captures people at the same time.

Photography: **Reskate Studio** | Material: **Acrylic paint, photo-luminescent paint** | Location: **Shenzhen, China**

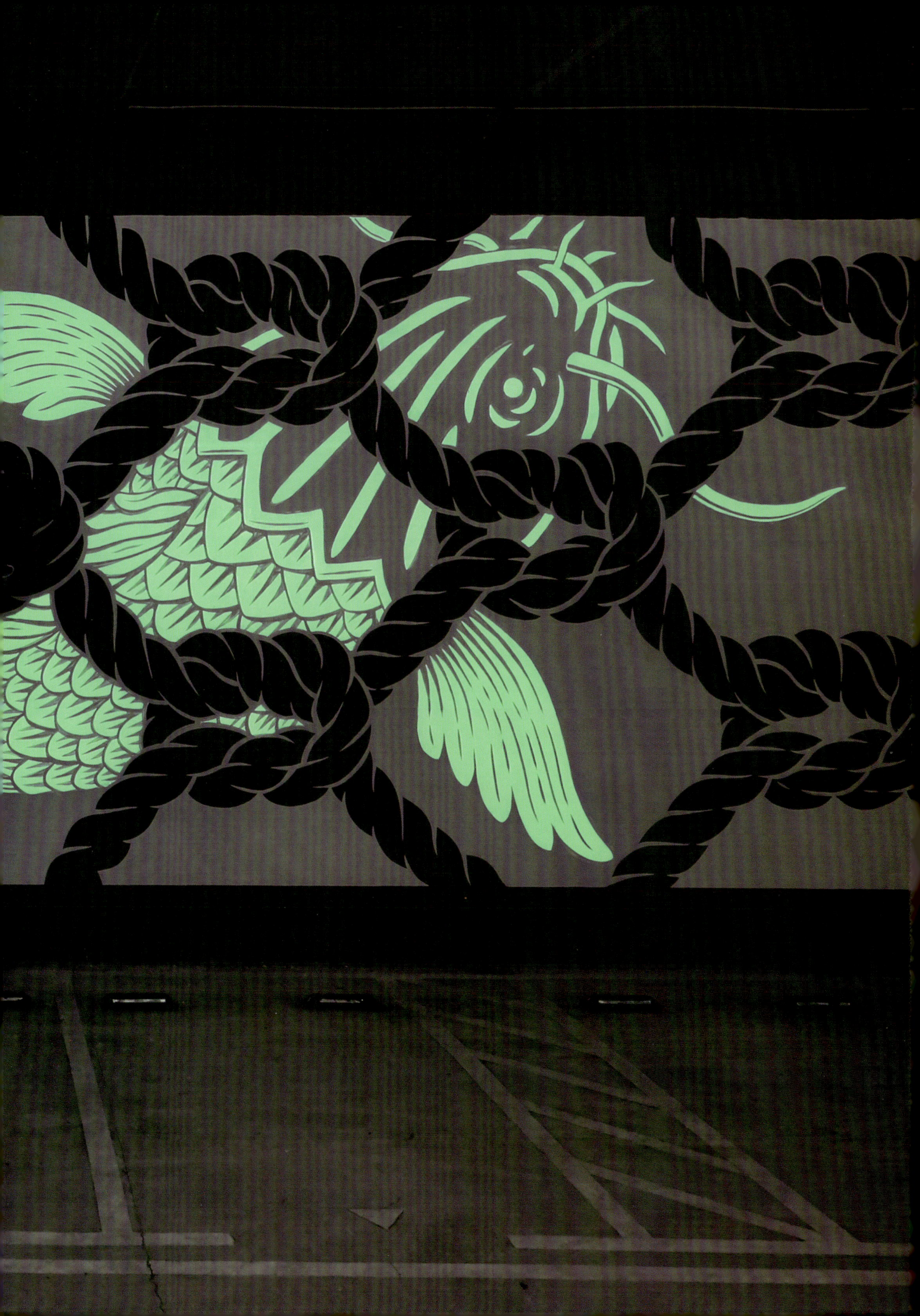

Harreman: Hizkuntza

The commercial extinction of the North Atlantic right whale (Eubalaena glacialis) in the Cantabrian Sea made the Basque sail to new destinations, which, as a result, created new languages such as Basque-Icelandic and Algonquin-Basque. This intervention is located in Patxa Place, where locals and visitors tend to gather, celebrate, and promote Basque culture.

Photography: **Reskate Studio**
Material: **Acrylic paint, photo-luminescent paint**
Location: **Baiona, French Basque Country**

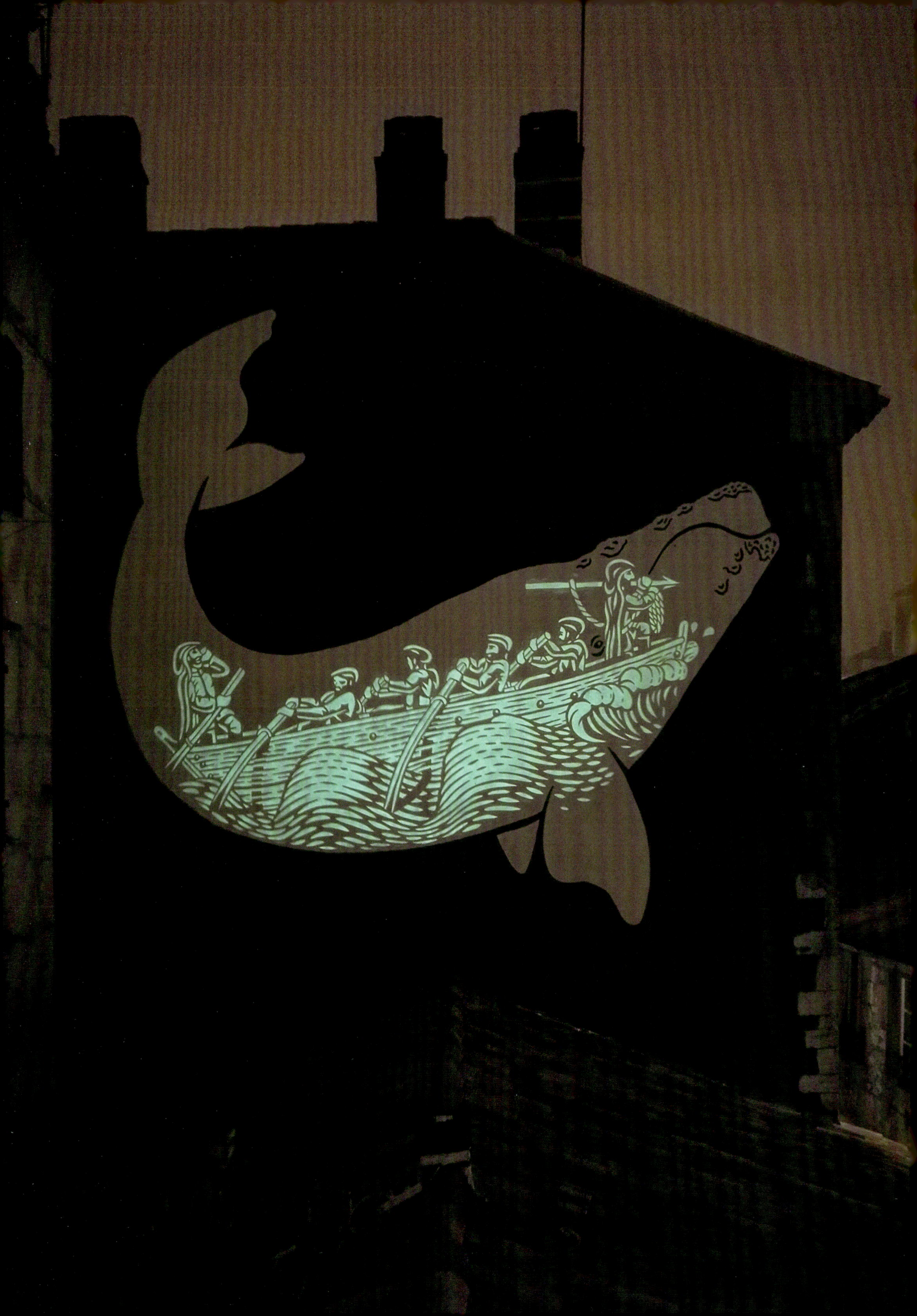

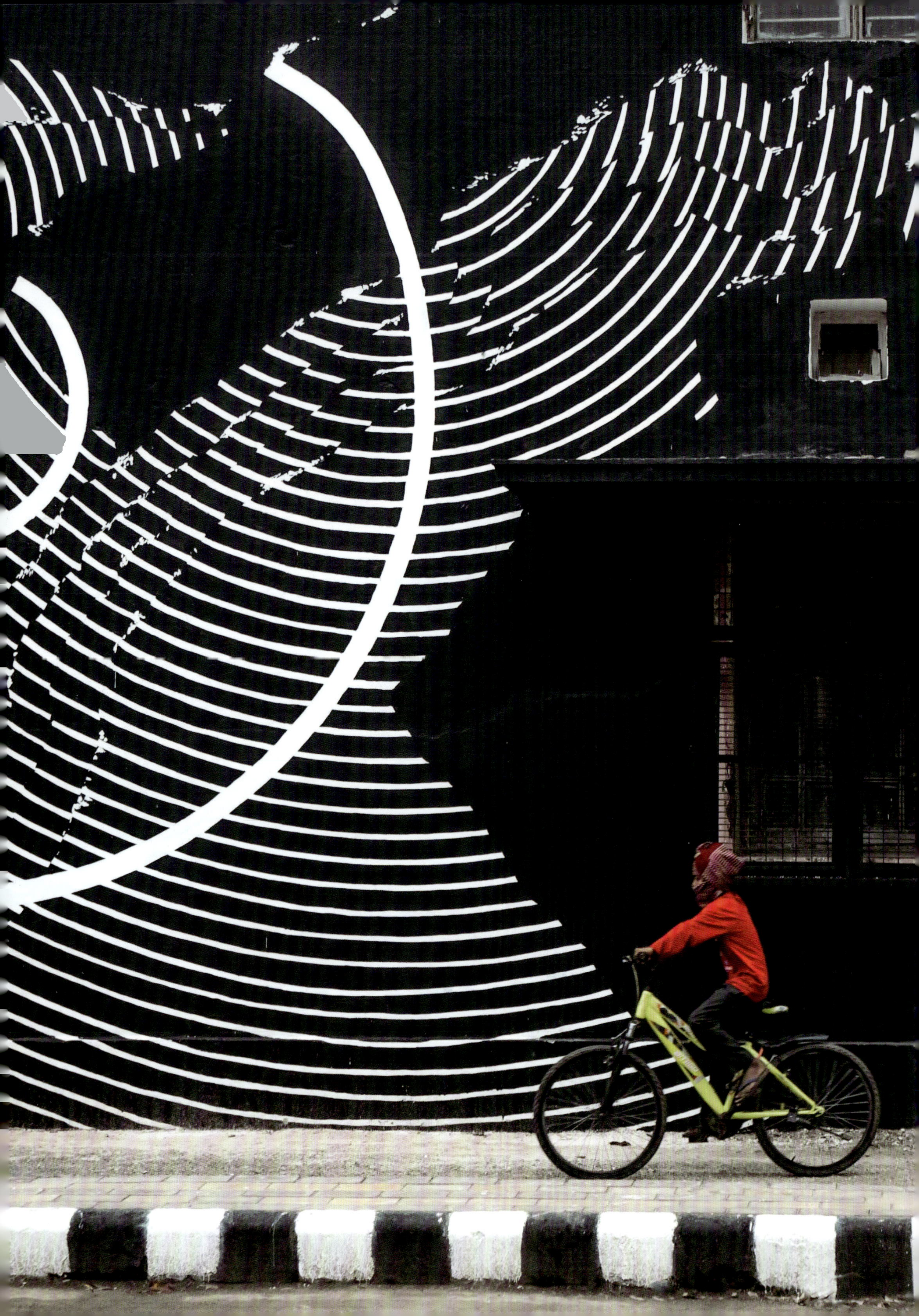

"I love larger scale pieces at the moment as it forced me to let go of a lot of the details I usually focus on in smaller works and shift my attention to textures and lines. I feel a bit freer to be loose and play with the composition on walls, as the shape, materials, and timing varies. It feels good to be a bit uncomfortable on a big scale."

Georgia Hill

Artist

Georgia Hill is an Australian multidisciplinary artist, specializing in type-based artworks that combine bold, monochromatic textures and lettering within experimental compositions.

Magnetic Labyrinth:
Monochromatic Textures on Walls

Originally from the Hunter Valley, Newcastle region, artist and illustrator Georgia Hill has achieved her fame in Sydney, Australia, where she is currently living and working. As a child, Georgia was given a lot of freedom to do the things she loved, as she said, "having chill, supportive, and proud parents who have let me blindly take this path and trust I will work hard enough to make it worthwhile." She grew up with an ambition to be an artist, architect, fashion designer, stylist, or any jobs that were related to art and creative mind. At the age of 24, Georgia moved to Berlin and thought she would achieve something there. It turned out to be an incredible challenge for her personally and emotionally, but also a rare opportunity to bury herself in detail-oriented pieces and gain confidence in her style. Now, as she flashes back, she feels happy that all the things she wanted to do have integrated into the frame of her current artworks.

Best known for her black-and-white lettering- and texture-based artworks, Georgia keeps exploring different things using a wide range of mediums and techniques, such as pen, ink, paint, or digital devices. "I've always loved texture and pattern, but it really took a long time for me to come into my own aesthetic, which has given my work more of an art direction rather than merely design- or client-oriented lettering. It is always shifting and changing, but I really enjoy being able to control that and focus on particular aspects or applications," explained Georgia. She always pays great attention to the details by ripping, layering, and playing with the textures. "I really love (and hate) that moment because to some extent, it is unpredictable—you never know if the second texture will get lost in the details on another layer," Georgia added, "but I love the idea that the result is all by chance, free of any digital or deliberate execution." On the other hand, she loves doing large-scale pieces on walls because it forces her to forget about the details and focus on the overall composition, shape, and materials, which gives her another experience of painting.

After creating various large-scale murals and making all the travels, nowadays, Georgia's works of art are more driven by introspection and feelings. "I really like that an element of a specific mural can be planned. It is about reacting or referring to the elements you see around—micro and macro details and impressions—that not just shape the way we draw but speak out our feelings," said Georgia. Besides, Georgia also finds inspiration from architecture, nature, fragments of conversations, or even shadows and interpret them to the details and varied contexts of her work.

Over the years, her instantly recognizable works of art have spanned galleries and small inner-city walls to 400-feet abandoned buildings across Canada, New Zealand, Iceland, Spain, Jordan, the United States, Japan, Indonesia, and across Australia's states.

Yehaan/This Must Be the Place

Large-scale mural created in collaboration with Hanif Kureshi for St+Art India, New Delhi, India. The St+Art India is a non-profit organization that works on art projects in public spaces. The aim of the foundation is to make art accessible to a broader audience by taking it out of the conventional gallery space and embedding it within the cities.

Photography: **Pranav Gohil** | Material: **Exterior acrylic on render** | Location: **New Delhi, India**

Goose Island, Chicago, USA

Full building mural created with the B_Line Chicago for R2 Developments. The B_Line is a mile-long street art corridor under a historic train line in Chicago's Fulton Market meatpacking district. It is an accessible, immersive art experience that began as a quest to resurrect one of Chicago's most rare displays of public art.

Photography: **Georgia Hill**
Material: **Exterior acrylic on render**
Location: **Chicago, Illinois, USA**

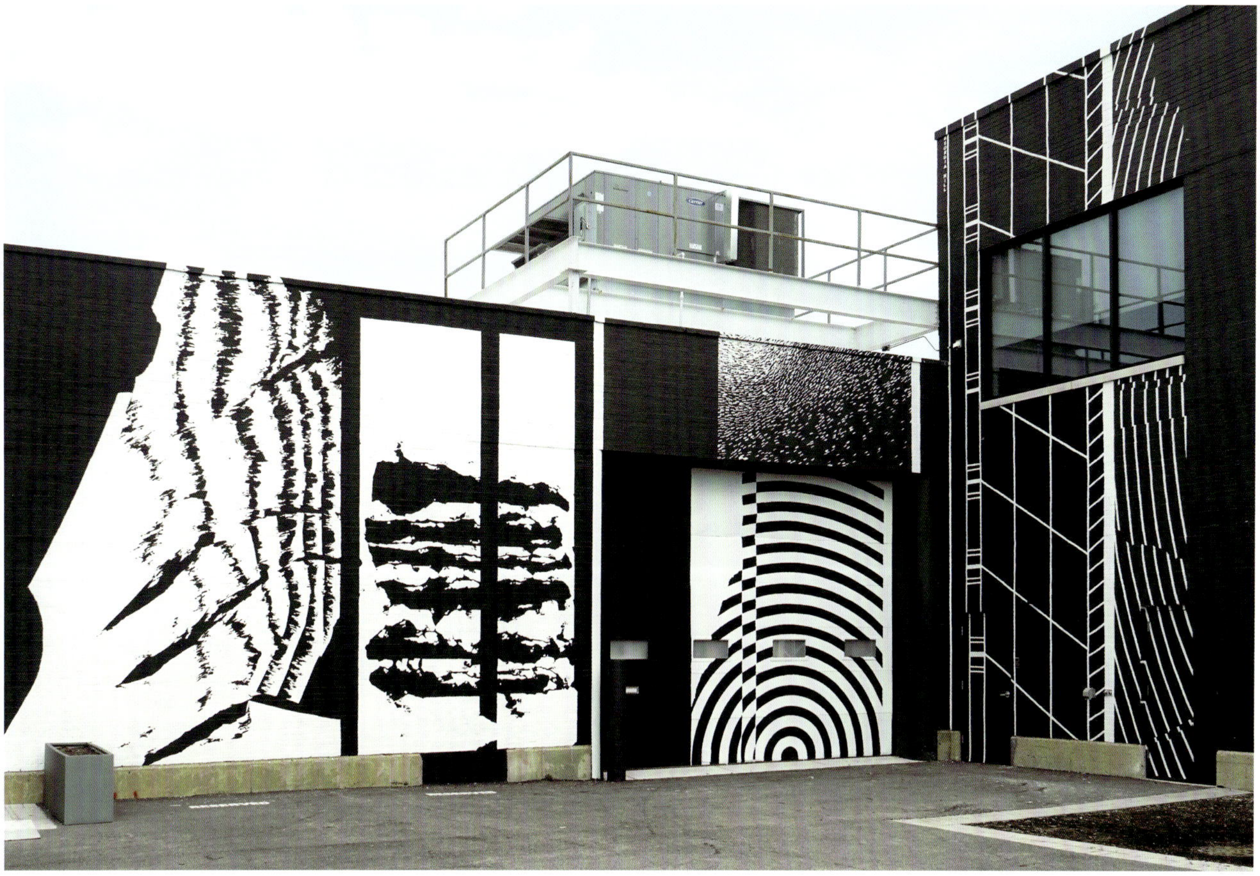

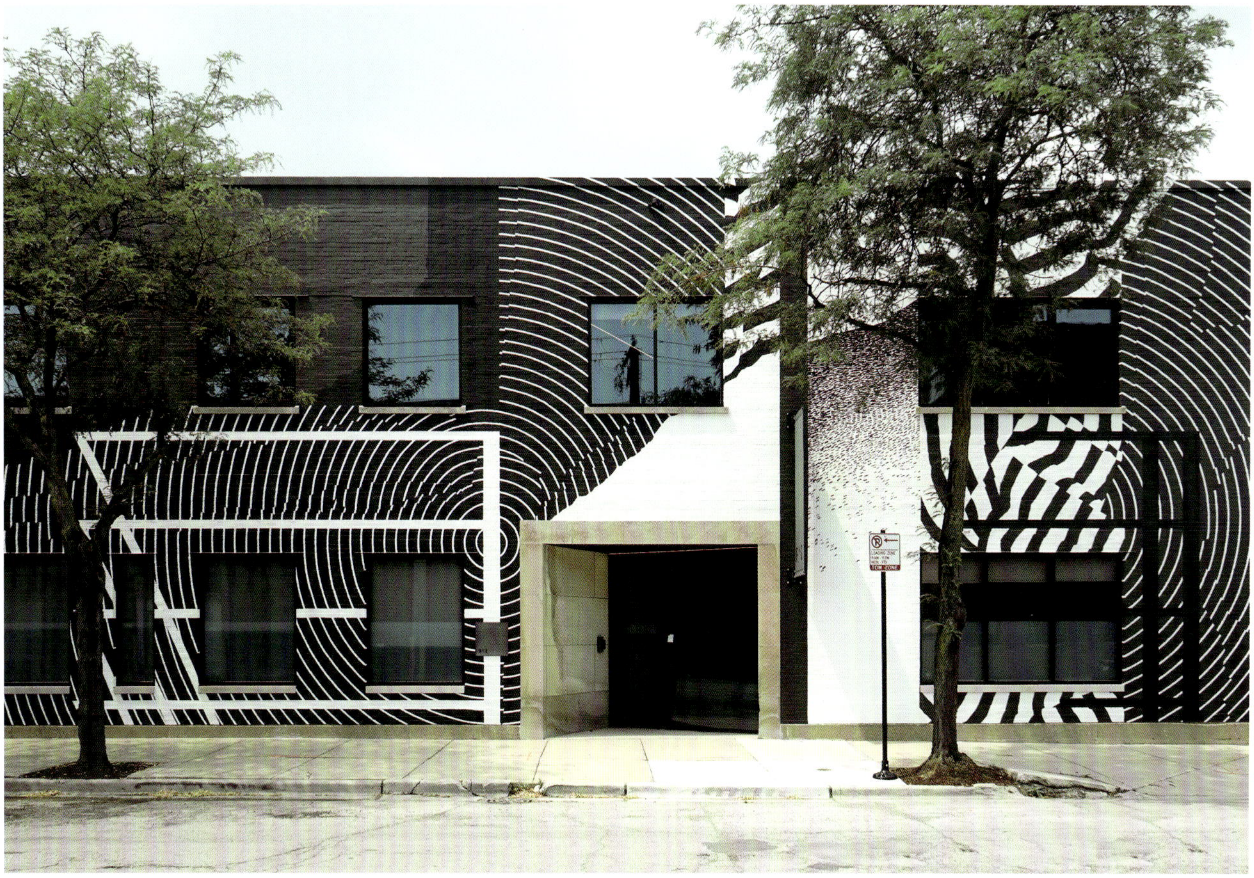

Bring It with You for Artding, Germany

Large scale mural created for the first Artding Mural Art Festival held in Erding, Germany, curated by Mr. Woodland. Artding is an upcoming street art festival in Erding.

Photography: **Fabian Klein** | Material: **Exterior acrylic on render** | Location: **Erding, Germany**

Index

Behin Ha

behinha.com

@behinhadesign

P. 076–083

Camille Walala

www.camillewalala.com

@camillewalala

P. 202–211

· 233 ·

Chiharu Shiota
www.chiharu-shiota.com
@chiharushiota
P. 040–047

Coryn Kempster and Julia Jamrozik
www.ck-jj.com
@ckandjj
P. 114–121

Eltono
www.eltono.com
@eltonogram
P. 194–201

Emmanuelle Moureaux
www.emmanuelle.jp
@emmanuellemoureaux
P. 010–019

Florentijn Hofman

www.florentijnhofman.nl
@studioflorentijnhofman
P. 106–113

Georgia Hill

www.georgiahill.com.au
@georgiahillbth
P. 226–232

Gabriel Dawe

www.gabrieldawe.com
@gabrieldawe
P. 020–029

Gordon Young and Why Not Associates

www.gordonyoung.net
www.whynotassociates.com
@whynotassociates
P. 132–139

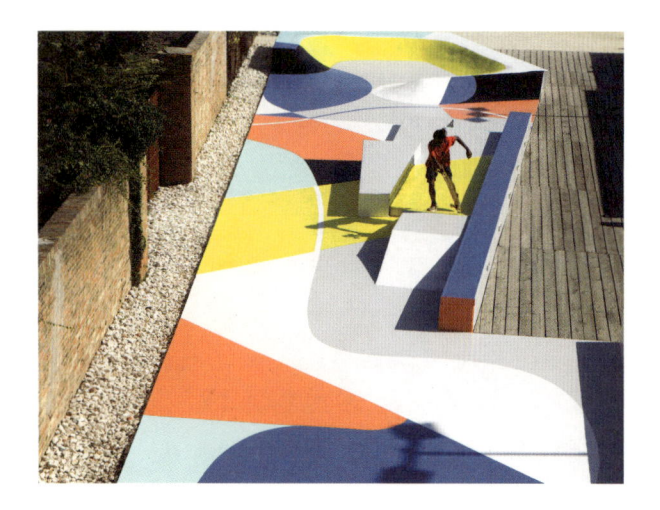

Gummy Gue
www.gummygue.com
📷 @gummy_gue
P. 162–169

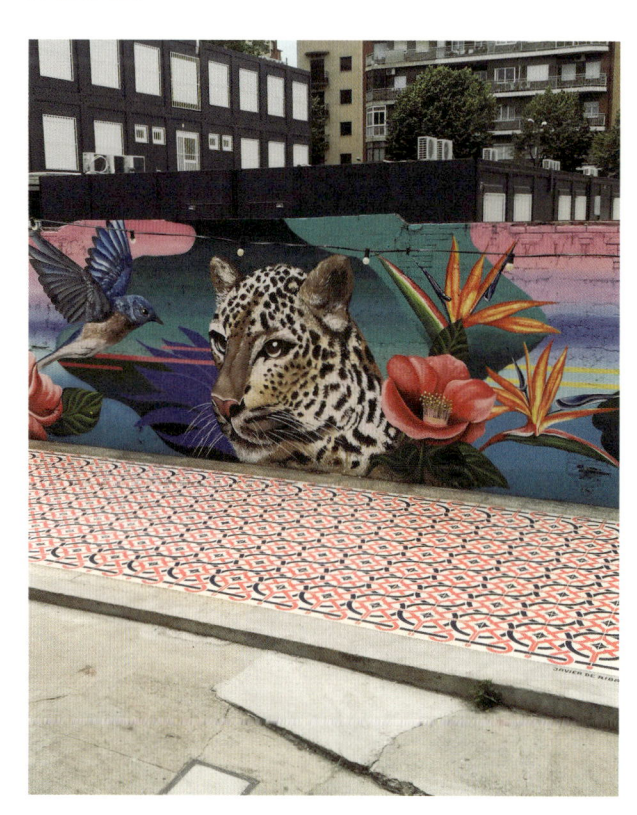

Janet Echelman
www.echelman.com
📷 @janetechelman
P. 048–055

Javier de Riba
www.javierderiba.com
📷 @javierderiba
P. 170–177

Kurt Perschke
www.redballproject.com
📷 @redballproject
P. 064–075

Luke Jerram

www.lukejerram.com

◉ @lukejerramartist

P. 056–063

MOMO

momoshowpalace.com

◉ @momoshowpalace

P. 186–193

Moradavaga

www.moradavaga.com

◉ @moradavaga

P. 122–131

Nómada Lab

www.nmdlab.com

◉ @nmdlab

P. 178–185

Paul Cocksedge Studio

www.paulcocksedgestudio.com
◯ @paulcocksedge

P. 084–095

Quintessenz

www.quintessenz.art
◯ @quinte55enz

P. 030–039

Reskate Studio

www.reskatestudio.com
◯ @reskatestudio

P. 218–225

Shirin Abedinirad

www.shirinabedinirad.com
◯ @shirin.abedinirad

P. 154–161

THEVERYMANY

theverymany.com
@theverymany
P. 096–105

XOMATOK

www.xomatok.com
@xomatok
P. 212–217

Vincent Leroy

www.vincentleroy.com
@vincent_leroy_studio
P. 146–153

Yong Ju Lee

www.yongjulee.com
@ylee2345
P. 140–145

Acknowledgments

We would like to thank all of the artists involved for granting us permission to publish their works, as well as the photographers who have generously allowed us to use their images. We are also very grateful to many other people whose names do not appear in the credits but who made specific contributions and provided support. Without these people, we would not have been able to share these beautiful works with readers around the world.